D1590847

TO HOLD AND TEACH THE CATHOLIC FAITH

TO HOLD AND TEACH THE CATHOLIC FAITH

The Faithful Exposition of Sacred Doctrine

KELLY BOWRING, STD

ST PAULS

Alba House

Library of Congress Cataloging-in-Publication Data

Bowring, Kelly
　To hold and teach the Catholic faith: the faithful exposition of sacred doctrine / Kelly
Bowring.
　　　　　p. cm.
　Includes bibliographical references.
　ISBN 0-8189-0999-4
　1. Catholic Church—Doctrines—Study and teaching. 2. Catholic Church—
Catechisms. I. Title.

BX1751.3.B69 2006
230'.2—dc22
　　　　　　　　　　　　　　2005026819

Produced and designed in the United States of America by the
Fathers and Brothers of the Society of St. Paul,
2187 Victory Boulevard, Staten Island, New York 10314-6603,
as part of their communications apostolate.

ISBN: 0-8189-0999-4

Printing Information:

Current Printing - first digit 　1　2　3　4　5　6　7　8　9　10

Year of Current Printing - first year shown

2006　2007　2008　2009　2010　2011　2012　2013　2014　2015

Dedicated to

Benedict XVI

The Evangelizer of the New Millennium

who says:

"The purpose of our lives is to reveal God to men."

"The Church by her nature is missionary; her primary task is evangelization.... At the beginning of the third millennium, the Church feels with renewed force that Christ's missionary mandate (the joy of *proclaiming and witnessing* to all the Good News of Christ the Savior) is of more current importance than ever."

"Dear brothers and sisters, at the beginning of the third millennium, how necessary it is that the *whole* Christian community proclaim, teach and witness integrally, unanimously and in agreement the truth of the Catholic Faith, of the doctrine and of morality!
All Christians — children, youths and adults, families and communities — docile to the action of the Holy Spirit, [are called to] become catechists and evangelizers in all environments, helping others to encounter Christ.
We ask this with confidence of the Virgin Mother of God, star of evangelization."

Table of Contents

Foreword

by
J. AUGUSTINE Di NOIA, OP

UNDERSECRETARY OF THE
VATICAN CONGREGATION FOR THE DOCTRINE OF THE FAITH

The *Catechism of the Catholic Church* contains nearly 3000 numbered paragraphs summarizing the essentials of Catholic doctrine as we find these expressed in the creed, in the Church's liturgy, in her moral teaching, and in her forms of public and private prayer. How can it be that something so simple — namely, the truth about God and his love for us — could become so complicated as to require such an elaborate compendium of doctrines?

One of the significant achievements of Kelly Bowring's fine book is to help us to present an intelligent answer to this question. What is more, this book demonstrates why having a solid Catholic understanding of this issue is so important for an authentic Catholic life.

In infusing the gift of theological faith in each of us in the sacrament of Baptism, the triune God gives us an intimate, personal knowledge of himself. The First Truth shares his own very knowledge of himself with us through the grace of faith. But, while God's knowledge of himself is simple — for he understands the Truth that he *is* in one simple act of vision — our knowledge of him is complex. To be sure, we know the First Truth who is God, but we cannot know him the way he knows himself. We are not, after all, God. We can only know him according to our ways of knowing. For this reason, we know the First Truth by knowing many individual truths about him.

Kelly Bowring's book both presupposes and explains this indispensable Catholic understanding of the place of doctrine in the life of each and every disciple of Christ. The failure — in catechesis, preaching and theology — to adhere to and expound the full truth of Catholic faith thus can have serious consequences in the life of faith itself. It's not just a theoretical matter. It is a matter of being true to the One who loves us. Being well-formed and faithful in the doctrines of the Catholic faith is crucial to being an authentic Catholic Christian person.

Taking the classical Thomistic approach, this book identifies among the causes of the crisis of faith a neglect of doctrine in the various ministries of evangelization and education in the Church, a rising climate of doctrinal dissent, and a corresponding decline of obedience and holiness of life. Bowring also recounts the measures which the teaching authority of the Church has taken in response to this problem. Then, after addressing the crisis of faith, Bowring advances a solution that relies on a creative retrieval of the account of doctrine advanced by St. Thomas Aquinas and important commentators in the Thomistic tradition — an account that has deeply influenced the Church's modern understanding of sacred doctrine.

Kelly Bowring is deeply convinced that the restoration of the faithful exposition of Catholic doctrine is central to authentic evangelization and the renewal of faith needed in our time, and strives to show how modern evangelizers must be authentic living witnesses of the truth of the faith for the success of the new evangelization. He argues persuasively that a movement to educate others on the meaning and significance of Catholic doctrine for all works of evangelization (catechesis and theology) is essential for the new evangelization, which must present Jesus Christ and foster an intimate relationship with Him through faithful adherence to the truths of his divine Revelation, as handed on by faithful living witnesses.

Kelly Bowring's goal in this book is to re-propose the faithful exposition of Catholic doctrine as the way to bring others into a sharing in the Truth, Jesus Christ, and in the mystery of his Revelation as contained in the doctrines of the faith. This task entails teaching the Word of God, which includes Scripture and Tradition, as expounded by the *Catechism of the Catholic Church*, in faithful obedience to the Magisterium. This book does not simply state this point, but explains why such a perspective is sound, and how it responds to the current crisis of faith.

The "deposit of faith" has for centuries been the Church's name for the body of truths about God, about creation, about the angels and us, about sin and redemption, about the incarnation, passion, death and resurrection of Jesus Christ, about the Church and the sacraments through which his divine grace flows to us, about the Blessed Virgin Mary and the saints, and about the commandments, beatitudes and virtues which, through the grace of the Holy Spirit, transform us into the image of Christ to share in the communion of the Father, Son, and Holy Spirit. These absolutely essential truths of our Catholic faith have found expression over the centuries in the doctrines of the Church. These truths together belong to the First Truth which is, in itself, the simplest thing of all, yet which is known by us in our ordinary way of knowing one thing at a time and over the course of time.

We are badly in need of an up-to-date account of doctrine's place in a complete education in faith.[1]

Christoph Schönborn

Faith is not given us in order that we preserve it, but in order that we communicate it. If we don't have the passion to communicate it, we don't preserve it.[2]

Luigi Giussani

The harvest indeed is great, but the laborers are few. Pray you, therefore, the Lord of the harvest, that He sends forth laborers.

Jesus Christ

---

[1] Joseph Cardinal Ratzinger and Christoph Schönborn, *Introduction to the Catechism of the Catholic Church* (San Francisco: Ignatius Press, 1997), 55.

[2] Address on the theme, "Rediscovering the True Face of the Parish," to the Pontifical Council for the Laity (11/24/04). This was the last statement in one of the last public addresses of Msgr. Giussani, founder of the ecclesial movement, *Communion and Liberation*, before he died on February 22, 2005.

Preface

The faithful have throughout the Church's history always aspired to receive, profess, practice, safeguard, and transmit the one true Christian Message of Jesus Christ, one that leads to a personal relationship with Christ Himself and to the eternal salvation He offers. Since the time of the Apostles, various methods and pedagogies have been tried and utilized, with varying success, to pass on the Faith. But, as we begin the third millennium of Christianity, there still remains among a majority of humanity a great hunger for holy wisdom and divine charity, for the Truth that will set them free.

The single Sacred Deposit of Faith (the *depositum fidei*)[3] of the Word of God, as contained in her sacred and revealed doctrines, has been and hence remains our primary means of contemplating God's truth on earth. Reason assists man to know God; but it does so as through a glass, only dimly seen. On the other hand, Revelation, and particularly sacred doctrine, when received with faith, reveals God to man as through a shining

---

[3] *Catechism of the Catholic Church*, 2nd ed., trans. United States Catholic Conference (1997), 84 (hereafter cited as CCC). Cf. also *Dei Verbum* (1965) 10 and 1 Tm 6:20.

[4] "'Sacred Tradition and Sacred Scripture make up a single deposit of the Word of God' (Vatican II, *Dogmatic Constitution on Divine Revelation* [*Dei Verbum*] 10), in which, as in a mirror, the pilgrim Church contemplates God, the source of all her riches" (CCC 97).

mirror.[4] Handing on the Faith, as well as that of all other forms of evangelization,[5] derives from Sacred Scripture foremost, Church documents like the new *Catechism of the Catholic Church*, and arguably, from other doctrinal resources like Aquinas' *Summa Theologiae*.[6]

But since Vatican II, due perhaps in part to secularized readings of *Gaudium et Spes*,[7] a cultural revolution within the Church sprung up such that anything that was characteristically pre-conciliar became suspect. Modes of religious dress, forms of prayer, the various devotions of piety, liturgical hymns that had been a part of the Church's cultural treasury for centuries, were not just dumped, but actively suppressed. And so it was with doctrinal teaching in handing on the Faith. In this period, for

---

[5] Initial distinctions should be made between *catechesis*, the passing on of the whole Deposit of Faith (Scripture and Tradition as authentically interpreted by the Magisterium), primarily properly to dispose a student, in faith, to receive the Sacraments; *theology*, which explains, defends and applies the principles of the whole Deposit of Faith, while also drawing new conclusions in a discursive (and argumentative/scientific) way — as a science of faith — in light of the revealed truths already known in the Deposit; *evangelization*, any and every proclamation of the Good News of the Kingdom of God as epitomized in and by Jesus Christ (which includes catechesis, theology, preaching, the liturgy; and the *kerygma*, the initial proclamation of the Mystery of Christ). Some of these concepts will be developed further in this book and are essential to understanding the meaning, role, and function of sacred doctrine.

[6] Joseph A. Komonchak, "Thomism and the Second Vatican Council," *Continuity and Pluralism in Catholic Theology*, ed. Anthony J. Cernera (Fairfield: Sacred Heart University, 1998), 57, 59. Noteworthy also, though not in the scope of this investigation, is that the Church has continually cited Aquinas as a pre-eminent source of Christian Philosophy (not just Theology), and that theology and philosophy work together in unison. What I propose is a philosophical-theological synthesis, and thus, Athens and Jerusalem, the Academy and the Church, united with Rome, acting in unison for the advancement of human knowledge united to divine truth in the work of all evangelization.

[7] The popular interpretation of this Vatican II document was that it represented an acknowledgment on the part of the Church that modernity is necessary and that it is the will of the Holy Spirit that Catholics accommodate their practices and culture, including its religious education, to modernity's spirit as quickly as possible. But, John Paul II argued that the document needs to be read from the perspective of Paragraph 22. In summary, this paragraph says that the human person needs to know Christ, and His truths, in order to have self-understanding.

many church leaders and theologians, the truths of divine Revelation which had formed centuries of the faithful and raised up Saints, were abandoned, and even suppressed, and instead replaced with personal opinion, subjective experience (more emotional than doctrinal), and avant-garde theories. To be a lay Catholic leader in many parishes in this period, one had to advocate the American pop culture more than the Creed.

This has led to a crisis of faith at the beginning of the third Christian millennium. The words of the Servant of God John Paul II in 1982 at Santiago de Compostela and declared again by Benedict XVI at the beginning of his pontificate, seem to resound appropriately here: "I send to you [the Church of today] a cry full of love: Return to yourself. Be yourself. Discover your origins. Revive your roots. Revive those authentic values that made your history glorious and your presence beneficial among the other continents."[8] Restore sacred doctrine and form evangelizers who are authentic living witnesses of the Faith to impregnate and form the Saints of the third millennium.

In writing this book, I came across a short story that I think sets the context for this book's twofold theme. This story by Harold Gardiner, which appeared in *America* in December 1944, tells of a paratrooper in a plane who contemplates his mission to go into a world torn by war and battle to do good and to ultimately save lives. The serenity and clarity of his present position, high in the sky, is contrasted with the chaos, danger and suffering that he will soon encounter on the ground. But he has no regrets; he volunteered for this mission, he knows what it will cost, but he is confident of success. The story concludes:

> He rose and stepped to the edge... He looked out and up once more to the dear infinity of clarity and peace that he loved. He was to leave it for a while, but he

---

8 Sunday Angelus (7/24/05), Zenit News.

knew he would seek it out again, so it was not good-bye...

From out the high world of clearness and peace, rocketing down, down to the low world of murkiness and tumult — he leaped...

This story reflected in a symbolic way the moment a long time ago when God became man and was born of the Virgin Mary in Bethlehem, leaping from Heaven and coming among us to share the good news for our salvation, and ultimately to die for His cause.

This story, I think, also reflects our mission today to become paratroopers of faith who are called to leap into our world with the good news of truth and love. World War II is now long past, Bethlehem even longer, but this same mission still exists, and perhaps is more needed, for the world is more deprived today than ever before. This is the call to each and every person who reads this book, to imitate the divine Paratrooper — to be the good evangelizer who brings the good news of Christ's sacred doctrine into this modern world torn apart by a spiritual war of vast destruction, from within and from without. Our mission is to become today's paratroopers of Christ.

TO HOLD AND TEACH THE CATHOLIC FAITH

Biblical Abbreviations

OLD TESTAMENT

Genesis	Gn	Nehemiah	Ne	Baruch	Ba
Exodus	Ex	Tobit	Tb	Ezekiel	Ezk
Leviticus	Lv	Judith	Jdt	Daniel	Dn
Numbers	Nb	Esther	Est	Hosea	Ho
Deuteronomy	Dt	1 Maccabees	1 M	Joel	Jl
Joshua	Jos	2 Maccabees	2 M	Amos	Am
Judges	Jg	Job	Jb	Obadiah	Ob
Ruth	Rt	Psalms	Ps	Jonah	Jon
1 Samuel	1 S	Proverbs	Pr	Micah	Mi
2 Samuel	2 S	Ecclesiastes	Ec	Nahum	Na
1 Kings	1 K	Song of Songs	Sg	Habakkuk	Hab
2 Kings	2 K	Wisdom	Ws	Zephaniah	Zp
1 Chronicles	1 Ch	Sirach	Si	Haggai	Hg
2 Chronicles	2 Ch	Isaiah	Is	Malachi	Ml
Ezra	Ezr	Jeremiah	Jr	Zechariah	Zc
		Lamentations	Lm		

NEW TESTAMENT

Matthew	Mt	Ephesians	Eph	Hebrews	Heb
Mark	Mk	Philippians	Ph	James	Jm
Luke	Lk	Colossians	Col	1 Peter	1 P
John	Jn	1 Thessalonians	1 Th	2 Peter	2 P
Acts	Ac	2 Thessalonians	2 Th	1 John	1 Jn
Romans	Rm	1 Timothy	1 Tm	2 John	2 Jn
1 Corinthians	1 Cor	2 Timothy	2 Tm	3 John	3 Jn
2 Corinthians	2 Cor	Titus	Tt	Jude	Jude
Galatians	Gal	Philemon	Phm	Revelation	Rv

CHAPTER ONE

The Doctrinal Crisis in the Church Today

A. INTRODUCTION TO THE CURRENT ISSUES

Religious heterodoxy and dissent have always been present within Christian history and the history of salvation. Even from the beginning, the serpent twisted God's truth, saying to Eve, "You will not die. For God knows that when you eat of it [the fruit of the tree of good and evil] your eyes will be opened, and you will be like God, knowing good and evil" (Gn 3:4b-5). Later, the prophets warned of false teachers who "speak visions of their own minds, not from the mouth of the Lord" and who end up leading God's people "astray with their lies and their reckless-ness" (see Jr 23:9-40; also Dt 13:2-6; Jr 14:13-16; Ezk 13:1ff). Our Lord too repeatedly warned about the false teachers who will lead many to spiritual ruin (see Mt 24:11; Mk 13:22; Jn 10:12). They have been present even from the birth of the Church. St. Paul calls them *false brothers* and *false apostles* (Gal 2:4; 2 Cor 11:26; 1 Cor 11:13), and St. Peter calls them *false doctors* (2 P 2:1).[1] St. Jude says, "They pervert the grace of our God into licentiousness" (v. 4). From the time of the Arians as

---

[1] Commenting on 2 Peter 2:1, St. Hilary of Arles states: "They revile the way of truth because they have turned orthodox doctrine into heresy, or because they have rejected the rule [of faith] given to them at their baptism, or because they have abandoned the way of truth" (PL Supp. 3:110).

well, false doctrine has been present and re-presented throughout the Church's history.

Today, the spread of the sickness of erroneous religious teaching seems more prevalent than ever. One Saint spoke of the present times, saying, "Never has the world been so corrupt as it is now, for never has it been so cunning, so wise in its own way, and so crafty. It cleverly makes use of the truth to foster untruth, virtue to justify vice, and the very maxims of Jesus Christ to endorse its own so that even those who are wisest in the sight of God are often deceived."[2] There is a state of doctrinal and moral confusion in the Church that has resulted in part from the agendas of these planters of the cockle-seeds of erroneous teaching.[3] Analyzing the crux of today's crisis of faith, two theologians have recently felt compelled to conclude that for many today "Knowledge and acceptance of 'Catholic doctrine' itself [is] no longer universally considered to be an essential and indispensable requirement of being Catholic."[4]

When doctrinal error replaces orthodoxy (true content) and orthopraxis (right teaching method), dissent spreads as quickly as a plague. Suggesting what might be a cause of our modern

---

[2] Louis Marie de Montfort, *The Love of Eternal Wisdom*, from Rosemary Guiley, *The Quotable Saint* (New York: Checkmark Books, 2002), 39. St. Louis also taught that the worst times create the Church's greatest saints. In *True Devotion to Mary* (nos. 35, 46), St. Louis prophesied that the formation of the greatest saints of the end times would come from Mary; and the army of souls consecrated to Mary will be her instrument in defeating the Devil and his Antichrist. As Satan gains power in the world, so much more shall the new Eve, with her spiritual children, triumph over him and crush his head.

[3] See Mt 13:24-43. The Fathers of the Church understood this parable of Jesus to be a metaphor for false doctrine (St. John Chrysostom, *Homilies on St. Matthew*, 47; St. Augustine in *Catena Aurea*). Cockle-seed resembles wheat so closely that even farmers have difficulty distinguishing it from wheat until the stalks begin to mature; it is quite toxic to humans. Like the cockle-seed, false doctrine can be difficult to distinguish at first, for the devil likes to mask falsehood with truth (Chrysostom), but as the fruits become known, a small error in the beginning becomes a great one in the end (Aquinas).

[4] Msgr. Michael Wrenn and Kenneth D. Whitehead, *Flawed Expectations* (San Francisco: Ignatius Press, 1996), 36.

crisis, the Venerable Cardinal Newman a century ago described the consequence when a slacking off of morals is permitted among God's people, as follows: "When the spirit of morals of a people are materially debased, varieties of doctrinal error spring up as if self-sown, and are rapidly propagated."[5] A deprivation of doctrine has led to a crisis of morals.[6] A deprivation of morals has led to a crisis of faith. The crisis of faith has in turn led to the further decline of morals, and so the cycle is continuing.

Such was the case at the time of the first centuries of Christianity, and such is the situation of faith again today. Our Lord, through His living Word, warns us even today to "beware of false prophets, who come to [us] in sheep's clothing but inwardly are ravenous wolves" (cf. Mt 7:15-20). From among our own they present themselves as our teachers. We go to them for light but find darkness; for strength but find doubt and weakness; for truth but find lies. "The preachers of false reform and doctrine bring nothing but separation from the life-giving vine-stem of the Church, the bewilderment and perdition of souls…. In this gospel passage Our Lord warns us to be prudent and on our guard against these lying teachers and their deceitful doctrines. It is not always easy to detect them, for sometimes bad doctrine comes with the appearance of being good."[7] St. Paul speaks also concerning "some who trouble you and want to pervert the gospel of Christ," only to then boldly admonish, "But even if we, or an

---

[5] John Henry Newman, *The Arians of the Fourth Century* (London: n.p., 1833), 20.

[6] One does not have to look far to see the moral decay of the past forty years, which along with the watering-down and distortion of the doctrines of the Faith includes: the abandonment of Confession and the decline of worthy reception of the Eucharist, failure to accept and teach sexual morality that has also led to actively promoting contraception, the acceptance of divorce and the abuse of the annulment process, the neglect of parents in catechizing their children in the true Faith, the acceptance of hedonism including the practices of pornography, homosexuality, abortion, immoral reproductive techniques, and euthanasia.

[7] Francis Fernandez, *In Conversation with God*, vol. 3 (New York: Scepter, 1994), 659.

angel from heaven, should preach to you a gospel contrary to that [of Christ's Church], let him be accursed" (Gal 1:6-8).

This is the post-modern climate the Church finds herself in at the beginning of the third Christian millennium. Perhaps Newman foresaw our times when he bemoaned: "It is a miserable time when a man's Catholic profession is no voucher for his orthodoxy, and when a teacher of religion may be within the Church's pale, yet external to her faith."[8] And more recently, Paul VI saw our times concerning the crisis of doctrine as well, stating:

> This concern for the faithful preservation of Christian doctrine, which was given such a solemn declaration at the beginning of Vatican II, must continue abidingly in these times which have followed upon the same Council. Indeed, those who have received the mandate in the Church of God to propagate the Gospel message and to teach and guard the deposit of faith must do so even more vigilantly because the dangers for this same deposit have become both more numerous and more serious. In fact, we must say these dangers have become immense because the general mentality of the day is alienated from religion. But even more so because of a particular reason full of deceit: the fact that in the very bosom of the Church works of not a few teachers and writers have been published, which, while proposing to express Catholic teaching in new ways and modes, nevertheless frequently desire more to accommodate the dogmas of the Faith to profane patterns of thought and speech than to

---

[8] John Henry Cardinal Newman, *The Idea of a University*, Part II, University Subjects, "A Form of Infidelity of the Day," Section 2, Its Policy, no. 1 (London: Longmans, Green and Co., 1893), 392-393.

obey the norms of the Church's Magisterium. It results from this, and it is an opinion widely dissemi-
nated, that the principles of the true doctrine may be
neglected, and that each person by private judgment
and according to natural propensity may select what
each one wishes from the truths of the Faith, and reject the rest.[9]

In essence, according to Msgr. Eugene Kevane, what has happened today is the formation of "a *new hermeneutic* [*of doctrine*],
one which gives true doctrine a new meaning 'far from the genuine tradition of the Church.'"[10] These false teachers of faith are
most conspicuous because they indistinctively use a content
deprived of its legitimate sources.[11] James Hitchcock explains
in more detail the scenario of our day:

> ...the purpose of much of postconciliar religious edu-
> cation, whether recognized as such or not, has been
> to create a situation in which no one is deeply attached
> to any particular set of beliefs.... The doctrines for

---

[9] Paul VI, AAS (Nov. 30, 1967), 965-966. Such thinking has not abated in our day
either. Concerning the requirement for theology professors to teach in conformity
to the Magisterium, DePaul University (a Catholic college in Chicago) religious
studies professor Jeffrey Carlson stated in dissent, "In the university we proceed
from the idea that no idea stands alone. Certainly one of the voices should be the
official teachings developed by the magisterium of the Catholic Church.... But
we invite students to consider multiple candidates for truth." Quoted in Julia
Lieblich, "Catholic colleges mum on teacher 'loyalty oath,'" *Chicago Tribune* (June
7, 2002), Section 2, p. 11.

[10] Eugene Kevane, "Introduction," in *Teaching the Catholic Faith Today* (Boston: St.
Paul, 1982), lxiii (italics added).

[11] This may well be the case for theology as well as catechesis. John Paul II explains
that a theology devoid of its sources is no theology at all: theology is a rational
discipline whose "object is given by Revelation, handed on and interpreted in the
Church under the authority of the Magisterium, and received by faith. These giv-
ens have the force of principles. **To eliminate them would mean to cease doing
theology**" at all. CDF, *Donum Veritatis* (Vatican City, 1990), 12 (emphasis mine).

which so many martyrs have joyfully accepted death — the divinity of Christ, the Real Presence, the authority of the papacy — are now treated as speculations of a merely secondary importance, readily adjustable to fit the presumed needs of the time.[12]

Perhaps this crisis is most evident within the current state of catechesis (process of handing on the Faith). Catechetics (teaching teachers how to catechize) and catechesis itself are today, in many Catholic schools and dioceses, deficient of sound doctrine because some religion teachers are ignoring or rejecting the primary magisterial texts from which sacred doctrine is imparted. The Congregation for the Clergy's *General Directory for Catechesis* (GDC) summarizes the effects of the problem, stating, "Youth catechesis must be profoundly revised and revitalized... [because] the first victims of the spiritual and cultural crisis gripping the world are the young."[13] The GDC goes on to blame as one of the sources of the crisis, that of a "weakness in the catechesis which they have received."[14]

In recent decades, some teachers have been emphasizing relativistic, subjective, and/or overly experiential approaches to the Faith which focus on "a vapid, non-biblical, overly-psychologized catechesis that has reduced Jesus to a 'warm fuzzy.'"[15] Others have organized the Faith in such a way as to cause an over-compartmentalization of the various topics of the Faith within catechesis, emphasizing some doctrines, while de-empha-

---

[12] James Hitchcock, *Catholicism and Modernity* (New York: Seabury Press, 1979), 110-111.

[13] Congregation for the Clergy, *General Directory for Catechesis* (Washington, DC: USCC, 1998), 181.

[14] GDC 182.

[15] Francis D. Kelly, *The Mystery We Proclaim*, 2nd edition (Huntington: Our Sunday Visitor, 1993), 36.

sizing or outright omitting others.[16] As well, some have consciously chosen to turn their backs on the classical tradition, especially the Fathers of the Church, and our Hellenistic patrimony, particularly as contained in scholasticism.[17]

The result of this new approach has been a de-emphasizing of certain central doctrines of the Faith, ones that these catechists happen to disagree with, such that the impact of this "inadequate catechesis has been to produce in young people 'a new illiteracy' with regard not just to the information content of the faith but to its most basic and fundamental concepts" of doctrine.[18] Though some 'teachers' of the Faith have caused the doctrinal crisis of our day and even advocate further abnegation, the Church will not concede.[19]

---

[16] Ratzinger and Schönborn mention these issues in *Introduction to the Catechism*. Concerning over-compartmentalization, see page 7 of their book, which we will also discuss later in this book. Concerning overly experiential approaches, Ratzinger states, the faith is since the 1960s often presented as "selected reflections of partial anthropological experiences" (40-41).

[17] Avery Dulles, "Vatican II and Scholasticism," *New Oxford Review* 57 (May 1990), 8. He explains the reasons for this, which includes abuses in the following areas — pastoral emphasis, freedom, modernization, ecumenism, and inculturation.

[18] Francis D. Kelly, op. cit., 36.

[19] With regard to the Church Fathers (and Doctors), see DV 8. John Paul II stated as well, "There can be no true formation of Christian understanding without constantly drawing on the tradition of our Fathers in the faith.... One of the chief merits of the Fathers, and the reason for their permanent value, lies in their having perceived and demonstrated in their time the unity of the Old and New Testaments in the person of Christ... the Fathers are also responsible for the origin of theological reflection and the first great dogmatic formulations.... They were the first theologians, for they were able to examine the Mystery of Christ by drawing on ideas borrowed from the thought of their time...." (John Paul II, Address, Rome, 10/30/93).

B. A Crisis of Doctrine

Along with the great breath of fresh air (*aggiornamento*) that Vatican II brought to the Church and the authentic Vatican II reforms that came with it, there began almost immediately after the Council other forms of 'reform' that have since not been as fruitful. Many modernizers in the work of evangelization went too far in pursuit of change, seeking to transform their orbits of influence by conducting radical revisions of catechesis and theology based on the 'spirit of Vatican II' *as they understood it*, but really in ways Vatican II never authorized.[20] John Mallon, former editor of Oklahoma City's diocesan weekly, the *Sooner Catholic*, summarizes the snobbish attitude of superiority that prevails among modern religious dissenters:

> The implication is that if you accept the authority of the Magisterium you are an unthinking, unwashed peasant who is an embarrassment to the Catholic Church — at least the "American" Catholic Church.
>
> And this perhaps is what is most offensive about theological dissent: the inherent snobbery of it all. The smug attitude of superiority that reeks throughout the entire Culture of Dissent. The constant sniffing at the Chair of Peter as the source of Christ's authority on earth — which ultimately adds up to unbelief....
>
> The issue here is not open debate or even thoughtful criticism, but defiance.... The image of dissident

---

[20] Concerning the false spirit of Vatican II, see Michael J. Wrenn, *Catechisms and Controversies: Religious Education in the Postconciliar Years* (San Francisco: Ignatius Press, 1991), 51. Though *aggiornamento* was a true fruit of Vatican II, much of the crisis in theology and catechesis that has ensued since the Council is perhaps due to an imbalance of applying an *aggiornamento* approach while at the same time abandoning the primary sources of the Faith.

Catholics as crusading windmill-tippers is getting tiresome.[21]

Mallon points out also that today's dissenters often try to position themselves as self-proclaimed prophets being ignored or victimized by orthodox Catholics, who to them are the modern-day Pharisees. "A whole school of thought... strangely grew up after Vatican II that held that believing 'doctrine' was not only *not* essential to being a Christian but was in some sense an *obstacle* to being one. 'Doctrine', held to be arid and boring, was deliberately downplayed in religion books, and Christian 'experience' was substituted for it.... Doctrine, which was nothing else but a systematic statement and development of the saving truths Jesus had revealed, was nevertheless, somehow, 'out,'"[22] report Msgr. Michael Wrenn and Kenneth D. Whitehead in their book, *Flawed Expectations*, on the reception of the *Catechism of the Catholic Church* in the United States. But, as Archbishop Charles Chaput points out, while "becoming a Christian is never *merely* an act of loyalty to an institution, or agreeing with a body of doctrines... (Nevertheless) doctrines are vitally important because they organize, clarify, and ensure the proper transmission of God's truth... the teaching of the Church is the teaching of Christ."[23]

It's true that teaching the Faith in the decades leading up to Vatican II had in some circles focused legalistically more on memorizing long question-and-answer lists of the doctrines of the Faith than on living in a personal relationship with Jesus

---

[21] "The Thomas Reese Affair," *Inside the Vatican* magazine, June 2005.
[22] Wrenn and Whitehead, 36.
[23] *Living the Catholic Faith* (Cincinnati: Servant, 2001), 16.

Christ, assisted by theological faith.[24] Thus, these original reformers sought to address this real problem in pre-Vatican II catechesis by organizing a renewal. Unfortunately though, things did not go as originally planned. As with many reforms, the imbalance of emphasis on the one extreme — rote memorization over internalization and conversion — was simply, though perhaps unintentionally at first, replaced with another extreme — an over-emphasis on personal, experiential self-awareness and growth accompanied by a relativistic perspective of God that neglected the reality and importance of His Revelation and of the Church's doctrine.

Noted theologian, Dr. Scott Hahn, discusses certain pivotal theologians in the United States during this period "whose writings at times seemed to reflect a somewhat reactionary antischolastic attitude [of whom]... [t]he most influential, catalytic figure is undoubtedly Gabriel Moran."[25] Hahn states that such theologians emphasized an "ongoing revelation" with stress on "personal experience" within catechesis, as exemplified by Moran's *Design for Religion*. In this book, Moran gives a description of Revelation that fails to acknowledge the divine source of Tradition, stating: "None of the statements, including those in the bible or church councils, is God's revelation."[26] Instead, Moran elsewhere defines Revelation as merely "the conscious

---

[24] It is important in this context to make a distinction between theological faith and personal belief. "[Theological] *faith is a gift from God, a supernatural virtue infused by Him....* Believing with [theological] faith is possible only by grace and the interior helps of the Holy Spirit.... Trusting in God and cleaving to the truths he has revealed are contrary neither to human freedom nor to human reason.... [Faith requires] full submission of... intellect and will to God who reveals" and to the truths of his Church (CCC 153-154). "The distinction between *theological faith* and *belief*... must be *firmly held*. If [theological] faith is acceptance in grace of revealed truth... then [personal faith or] belief... is religious experience still in search of the absolute truth and still lacking assent to God who reveals himself" (Congregation for the Doctrine of the Faith, *Dominus Iesus* (2000), #7).
[25] Scott Hahn, "Prima Scriptura," *The Church and the Universal Catechism.* Ed. by Anthony Mastroeni (Steubenville: Franciscan U. Press, 1992), 106-107.
[26] Gabriel Moran, *Design for Religion* (New York: Herder and Herder, 1971), 46.

experience of people" in the Church today.[27] The emphasis on this approach, that of what Stuart Swetland has called "an insipid, creedless, doctrineless, non-cognitive catechesis,"[28] has become normative in some modern catechetical circles. According to Msgr. Swetland: "Due to the influence of prominent religious educators like Gabriel Moran the idea of ongoing revelation became accepted by the catechetical establishment."[29]

The statistics are alarming[30] and the results are startling, as exemplified by Nancy Nos in an April 1992 article in *First Things* entitled "Teach Me: A Catholic *Cri de Coeur.*" She writes, "...the Catholic Church in the United States is committing suicide through refusal to educate its people.... We do not know even the fundamentals of our religion." Msgr. George A. Kelly, author of *Who Should Run the Church: Social Scientists, Theologians or Bishops*, sums up the game plan of these new catechists when he states: "The great cop-out of this era is not to answer questions [of faith and morals] at all. This explains the great decline of catechisms [from the 1970s through the 1990s]. They provide answers which some of us do not like."[31]

The result of this organized catechetical revolution, however, has been the establishing of a 'new catechesis' that has become in effect, not a solution to a problem, but its antithesis:

---

[27] Gabriel Moran, *Theology of Revelation* (New York: Herder and Herder, 1966), 120.

[28] Stuart Swetland, "Catechetical Content for Our Culture," *The Church and the Universal Catechism* (Steubenville: Franciscan U. Press, 1992), 124. For an example of this approach in practice, see Thomas Bokenkotter, *Essential Catholicism: Dynamics of Faith and Belief* (New York: Doubleday, 1985), 34-38.

[29] Swetland, 126.

[30] Ibid., 120. Some examples include the following: a late 1980s study by the National Catholic Education Association (NCEA) showed how high school juniors and seniors scored in the four areas tested: Christian Doctrine 59%, Christian Life 65%, Sacred Scripture 61%, Religious Terms 59%; and a 1992 Gallup poll showed that only 30% of Catholics could identify the correct Catholic understanding of Jesus' Real Presence in the Eucharist when confronted with a choice between Catholic, Baptist, Lutheran, and Calvinist statements of doctrine.

[31] George Kelly, *Who Should Run the Church: Social Scientists, Theologians or Bishops?* (Huntington, IN: Our Sunday Visitor, 1976), 167.

no longer is emphasis placed on doctrine at all, much less memorizing it. Some proponents of the new catechesis have gone so far as to shun all doctrine-based instruction as antithetical to the proper development of the students' spiritual prosperity. Others have tried to adopt fashionable importations from secular culture which have been in reality more cultural relativism than authentic inculturation.[32] In this period, religious formation being previously called the Confraternity of Christian Doctrine (CCD) was renamed in many circles Continuing Christian Education (CCE). Perhaps to some of these revolutionists, the change from 'D' to 'E' was a change from emphasis on objective "doctrine" to that of subjective and relativistic personal "experience," which for them even sought to render doctrine irrelevant.

One of the pioneers of this new catechetical movement, Father Gerard S. Sloyan, a mentor of Gabriel Moran, has criticized the traditional doctrine-based "textbook catechetics" as having been "removed from the spirit of Christ's preaching, slightly repellant to the youthful mind."[33]

Father Berard Marthaler, a contributor to *The Universal Catechism Reader* (1990, edited by Thomas J. Reese, SJ) — a text on the philosophy of the modern catechetical movement which was organized to criticize the new *Catechism of the Catholic Church* — criticized the "old style" of catechizing by stating that "more is required of Christian education than the handing on of shopworn formulas, tired customs, and trite devotions."[34]

---

[32] Msgr. Wrenn explains: "Religious education too often has been compromised, as too often theology has been compromised over the same period (since *Humanae Vitae* was issued), by fashionable importations from 'the world'; these importations have not always been compatible with the authentic Catholic faith as handed down" (*Catechisms and Controversies*, 76).

[33] Father Gerard S. Sloyan, "Religious Education: From Early Christianity to Medieval Times," in Michael Warren, ed., *Sourcebook for Modern Catechetics* (Winona, MN: St. Mary's Press, 1983), 127.

[34] Father Berard Marthaler, "The Modern Catechetical Movement in Roman Catholicism: Issues and Personalities," in ibid., 278. Father Thomas Reese, SJ, mentioned here, resigned as editor of *America* magazine in protest to the election of Cardinal

These proponents of the new catechesis have rejected the traditional methodology of a doctrine-based approach to catechesis. One influential text used to train catechists in this period dismissed the use of doctrine by stating, "Teachers realize that today's adolescents will not accept canned truths.... One cannot 'teach them religion' in the sense of inculcating any kind of Catholic ready answers."[35] Together, these proponents of the new catechesis have sought a new form of catechesis essentially devoid of doctrine, whereby formulas and devotions have been sidelined in the modern catechetical movement.

The primacy of the need for objective divine Revelation in the ministry of catechesis began to be sidelined as well shortly after Vatican II. One of the General Conclusions of the International Catechetical Study Week (1968) in Medellin, Colombia, for example, shifted the focus from Revelation to personal subjective aspirations, stating:

> Catechetics today, in accordance with a more adequate theology of Revelation, realizes that the first place to look when seeking God's design for contemporary man is the area of history and authentically human aspirations. These are an *indispensable part* of the contents of catechetics.[36]

This statement, while properly inductive in its catechetical focus, also shows evidence of the beginning of a new *emphasis* that began at this time within the catechetical endeavor, namely on

---

Ratzinger as Pope Benedict XVI in April 2005, and also following a letter from the CDF requesting his resignation for having been a long-time advocate of the dissent.

[35] Mary Perkins Ryan, ed., *Helping Adolescents Grow Up in Christ* (New York: Paulist Press/Deus Books, 1967), Foreword.

[36] Luis Erdozain, "The Evolution of Catechetics: A Survey of Six International Study Weeks on Catechetics," in Warren, ed., *Sourcebook*, 101.

an anthropocentric approach to faith development. Though the inductive method is a valid approach to catechesis, however, the shift of emphasis upon it later went too far, leading to a de-emphasis of the objective doctrine and moral truth of God's authoritative Revelation and instead focusing on man's aspirations of who *he thinks* God is and what *he thinks* God wants from a subjectivist and relativistic perspective. Such new perspectives eventually led to a further crisis "in which catechesis was reduced to a species of 'pop psychology.'"[37]

Catechesis has been in a state of crisis, as Wrenn and Whitehead explain in *Flawed Expectations*, because "The truths and indeed the relevance of many of the Church's ancient beliefs [are] increasingly being subjected to widespread denigration and even denial, often from inside as well as from outside the Church.... [S]ome of these Neomodernists [view] already established and firm Church *doctrines* as out of date and as hindrances to the Church's relationships with the modern world and with other Christians."[38]

All of this considered, it may be acknowledged that the dissemination of heresy sometimes has had a positive effect upon the development of doctrine itself. It is as if God had a plan despite the attempts of religious dissenters, as St. Paul explains: "We know that in everything God works for good with those who love him" (Rm 8:28). As in past centuries, in the current crisis of faith, widespread erroneous teachings have actually become the impetus used by the Church to sharpen and clarify her doctrine and have become opportunities for her to grow in her understanding of revealed truth. John Hardon, SJ, discusses the contribution of heresy to the development of doctrine, stating, "There is a mysterious sense in which we can thank God's providence for drawing so much good and so much depth of truth

---

[37] Francis D. Kelly, 30-31.
[38] Wrenn and Whitehead, *Flawed Expectations*, 25, 29.

from the errors promulgated by those who deny a mystery of the faith. In God's providence, each error provided an opportunity for the Church's teaching to become even more clear and more specific. In other words, heresy has contributed immensely to the sanctification of the Church."[39] This being so, the crisis itself has been a reality far too troubling for the Church to ignore.

Since the time these new approaches have begun to be introduced, together with their new methods, the Church has attempted to counter their influence by issuing official catechetical documents addressing these issues. One such magisterial document, the *Credo of the People of God* (1968), is a comprehensive profession of the Faith, by Pope Paul VI, for our modern times. But, as usual, its reception was mixed. A *Commonweal* Magazine editorial in July 1968 summed up the reaction of some of the catechetical groups in the United States at that time:

> There cannot be many Catholic biblical theologians left who would be willing to speak of an 'original offense' committed by someone named 'Adam.' There cannot be many sacramental theologians left who would say that the doctrine of the real presence is 'very appropriately called by the Church transubstantiation.' There cannot be many liturgists to glorify adoration of the 'Blessed Host.' There cannot be many ecclesiologists left who would give the biblical image of the Church as 'Body of Christ' primacy over other images. There cannot be many dogmatic theologians left who would care to speak of those who refuse God's love and pity as 'going to the fire that will not extinguish.' In sum, there cannot be many theologians left who would be able to assent to a message and a

---

[39] *With Us Today* (Ypsilanti, MI: Ave Maria University Communications, 2000), 17.

'new Credo' whose content not only fails to reflect even Vatican II, but even more fails to admit what has happened to theology since then.[40]

The content of catechesis in the United States began in some ways to be no longer in the hands of the teaching authority of the Church, but began to be greatly influenced by outspoken religious leaders in the theological and catechetical arena, as their reaction to *Humanae Vitae* would also demonstrate later in that same year. While it is a welcomed occurrence for the laity to have gotten involved in Church leadership, beginning in the 1970s, some of their new philosophies ultimately worked to change the course and content of many religious texts used in teaching the Catholic Faith for decades to come.[41]

Again, the Apostolic See responded by issuing the *General Catechetical Directory* (1971), which had been previously mandated by the Fathers of Vatican II.[42] The GCD emphasized the importance of assimilation, memorization, and a cognitive learning of the sacred doctrines of the Faith. It spoke of "errors which are not infrequently noted in catechetics today… [which can be] avoided only if one starts with the correct way to understanding the nature and purpose of catechesis and also the truths which are to be taught by it."[43]

But the American catechetical leaders responded to the Apostolic See quickly, and thus exposed their own agenda, by mis-

---

[40] Editorial, "The Pope's New 'Credo'", in *Commonweal*, July 12, 1968.

[41] For details on a study on doctrinal errors and deficiencies prevalent in religion textbook series in the United States in 1970 (discussing texts published by W.H. Sadlier, Benzinger Brothers, Allyn and Bacon, and the Paulist Press), see *Our New Catechisms: A Critical Analysis* (New Rochelle, NY: Catholics United for the Faith, December 8, 1970).

[42] Vatican Council II, *Christus Dominus* (1965), 44.

[43] Congregation for the Clergy, *General Catechetical Directory* (Washington, DC: United States Catholic Conference, 1971), Foreword.

interpreting the GCD, claiming that it advocated "another step away from book-centered catechesis by twice stating that the role of catechists is more important than texts."[44] The catechetical directors of the National Conference of Diocesan Directors of Religious Education (NCDDRE) also responded to the GCD by publishing their own commentary on it, called *Focus on American Catechetics: A Commentary on the General Catechetical Directory* (1972). While claiming that the GCD contained simply the "theological viewpoints" of some, they stressed that it was not official Church "legislation." The NCDDRE document went on to claim that Revelation is a "process" that evolves, and that the educator should "not see his task as primarily transmitting unspoiled doctrines from the deep freeze of the past, but rather as helping the student reflect on *his own experience.*"[45]

Their views expressed a major shift from sound doctrine to relativistic experience as the focus of catechesis. *Focus* went on to claim, "while there may remain some confusion in regard to the GCD's position on the use of [doctrinal] formulas, it is evident that the document does not intend that educators return to the discredited methodology of yesteryear."[46] They essentially re-worded the official Church document to state exactly what the document did not intend to be stated — namely, that doctrine is to be sidelined and replaced with the process of discovering God primarily through one's own personal experiences. Then, at the end of the commentary, *Focus* made various suggestions in its Notes section (pp. 100-101) on further reading which provided a list of other questionable theologians, like

---

[44] Father Berard Marthaler, "The Genesis and Genius of the *General Catechetical Directory*," in Warren, *Sourcebook*, 253.

[45] Revs. Thomas F. Sullivan and John F. Meyers, *Focus on American Catechetics: A Commentary on the General Catechetical Directory* (Washington, DC: National Catholic Education Association's National Conference of Diocesan Directors of Religious Education, 1972), 24-25, emphasis added.

[46] Wrenn, *Catechisms and Controversies*, 169.

Father Charles E. Curran, a professor at Catholic University of America until he was dismissed as a result of the decision of the Congregation of the Doctrine of the Faith that he was no longer a Catholic theologian; Gregory Baum concerning the topic of revelation, emphasizing the notion of an "ongoing" revelation; John Dedek in support of the fundamental option theory; and Richard P. McBrien who argues that the Church and the Kingdom are not synonymous.

Following the style of *Focus*, shortly afterwards, the United States Catholic Conference published *A Study Aid for Basic Teachings for Catholic Religious Education* (1974). It consisted of a list of recommended books for religious educators. A sampling of its authors contains some well-known dissenting theologians like Gabriel Moran who writes: "Christ does not supply any ready made answers for the questions of contemporary man.... He gives no revealed doctrines about God nor any revealed precepts for leading a proper life"; Bernard J. Cooke who writes: "Christian faith is not the acceptance of a body of doctrines nor is it the observance of laws"; Gerard S. Sloyan who writes: "Seeking moral guidance through our Roman Catholic Church alone is an appeal which we are not wise to make in any Christian matter, doctrinal or moral"; Piet Schoonenberg, who writes about original sin: "The notion that the whole human race has descended from one couple seems a presupposition based on an outdated picture of the world," which thus leads to a discrediting of the doctrine of original sin; and Robert Nowell who writes: "The very existence of the devil and his attendant demons, and thus the existence of a class of damned persons other than human beings, has now become open to question."[47] These are a sample of the theologians and their views from the recommended reading list of this catechetical "study aid." And for some scholars,

---

[47] Ibid., 175-176.

initial *dissidence* later lead to outright public *deviance* to Church doctrine.[48]

Many catechetical texts were greatly influenced by these new theologies. One such student religion textbook, *Christ among Us* (1975), by Anthony Wilhelm, was popular for about a decade until the Congregation for the Doctrine of the Faith (CDF) requested that the book's *Imprimatur* be removed. Harper and Row decided immediately to republish the book, and it has continued to sell very well, and has been called "the nation's most widely used introduction to Catholicism" by the *New York Times* and "a fine piece of scholarship" by the Catholic News Service of the United States Bishops, as portrayed in a *Commonweal* magazine ad in 1990.[49]

When the United States Bishops issued the *National Catechetical Directory, Sharing the Light of Faith* (1979) a few years later, the authors of *Focus on American Catechetics*, the NCDDRE, again published a commentary, called *Discussion Guide to Sharing the Light of Faith*, in which they raised issues, this time concerning the NCD's teachings, and then went on to counter its statements by suggesting other dissenting perspectives for recommended reading.[50]

---

[48] From 1978-1980, dissident sexual ethics "scholar" Anthony Kosnik, who wrote *Human Sexuality* (Paulist Press, 1977) and later left the priesthood was listed by the USCC as an ethics contributor. His views included that "fornication, adultery, homosexuality, sodomy, and bestiality" were not "intrinsically evil acts," but merely "sexual taboos." He fought for his cause even through 2004, when he picketed publicly outside a church in Michigan in favor of same-sex marriage. Also included were Fr. Kevin O'Rourke (who supported euthanasia; he became a well-known advocate for the removal of nutrition and hydration from cognitively disabled people who are not otherwise dying, as with the well-known case of Terri Schiavo in Florida in May 2005) and Sidney Callahan (who became an advocate for homosexual marriage in 1994 and for contraception after being part of the Papal Birth Control Commission advising Paul VI not to write *Humanae Vitae*). These three participated as Catholic theologians in the USCC sponsored Reformed-Catholic Dialogue during this time, which lead to the publication of *Ethics and the Search for Christian Unity* (1980).

[49] Ibid., 124-125.

[50] See ibid., 186-193.

With all of this in the air in the United States at the end of the 1970s, a new pope was elected who would soon show a great interest and influence in catechesis. Soon after becoming Pope, John Paul II issued his Apostolic Exhortation, *On Catechesis in Our Time* (*Catechesi Tradendae*, 1979) to begin to address the crisis within contemporary catechesis. In this document, he states:

> One of the major features of the renewal of catechetics today is the rewriting and multiplication of catechetical books taking place in many parts of the Church today.... But it must be humbly and honestly recognized that this rich flowering has brought with it articles and publications which are ambiguous and harmful to young people and to the life of the Church... and catechetical works which bewilder the young and even adults, either by deliberately or unconsciously omitting elements essential to the Church's faith, or by attributing excessive importance to certain themes at the expense of others, or, chiefly, by a rather horizontalist overall view out of keeping with the teaching of the Church's magisterium.[51]

The Church has not been oblivious to the sentiments of these modern catechists and theologians. John Paul II also commented on theologians' lack of faith in catechism-based doctrinal evangelization in *Crossing the Threshold of Hope*, saying: "Some theologians, at times whole groups, spread the notion that there was no longer a need for a catechism, that it was an obsolete means of handing down the faith, and therefore should be

---

[51] John Paul II, Apostolic Exhortation: *On Catechesis in Our Time* [*Catechesi Tradendae*] (1979), 49.

abandoned."[52] And this observation is from the Great Initiator of the New Evangelization, who himself has been called "[t]he greatest evangelist in recent times," according to Cardinal Cipriano Calderón, former vice president of the Pontifical Council for Latin America.[53] Cardinal Calderón also has termed John Paul II the "Angel of the New Evangelization, of the planetary evangelization." John Paul, the hero of modern evangelization, clearly saw the great necessity of catechism-based doctrine for success in handing on the Faith in our times. As the greatest Catholic hero of youth in modern times, at the 1993 World Youth Day in Denver, he told the young people: *"Do not be afraid* to go out on the streets and into public places like the first apostles who preached Christ and the good news of salvation in the squares of cities, towns and villages. This is no time to be ashamed of the Gospel.... It is the time to preach it from the rooftops."[54]

But even after the *Catechism of the Catholic Church* was issued, and despite its being a bestseller among the faithful, the catechetical establishment's reaction in the United States was less than enthusiastic. One example of their handling of this was the issuing of a commentary and supplemental video series on the *Catechism* by Brennan Hill and William Madges, two professors of the theology department at Xavier University in Cincinnati, Ohio. Their book, *The Catechism: Highlights and Commentary*,[55] re-published in part in *The Religion Teacher's Journal*, and hailed by *The Catechist* magazine, was written with the self-proclaimed goal of placing "the teachings of the *Catechism* into

---

[52] John Paul II, *Crossing the Threshold of Hope* (New York: Alfred A. Knopf, 1994), 164-165.

[53] ZENIT News (April 16, 2005).

[54] Accessed online at http://www.catholic.org/printer_friendly.php?id=2049&section =Featured+Today (April 16, 2005).

[55] Brennan Hill and William Madges, *The Catechism: Highlights and Commentary* (Mystic, CT: Twenty-Third Publications, 1994).

dialogue with other trends in contemporary theology," while in actuality, distorting the meaning of much of the *Catechism* itself.[56]

To address the doctrinal crisis in America, the United States Bishops have followed the lead of the Apostolic See in reforming the field of catechesis, establishing the Ad Hoc Committee to Oversee the Use of the Catechism, later becoming the Office

---

[56] Wrenn and Whitehead, 172; Chapter 5 of their book is a critique of the Hill and Madges commentary. Concerning this commentary, Wrenn and Whitehead conclude: "Unfortunately, the circumstances are not normal when what purports to be a 'commentary' on an authoritative Church document actually serves to undermine and even contradict the same document — and nevertheless remains perhaps one of the most recommended and frequently used of all instruments in the United States for training DREs, teachers, and catechists in the significance and contents of the *Catechism*.... This is a situation that should be considered intolerable by the Church" (186).

Other *Catechism* commentaries that are critiqued as seriously flawed by Wrenn and Whitehead in detailed chapters of their book, *Flawed Expectations*, include *Commentary on the Catechism of the Catholic Church*, edited by Michael Walsh (Collegeville, MN: Liturgical Press, 1994), in Chapter 6; *Exploring the Catechism*, written by Jane E. Regan et al. (Collegeville, MN: Liturgical Press, 1994) and *The New Catechism: Analysis and Commentary*, edited by Andrew Murray (Manly, Australia: Catholic Institute of Sydney, 1994) in Chapter 7; and *The People's Catechism: Catholic Faith for Adults*, edited by Raymond Lucker et al. (New York: Crossroad, 1995) in Chapter 8.

Having provided examples of flawed commentaries, it is important also to mention that there have been several *Catechism* commentaries published in English since 1994 that are faithful to the *Catechism*. Some include: *Essentials of the Faith: A Guide to the Catechism of the Catholic Church*, by Alfred McBride, O Praem (Huntington, IN: OSV, 1994), *A Concise Companion & Commentary for the New Catholic Catechism*, by James Tolhurst (Leominister, Herefordshire, United Kingdom: Gracewing and Westminister, MD: Christian Classics, 1994), *The Splendor of Doctrine: The Catechism of the Catholic Church on Christian Believing*, by Aidan Nichols, OP (Edinburgh, Scotland: T&T Clark, 1995), *New Vision, New Directions: Implementing the Catechism of the Catholic Church*, by Robert J. Hater (Allen, TX: Thomas More, 1994), *The New Catholic Catechism: Workshop Resources*, by Sr. Mary Ann Johnston (Washington, DC: NCEA, nd), *A Moment of Grace*, by Cardinal John O'Connor (San Francisco: Ignatius Press, 1995), *The Faith*, by John A. Hardon, SJ (Ann Arbor: Charis, 1995), *The Truth Will Set You Free*, by Michael Mazza (West Allis, WI: Veritas Press, 1995), *The Love That Never Ends: A Key to the Catechism of the Catholic Church*, by J.A. DiNoia, OP, et al. (Huntington, IN: OSV, 1996), *Catholic Christianity: A Complete Catechism on Catholic Beliefs Based on the Catechism of the Catholic Church*, by Peter Kreeft (San Francisco: Ignatius Press, 2001) and *Living the Catechism of the Catholic Church* 4 vols., by Christoph Schönborn, OP (San Francisco: Ignatius Press, 1995-2002), *Living the Catholic Faith*, by Charles Chaput, OFM Cap. (Cincinnati: Servant, 2001).

for the Catechism. Among its responsibilities,[57] this Office evaluates the various catechetical publishers' resources to verify if they are in conformity with the Church's doctrine and with the *Catechism of the Catholic Church*. Although the Office publishes only a list of catechetical texts which they have actually approved, they have made it known that they have discovered a pattern of doctrinal deficiencies and errors, which they state is rather common among the catechetical series they have reviewed. Archbishop Daniel Buechlein, Consultant to the Office, while addressing the June 1997 General Assembly of Bishops, listed ten such deficiencies,[58] which are summarized as follows:

1. There is insufficient attention to the Trinity and the Trinitarian structure of Catholic beliefs and teachings.
2. There is an obscured presentation of the centrality of Christ in salvation history and an insufficient emphasis on the divinity of Christ.
3. There has been an indistinct treatment of the ecclesial context of Catholic beliefs and magisterial teachings.
4. There is an inadequate sense of a distinctively Christian anthropology.
5. There is insufficient emphasis on God's initiative in the world with a corresponding overemphasis on human action.

---

[57] The objectives of the Office for the Catechism are:
   1. To advise the bishops on matters related to the *Catechism of the Catholic Church*;
   2. To review works that use the copyrighted text of the *Catechism* as to their consistency with the *Catechism*;
   3. To oversee the use of the *Catechism of the Catholic Church*, especially in the revision of catechetical materials presently in use and in the development of new catechetical materials. This is accomplished by the review of catechetical materials voluntarily submitted to the Ad Hoc Committee as to their conformity with the *Catechism of the Catholic Church*;
   4. To monitor the feasibility and advisability of developing a national catechism/ catechetical series;
   5. To oversee the development of the national adult catechism.
[58] Archbishop Daniel Buechlein, *Oral Report to the General Assembly of Bishops,* June 19, 1997, [Document on line] http://www.nccbuscc.org/catechism/document/ oralrpt.htm (Internet), accessed July 24, 2001.

6. There has been an insufficient recognition of the transforming effects of grace.
7. There has been an inadequate presentation of the Sacraments.
8. There is a deficiency in the teaching on original sin and sin in general.
9. There has been only a meager exposition of Christian moral life.
10. There has been an inadequate presentation of eschatology.

The Bishops' Committee also notified catechetical publishers in November 1998 that certain usages of terms that are in conformity with the *Catechism* would have to be observed in order to obtain approval.[59] They include:

1. The use of Personal pronouns for God like "He."
2. The use of "Old" and "New" for each division of the Bible instead of Hebrew and Christian.
3. The use of BC (before Christ) and AD (*Anno Domini*) instead of BCE (before the Common Era) and CE (Common Era).
4. The specific statement of the need for First Penance before First Holy Communion in texts that address this topic.

Many catechetical publishers in the United States have reacted to the bishops' call for conformity of doctrine with enthusiasm, rewriting their previous texts or publishing new ones.[60]

---

[59] http://www.nccbuscc.org/catechism/update/update1st.htm (Internet), accessed January, 2002.

[60] A complete listing of approved texts can be found at http://www.usccb.org/catechism/index.htm, and clicking the most recent *Catechism Update* (Internet), accessed July, 2005. For a discussion of specific catechetical texts which contain errors and deficiencies since the *Catechism*'s release, and specifically analyzing these 14 points, see my doctoral dissertation: *The Holy Keeping and Faithful Exposition of the Deposit of Faith: A Hermeneutic of Sacred Doctrine within the Ministry of Catechesis*, Angelicum, Rome, 2002.

Along with the *Catechism,* and to give Catholics and non-Catholics more easy access to the basic and essential tenets of the Catholic Faith, in 2005, the Holy See issued the *Compendium of the Catechism of the Catholic Church.* The United States Bishops' Office for the Catechism has also sought to contribute to the renewal of catechesis by seeking to issue a National Adult Catechism and a National General Directory, with the goal of adapting their corresponding Magisterial documents (the CCC and the GDC) to the different socio-cultural-ecclesial contexts of the United States and to the peculiar characterizations of different age-groups (child, adult, elderly), as well as to various pedagogical factors and methodological and didactic applications. But, as some in the catechetical field have initially responded with discontent, having hoped for their revisionist perspectives to be included in these newer Church documents, others have understood the harmony between these documents and the *Catechism* itself. Soon after Pope Benedict XVI presented the *Compendium,* Msgr. Scenico, head of the Congregation for the Doctrine of the Faith's office of catechesis spoke about this, saying: "The Church [has] a duty to proclaim the faith incarnated by Jesus Christ: 'Go and preach, I will be with you' — this is what Christ said. To presume that the Church should say something else (in the *Compendium* than she did in the *Catechism*) would be to misunderstand the reality of the Church. And if the Church did not behave according to what she has received from Jesus Christ, then she would betray Jesus Christ."[61]

Such desires for 'alternative' catechesis and attempts to introduce such perspectives to the faithful have not been limited to the United States. The Dutch Catechism (*De Nieuwe Katechismus*), published in 1966 and sold in the United States as *A New Catechism: Catholic Faith for Adults,* was one of the first texts of the new catechesis. Concerning its flaws, a Vatican

---

[61] Interview, *National Catholic Register* (7/17/05), 10.

commission of cardinals eventually issued a 10-point declaration of required changes needed to correct the deficiencies and errors regarding doctrines that were misstated, distorted, or omitted in this catechism of the Netherlands.[62] According to Msgr. Wrenn, "These ten points constitute practically a summary of some of the major doctrinal errors of the present day [and] would appear in many places in the ensuing years, especially in some of the new religion textbooks."[63]

With the onslaught of doctrinally deficient catechetical materials that have been published since the 1960s, one wonders what has been the underlying agenda of these proponents of the new catechesis.

---

[62] "Declaration on 'A New Catechism'" was issued by the papal commission of cardinals on October 15, 1968, and is summarized in Wrenn, *Catechisms and Controversies*, 144-146. The ten subject headings are as follows:
1. Points Concerning God the Creator — that He created human souls and a realm for the angels.
2. The Fall of Man in Adam — clearly stating that man rebelled against God in the beginning.
3. The Conception of Jesus by the Virgin Mary — regarding the perpetual virginity of Mary.
4. The "Satisfaction" Made by Christ Our Lord — this doctrine needed to be proposed without ambiguity.
5. The Sacrifice of the Cross and the Sacrifice of the Mass — clearly stating that the Sacrifice of the Cross is perpetuated in the Eucharistic Sacrifice.
6. The Eucharistic Presence and the Eucharistic Change — regarding the doctrine of transubstantiation, the consecration of bread and wine into the very Body and Blood of Christ.
7. The Infallibility of the Church and the Knowledge of Revealed Mysteries — regarding the truth in maintaining the doctrine of the Faith and explaining it always in the same sense.
8. The Ministerial or Hierarchical Priesthood and the Power of Teaching in the Church — regarding that participation in the priesthood of Christ by the ordained which differs in essence from the priesthood of the faithful; the teaching authority belongs directly to the Holy Father and the bishops joined to him in hierarchical communion.
9. Various Points concerning Dogmatic Theology — regarding the contemplation of the trinity, the efficacy of the sacraments, and the souls of the just in purgatory.
10. Certain points of Moral Theology — regarding the existence of moral laws, which bind our consciences always and in all circumstances; regarding conjugal morality and the indissolubility of marriage.

[63] Ibid., 146.

C. Toward a Solution to the Crisis of Faith

At the heart of today's crisis of faith[64] is the place of doctrine and its role in spreading the Faith. Many catechetical leaders in the United States have been undermining the meaning and redefining the function of doctrine, while instead emphasizing a creedless, content-less, non-cognitive, and non-deductive form of overly-experiential catechesis. This new form of teaching is not one that emphasizes the shared living witness of the teacher in relationship with the living God and His Church, but instead relies excessively on the subjective, autonomous, and personal experience of the teacher, and on those of the individuals being taught. Though experience is a vital aspect of good pedagogy, and "catechesis should be concerned with making men attentive to their more significant experiences,"[65] the problem with such an imbalance of emphasis is that it neglects a more important pedagogical necessity, namely that catechesis "also has the duty of placing under the Gospel the questions which arise from those experiences, so that there may be stimulated within men a right desire to transform their ways of life."[66] "Education in faith," as Ratzinger (Pope Benedict XVI) and Schönborn explain, "is more than merely 'experience,' 'existential concern' and 'emotional awareness'";[67] it must be impregnated with objective Revelation in the form of doctrinal truth, systematically presented with the love of Christ (Eph 4:15).

Authentic catechesis concerns itself with *both* personal experience and the living Word of God. Essentially, catechesis "must be illumined by the light of revelation."[68] Catechesis must

---

[64] For a summary of the issues surrounding the crisis of faith, see Ratzinger's *Introduction to Christianity*, Chapter 1.

[65] GCD 74.

[66] Ibid.

[67] Ratzinger and Schönborn, *Introduction to the Catechism*, 55.

[68] GCD 74.

also strive to maintain a balance between orthopraxis (right practice) and orthodoxy (true belief). About this, John Paul II explained: "It is also quite useless to campaign for the abandonment of serious and orderly study of the message of Christ in the name of a method concentrating on life experience.... Authentic catechesis is always an orderly and systematic initiation into the revelation" of God.[69] Such is the proper function of catechesis, the balance of doctrine and experience, one that was so masterfully exemplified in the past by great teachers like St. Thomas Aquinas.

Advocates of this new form of catechesis have sought to omit from their catechesis much of the Deposit of Faith, the doctrines of the Faith as found in the Church's catechetical resources and catechisms, seeing them as outdated — left over from a failed pre-Vatican II system of teaching. This kind of thinking is exemplified by the following writing from a catechetical professional who has a doctorate in religious education:

> Those who still stand by the catechism are finding it lonely business. Religious educators simply have found better ways, such as using films and filmstrips, devising new printed materials, new audio-visuals, new tapes, and creating a variety of other learning tools in great bulk which take more account of life experiences [and] new theological insights. A number of new trends have made the catechism obsolete as a teaching tool, especially for the young. Some of these are... the trend toward much later first confession (because) the whole doctrine of sin is undergoing extensive revision. Morality is being rethought and teachers aren't so quick to portray human actions as right or wrong, and if wrong, as seriously wrong. Religious education

---

[69] CT 22.

is more people-oriented, stressing charity and personal
commitment to people rather than faith in abstract
doctrines.[70]

Unfortunately, one resulting effect of thirty years of this
new catechesis is that there has been a "Missing Person" in
catechesis,[71] and without Him and His message, a loss of the sense
of a need for conversion. Jesus Christ must again be the focus of
teaching the Faith.

The post-Vatican II catechetical movement has had great
effects on the young people, but the results have been mixed.
The fruits of the modern catechetical revolution have long been
under scrutiny, with generations of Catholics now suffering religious illiteracy concerning the doctrines of the Faith and thus
concerning the Truth who is Jesus Christ Himself. Instead of
growing in the Faith within the solid bedrock of doctrinal
catechesis, the Apostolic See's *General Directory of Catechesis*
contends that today, many young people "have lost a living sense
of the faith."[72]

Even further, many young people today "no longer consider
themselves members of the Church, and (instead) live a life far
removed from Christ and His Gospel."[73] The current state of af-

---

[70] Quoted in Eugene Kevane, *Catechism of Christian Doctrine*, ed. Eugene Kevane
(Arlington: Center for Family Catechetics, 1980), 122.

[71] Francis D. Kelly summarizes the results of the new religious education prevalent
in many circles of the United States over the past four decades in *The Mystery We
Proclaim*, 37-40. He lists the problems of catechesis, in need of critical evaluation
and reform, as follows:
 1. Too much emphasis on process and not enough on product (Christ and His
 teaching).
 2. Too little truth and a great deal of opinion (relativism).
 3. There is a "missing person" in today's catechesis (Jesus).
 4. A loss of the power of the biblical drama of salvation (salvation history).
 5. An inadequate and superficial ecclesiology.

[72] GDC 58.

[73] Ibid.

fairs has contributed to many of the problems facing young people decades after the 'catechetical renewal' began — some of which include the rise of secular materialism, the widespread degradation of human life, societal attitudes that are plagued by hedonism (excessive, amoral pursuit of immediate self-gratification and pleasure which promotes using others as objects), an overall moral decay within a secularized society that has led to the breakdown of the family and to the lack of religious instruction in the home, the embracing of relativism (belief that everything is mere opinion in a world devoid of truth[74]), and the rise of New Age philosophies which have sought to satisfy young people's innate search for life's meaning but only left them wanting and unsatisfied in a whirlpool of superficiality.

Regardless of whether these issues are directly related to the crisis of sound teaching in the work of evangelization, it is incontestable that all the answers to life previously provided by sound religious instruction, one based upon sacred doctrine, are no longer present in the new catechetical approaches that have dominated in recent years. As a result, many young people have been forced to seek these answers elsewhere or abandon them altogether in a world of ignorance, skepticism and doubt. The harm caused by ignorance of doctrine was perhaps foreseen even by St. Pius X, the first catechetical pope of the twentieth century, in his *Catechism on Christian Doctrine*, in which he said, "...the greatest part of the evils which afflict the Church arises from the ignorance of her teaching and her laws."[75] Our foe is clearly religious ignorance of sound, saving doctrinal truth.

Alfred McBride, O Praem., sums up the situation of the current crisis in evangelization:

---

[74] About this, Francis D. Kelly states, "Overcoming the dominant subjectivity of our culture is a first step and a great challenge for catechesis" (*The Mystery We Proclaim*, 1st edition, 119).

[75] Pius X, Letter of October 18, 1912, AAS (1912), 690.

The chaos in religious education today has resulted from an agenda that pretended to implement Vatican II, but in fact subverted it. We are now the heirs of the "bad theory leads to bad practice" syndrome. This bad theory was not taught by the Council or the Magisterium, but by certain theologians and catechetical writers.

Over a period of twenty-five years they gained — in many cases — influence and control of the departments of religion and religious education in Catholic colleges and universities, of the publishers of the most widely used religion textbooks, and of the middle management positions in dioceses and archdioceses. They were and are the major speakers at most religious education conventions. Through their books and articles and classroom indoctrination, they shape the minds of the leaders, who in turn pass this on to the classroom and volunteer teachers. They are not teaching Catholicism but rather a mélange of personal opinions that usually resurrect discredited nineteenth century liberal Protestantism and reflect New Age pieties.

Bad theory has led to bad practice. Wrong ideas have led to wrong consequences.[76]

According to Msgr. Francis D. Kelly, "Until Catholic catechesis has recovered its true purpose, it will continue to wander from one methodological fad to another and leave behind yet more religious illiteracy."[77]

---

[76] Alfred McBride, O. Praem., "Why We Need the New Catechism: Vatican II Promise and Post-Vatican II Reality," *The Church and the Universal Catechism*, ed. Anthony Mastroeni (Steubenville: Franciscan U. Press, 1992), 39-40.

[77] Ibid., 22.

Given the reality of the crisis, it is important neither to over-state the situation nor to neglect to balance the fact that the teaching of solid doctrine by faithful catechists is also alive and well in catechesis today. McBride continues the discussion by qualifying it as follows:

> Lest I unfairly paint too bleak a landscape, let me note that many diocesan and parish directors of religious education are exemplary leaders of catechesis today. Thousands of good-hearted and faith-filled lay volun-teer and classroom teachers are sharing the authentic faith of the Church.... They stand out as encourag-ing and positive signs in catechetics today. They de-serve our support, gratitude, praise, and prayers.[78]

The faithful have a right to *drink in the pure doctrine of faith*[79] from Mother Church "that [they] may suck and be satisfied with her consoling breasts; that [they] may drink deeply with de-light... and [they] shall suck, [they] shall be carried upon her hip, and dandled upon her knees. As one whom his mother com-forts, so I (the Lord) will comfort [them]" (Is 66:11-13). They have a right to receive not merely the wood, hay, and stubble of religious personal experience, but the gold, silver, and precious stones (1 Cor 3:12) of the true doctrines of the Faith.

Having presented the crisis of doctrine within catechesis, let's move toward a solution to the crisis by first focusing on sa-cred doctrine itself — what it is; from whence it first became a central part of the teaching of the Faith; and what its role is within the ministry of teaching the Faith today.

---

[78] Ibid., 40.
[79] Pius XI, at the canonization Mass of St. Thérèse.

CHAPTER TWO

The Meaning of Sacred Doctrine

To begin to understand what sacred doctrine is, we must start with the father of modern theology, St. Thomas Aquinas, and his systematic summary of sacred doctrine, the *Summa Theologiae*. We will see that the Church's modern understanding of sacred doctrine derives from these Thomistic foundations.

A. TEACHING DOCTRINE IN THE HISTORY OF THE CHURCH

Since the time of Christ, with the first century Apostles' Creed being "the oldest Roman Catechism,"[1] the Faith has always been presented in one form or another.[2] The Church has continually defended her children from heresies, apostasies, schisms and dissent, remaining ever vigilant in guiding her children to the Person of Christ by way of the doctrines of His Church.[3]

---

[1] CCC 196.

[2] From the beginning of Christianity, doctrines of the Faith have been handed down. Professor J.N.D. Kelly of Oxford stated in his *Early Christian Creeds*, 3rd ed.: "The early Church was from the start a believing, confessing, preaching Church.... It is impossible to overlook the emphasis on the transmission of authoritative doctrine which is found everywhere in the New Testament" (London: Longman, 1972, 7-8).

[3] Describing the importance of doctrine even for the early Church, Hilaire Belloc in "What Was the Church of the Roman Empire?" *Europe and the Faith* (NY: Missionary Society of St. Paul, 1920), explains that heretics fought the Church precisely because she had articulated exact doctrine from the beginning:
"These sects arose precisely because within the Catholic Church (1) exact doctrine, (2) unbroken tradition, and (3) absolute unity, were, all three, regarded as the necessary marks of the institution. The heresies arose one after another from

Throughout the centuries, while the preferred method of handing on the Faith systematically has varied — having included creeds, summaries (*summae*), and catechisms — the content of the Faith itself has remained ever the same. "From the beginning, the apostolic Church expressed and handed on her faith in brief formulae for all."[4] As the Editorial Commission of the *Catechism of the Catholic Church* points out:

> In the New Testament, the Gospels are the first great "Catechism" which was transmitted orally and then put to writing. Jesus "teaches" and "preaches" (Mt 9:35; Mk 1:21; Lk 21:37). The Sermon of the Mount (Mt 5:2) speaks of the "teaching to the disciples." This mission was handed over to Peter with the office of the "keys" which, in Hebrew mentality, meant, amongst others, the office of teaching. In the Acts and the Pauline Letters the word "to catechize" appears already as the instruction regarding the salvific action of God.[5]

the action of men who were prepared to define yet more punctiliously what the truth may be, and to claim with yet more particular insistence the possession of living tradition and the right to be regarded as the centre of unity. No heresy pretended that the truth was vague and indefinite. The whole gist and meaning of a heresy was that it, the heresy, or he, the heresiarch, was prepared to make doctrine yet more sharp, and to assert his own definition."

4 CCC 186. See also Rm 19 and 1 Cor 15:3-5. "The Church has always used formulations of faith which, in short forms, contain the essentials of what she believes and lives: New Testament texts, creeds or professions of faith, liturgical formulas, Eucharistic prayers. At a later period, it was considered useful to provide more ample explications of the faith in organic synthesis, through the catechisms" (GDC 119).

5 *Informative Dossier* (6/25/92), accessed online at http:// (7/22/05).

6 As defined at the Councils of Hippo and Carthage in the 390s, as stated earlier by Pope Damasus in 382, and later confirmed by Pope Innocent I in 405 AD, and definitely held in 1546 at the Council of Trent.

7 For more on the Church Fathers and their place in teaching the Faith today, see Congregation for Catholic Education, *Instruction on the Study of the Fathers of the Church* (11/10/89), in ND 267b-268.

In the patristic period, the first to eighth century, the canon of Scripture[6] and its commentaries were the focus of the Church Fathers.[7] The emphasis of the Church Fathers was chiefly apologetic, polemic, and positive, as the Church welcomed her first converts from paganism to Christianity and then fought off heresies from within, such as Arianism, Nestorianism and Monophysitism. Thus, the work of transmitting the Faith through Tradition focused mainly on Scripture commentary and on brief formulae and creeds of doctrine.[8] Besides the *Didaché* or "Doctrine of the Apostles" (c. 70-90), which contains some catechetical elements, St. Irenaeus, who was martyred in 202, wrote the first catechism, *The Proof of the Apostolic Teaching*, which contains a clear statement of the fundamental truths of Christianity.[9] St. Cyril of Jerusalem (315-386) wrote the first extended text on catechesis, called *Catechetical Instructions* (*Catecheses*), entailing twenty-four religious instructions on doctrine and morals[10] with a section entitled *On the Doctrine*, and St. Gregory of Nyssa (330-395) wrote *The Great Catechism* (*Catechetical Discourse*), an exposition of the Catholic Faith.

A major reference to the Deposit of Faith is made around Augustine's time, with St. Vincent of Lerins, in his famous *Vincentian Canon*, writing, "In the Catholic Church, every care should be taken to hold fast to what has been believed everywhere, always, and by all" (*Quod ubique, quod semper, quod ab omnibus*).[11] Asking about the possibility of progress in the religion of Christ, he continues, "We must make this reservation,

---

[8] See CCC 78, 186. Every sentence and word of the Church's formulas and creeds was carefully discerned in order to articulate the orthodox Catholic Faith in doctrinal propositions. Members of the Church suffered torture, exile, and even death in order to faithfully preserve and transmit the doctrines of the Deposit of Faith. Such faithfulness and religious fervor is needed again in our own day.

[9] John Laux, *Church History* (Rockford: TAN, 1989), 60.

[10] John A. Hardon, SJ, *Catholic Wisdom* (San Francisco: Ignatius Press, 1987), 47.

[11] Vincent of Lerins, *The Commonitories*, I, 2; in Rudolph E. Morris trans., *The Fathers of the Church* (New York: The Fathers of the Church, 1949), vol. 7, 270.

however, that the progress shall be a genuine progress and not an alteration of the faith. We have progress when a thing grows and yet remains itself: we have alteration when a thing becomes something else."[12] In this period, St. Augustine's *De catechizandis rudibus* tries to help deepen the faith of those converts who, though educated in worldly knowledge, were "rude" in the religious one. Later centuries would see the teaching of Church doctrine in the form of Lombard's *Sentences* and Thomas Aquinas' *Little Treatises* (*Opuscula*), which contain his catechetical instructions given during the last Lent of his earthly life. Doctrinal teaching was becoming more and more systematic leading up to the Council of Trent, as seen in the *Lay Folks Catechism*, written by the Archbishop of York in the fourteenth century (1357), which included sections on the Creed, the Sacraments, and morals.

In the Catholic Reformation of the sixteenth century, the primary means of spreading doctrinal renewal was the *Roman Catechism* of Trent and of St. Pius V, commissioned by the Trent Council Fathers "so that the faithful may be mindful of the Christian Profession which they made in their baptism, and be prepared for reading and study of the Holy Bible,"[13] and be educated in the divine truths. This *Catechism* followed the fourfold method of apostolic catechesis (Creed, Sacraments, Morality, Prayer), as derived from Acts 2:42, and made popular in the ninth century by Alcuin, Charlemagne's great scholar, who wrote *Exposition for Children in Questions and Answers*, which included sacred history and doctrine on the Sacraments, the Creed and the Our Father. The ordering of the *Catechism* of Trent, and all major catechisms since, is primarily theological-apologetic rather than biblical-historical. Later catechisms, like the famous German catechism of Joseph Deharbe, SJ, the *Baltimore Catechism*

---

[12] Ibid., I, 23, op. cit., 536-537.
[13] See A. Thiener (ed.), *Acta genuina ss. Oecumenici Concilii Tridentini* (1874), vol. I, 91.

in the United States, and the *Catechism of the Catholic Church* would also follow its structure.

In examining the ways the Faith has been taught in the Church's history, there are traditionally three distinguishable historical periods: the patristic period which focused on Scripture as its primary source; the scholastic period which popularized the use of *summae*; and the modern period which entails the use of catechisms.

Briefly examining each period, Garrigou-Lagrange, in his *The One God*, discusses the unique features of each which led to particular emphases in teaching the Faith. According to him, a systematic theology as we know it today did not yet exist in the patristic period, "except in certain works of St. Augustine[14] and St. John Damascene."[15] But as we move into the second period, commonly called the Scholastic period, which occurred during the Middle Ages and primarily took place after the Fourth Lateran Council (1215), education moved from the monastery (monastic) and cathedral schools to the universities. The universities began to offer four faculties: *theologia* (with philosophy), law (civil and canon), medicine (with physics), and arts (*trivium* and *quadrivium*).[16] *Theologia* was considered the queen of the sciences. It began in this period to utilize Greek philosophy to shed light on the doctrines of the Church.

The study of theology during this period was known as Scholasticism. "Scholasticism," according to historian and educator John Laux, "did not attempt to add anything to Divine Revelation or to teach new doctrines, but only to furnish a rational basis for Christianity by showing the harmony which exists between faith and reason, and also to reduce the doctrines contained in Scripture and Tradition to an orderly and definite

---

[14] Cf. *De Trinitate*, PL, XLII.
[15] Cf. *De fide orthodoxa*, PG, XCV, quoted by Reginald Garrigou-Lagrange, OP, *The One God*, trans. Dominic Bede Rose (St. Louis, MO: B. Herder, 1946), 1.
[16] Laux, 372-373.

system."[17] As the scholastic, systematic approach to passing on the Faith took shape, the theologians of this period followed the tradition of their predecessors in organizing the Faith into the fourfold approach — Creed, Sacraments, Morality, and Prayer — though in a less structured way than the catechisms to come would.[18] Fr. Robert Bradley, SJ, in his doctoral dissertation, *The Roman Catechism in the Catechetical Tradition of the Church*, explains:

> In the millennium between Origen and St. Thomas Aquinas the catechetical tradition had undergone many changes, exactly as the Church in all aspects of her life had changed. Underlying the changes, deep and recurring as they were, there remained, however, the identity of the faith. It was the same Church, reading the same Scriptures, handing on with them the traditions of the same teaching which formed her life. The continuity — and the consciousness of the continuity — were certainly there... what the Scholastics were systematizing was nothing other than what they had received from the Scriptures: the Scriptures as summarized by the Fathers in the great formularies which formed the core of the tradition — the Creed, the Commandments, the Our Father, and the formularies combined with actions called the sacraments.[19]

In this period, systematic, scholastic theology didactically and speculatively expounded and defended the Faith, deducing from it new theological conclusions as well. This was the age of

---

[17] Ibid., 374.
[18] The *Catechism of the Catholic Church* follows the traditional fourfold content of the Faith, which dates back to Acts 2:42.
[19] Robert Bradley, SJ, *The Roman Catechism in the Catechetical Tradition of the Church* (Lanham: University Press, 1990), 83.

the *summae*, "so called because each is a complete treatise on all subjects pertaining to theology, and according as these various subjects are considered under the light of the higher principles of faith and reason."[20] The most significant *summa* of this period is Aquinas' *Summa Theologiae*.

The third and most recent period, which began with the Council of Trent, has seen the scholastic technique of the *quaestio* replaced by a structure of exposition. The three catechisms of St. Peter Canisius, SJ, the "hammer of heretics," were among the first catechetical texts after the Council of Trent (the Canisian catechisms were written in 1555, 1556, 1558). His approach followed that of John Gerson, who wrote *On Leading the Little Ones to Christ* in the early fifteenth century, while chancellor of the University of Paris. Also soon after the Council of Trent, St. Charles Borromeo, Archbishop of Milan and one of the founders of the Confraternity of Christian Doctrine, had a significant role in the composition of the *Roman Catechism* of Trent,[21] chairing the papal commission that produced the manual.

These catechisms were structured with the purpose of making an exposition of Catholic doctrine, but Congar notes that they were "not an extremely systematic and dialectical elaboration, [as] the *Summas* of the Middle Ages" had been. Instead, Congar explains, the *Catechism* of Trent was "a kind of developed 'Christian doctrine' or an explanation of the datum of faith taken from positive expressions of the sources."[22]

While the *summae* followed a dialectical order of invention and proof, the catechisms took a more pedagogical approach of explanation or exposition.[23] In both cases though, the same goal

---

[20] Garrigou-Lagrange, 2.

[21] Laux, 483, 491.

[22] Yves M.-J. Congar, OP, *A History of Theology*, Trans. and ed. Hunter Guthrie (New York: Doubleday, 1968), 179.

[23] Ibid., 179-180.

was maintained, namely that of a unified and organized presentation of sacred doctrine with the various branches of theology grouped into a single whole.

Theology has in this last period become chiefly positive and critical according to Garrigou-Lagrange.[24] In this period, theology has sought to reach out to the Protestants as well as the rationalists, thus being polemic, positive, and apologetic. Protestants also initially organized their doctrine into single, straightforward manuals.[25] In Catholic teaching, the reason for the development of catechisms, besides giving a complete exposition of doctrine, was "the need to distribute systematically the different branches of theology which had sometimes been divided and subdivided to excess."[26] Overall, the third period has seen theology become a study and an exposition of a critical knowledge and defense of the Faith.

Apart from their development historically, the fact that a particular catechetical/theological resource (creed, *summa*, catechism) came from a certain period in Christian history does not diminish its viability in teaching the Faith today. Truth is truth. But, some think otherwise, as seen by the recent attempt to introduce a new mode of theological procedure, called by some 'evolutionism,' which has attempted a coup of all historical religious "truth," whereby there has been an attempt to dismiss religious truth as pre-modern theological "jargon." This evolutionism is a form of relativism. Garrigou-Lagrange discusses the situation as follows:

> According to this view, which is not infrequent today, among all the systems appearing in the course of

---

[24] Garrigou-Lagrange, 3.

[25] Martin Luther, in 1529, using the material of his catechetical sermons wrote his *Catechismus Maior*, as a guide to the preachers of his reform. Later he wrote another one for "children and simple people," which he even called *Enchiridion*.

[26] Congar, *A History of Theology*, 181.

time in accordance with the evolution of ideas, no system is absolutely true, but each is relatively true, that is, in opposition to another proceeding doctrine, or else to some other brief evolutionary period of the past. The way that, for instance, Thomism was relatively true in the thirteenth century in opposition to the doctrine of certain Augustinians, which it surpassed; but it too, is not absolutely but relatively false with respect to the subsequent system which, either as an antithesis or as a superior synthesis, is of a higher order in the evolution of ideas. Thus Scotism, coming at a later date, would be truer than St. Thomas' doctrine, and this by the momentum of its progress in the history of philosophy and theology.[27]

Having presented this view, he continues, "If it were so, nothing would be absolutely true, not even the principle of contradiction... none of the accepted definitions would be absolutely true.... There would be only relative truth.... Only relativity would be absolute."[28]

Garrigou-Lagrange counters this notion of absolute evolutionism by concluding instead that "in theology, however, we rely first upon proofs taken from the authority of Holy Scripture or divine tradition, or even the writings of the holy Fathers, and in the second place on arguments drawn from reason, while, of course, not neglecting the history of problems and their solutions."[29] Thus, again, we see the vital importance of Scripture and Tradition as the always relevant sources of content for all of evangelization, as they are in both the *Summa Theologiae* and the *Catechism of the Catholic Church*. Although the format and

---

[27] Garrigou-Lagrange, 11.
[28] Ibid., 12.
[29] Ibid., 13.

style of Aquinas' *Summa Theologiae* is seldom today employed as a methodology in teaching the Faith, the doctrines presented by both the Church Fathers and by Aquinas in the *Summa* remain as relevant today as the day they were first presented by them, though *our understanding* of the doctrines of Faith has indeed grown, in what is properly referred to as the development of doctrine.[30]

Undoubtedly, one of the most significant moments in the Church's developmental understanding of sacred doctrine occurred with the introduction of the masterful, comprehensive, and systematic work of St. Thomas' *Summa Theologiae*. But, given that this work of theology was written over 700 years ago, we may wonder if Aquinas' *Summa* is outdated today as a resource of doctrine, or can it still be helpful in a contemporary theological argument?

B. THE DOCTRINAL PURPOSE OF THE *Summa Theologiae*

St. Thomas, always thirsting to forge more deeply into the knowledge of truth and to find more adequate means to pass it on to his students, began writing his own *Summa* in around 1265-66. He had been sent to Rome to found a *studium*, a house of studies or priory school for theological students. At Santa Sabina, as previously with his students in Paris, he tried the first year to teach with Lombard's *Sentences*. But, St. Thomas decided to abandon it and make a subsequent effort at teaching in the best way and with the best theological content he could gather, by compiling all of his theological wisdom into his own *Summa Theologiae*.

In the Prologue of his *Summa*, St. Thomas seems to allude

---

[30] See CCC 94.

to the ongoing dilemma he himself faced in the theological endeavor of his day. Although he "wanted to contribute to the already long and remarkable tradition of the manualists in his order," he also "wanted to fill in the most conspicuous gaps"[31] found in the texts he had previously worked with. So with this in mind, he wrote in his Prologue:

> We have considered how newcomers to this teaching [the things of the Christian religion] are greatly hindered by various writings on the subject, partly because essential information is given according to the requirements of textual commentary or the occasion of academic debate, not to a second educational method, partly because repetitiousness has bred boredom and muddle in their thinking.[32]

St. Thomas, according to Thomist theologian, James Weisheipl, OP, thus gives three reasons why contemporary works of theology were insufficient and unsuitable for introductory level students of theology: (1) they were too verbose and detailed, (2) they were all unsystematic [or not properly systematic], and (3) they were too repetitious because they were unsystematic.[33] Drawing implications from the *Summa*'s Prologue, Victor White, OP, concludes that the purpose of the *Summa* is to assist the teacher in encountering "all men, beginners no less than the proficient, leading them from what they know and accept to what they do not [know and accept] of the universal truth. In other words, its whole orientation is evangelistic, 'pedagogical,' and...

---

[31] Ibid., 145.

[32] St. Thomas Aquinas, *Summa Theologiae*, Blackfriars edition (New York: McGraw-Hill, 1963), 3.

[33] James Weisheipl, OP, *Friar Thomas D'Aquino: His Life, Thought, and Work* (Garden City, NY: Doubleday and Co., 1974), 218.

it is 'scientific' only to the extent that scientific and logical methods may serve this evangelistic concern."[34]

The Sacred Scriptures and the writings of the Fathers were, and still are, the rule of Faith, "but training of [an evangelist] requires that beginners in the 'science' be aided by a systematic view of the whole of 'sacred doctrine.'"[35] Thus, as he stated he would, what follows the Prologue is a strictly logical and scientific discourse on the Deposit of Faith, which became known as the *Summa*.

Examining the *Summa* over many years, Garrigou-Lagrange concluded:

> The expositions and demonstrations are simple and clear, especially if they are compared with the sentences of Peter Lombard, and superfluous questions are avoided in accordance with the Angelic Doctor's plan as stated in the Prologue. Likewise, repetitions are eliminated, as much as possible, because subjects

---

[34] Victor White, OP, "Holy Teaching: The Idea of Theology According to St. Thomas," *Aquinas Papers No. 33* (London: Blackfriars, 1958), 7. He gives some commentary on the Prologue to demonstrate his point:

"Meanwhile we should notice that the remainder of the Prologue is likewise occupied with these needs of the learner; with the teacher-learner relationship. *Consideravimus namque huius doctrinae novitios, in iis quae a diverisis conscripta sunt, plurimum impediri.* The newcomer to catholic truth and the Christian religion is not only not helped by the books current in St. Thomas's time, he is positively hindered. In fact his needs are not considered, their contents and arrangement are dictated by purely professional interests — '*secundum quod requirebat librorum expositio*' (the Biblical commentaries) or '*secundum quod praebebat occasio disputandi*' (the *Questiones disputatae*). Then as now there seems to have been a lot of plain plagiarism *frequents (sic) repetitio*, and the effect for the learner, so far from being helpful and enlightening, is boredom and muddle *(fastidium et confusio)*. St. Thomas's own treatment and arrangement will be governed, not by the interests of the professional investigator (*ordo inventionis*), but he tells us, by the *ordo disciplinae* — the order of learning, pedagogical method. The requirements of the learner will be paramount. We can of course q estion whether St. Thomas has been successful in achieving his purpose, but he can leave us in little doubt what his purpose is."

[35] Weisheipl, *Friar Thomas D'Aquino*, 219.

are always treated in a general way before they receive special consideration, and St. Thomas does not refer his reader to what is to be said later on. In this simplicity and clarity, the Angelic Doctor evidently far surpasses not only his predecessors, but even Scotus and Suarez.[36]

St. Thomas set out to close the gaps, or at least the limitations so prevalent in thirteenth century doctrinal teaching. As Chenu remarks, St. Thomas saw that "the multiplying of questions and arguments, repetitions, [and] needless digressions" served only to "clutter up the mind and produce aversion for study."[37] But even more seriously, "the framework itself of the teaching system, whether the commentaries on the basic texts or the disputed questions, blocks out the highest demands of mind, which can express the full understanding of its object only if given free constructive rein."[38]

In St. Thomas' approach and intention, "the *Summa* is a book of the pupil,"[39] for the beginner. On the other hand, texts like the *Disputed Questions* are for the advanced student of theology. Even though the intended readers of the *Summa* are not meant to be already masters, the work itself is perfectly masterful. It is "the fruit that ripened out of the loftiest teaching in the medieval university."[40]

Only a saint like St. Thomas could have written the great summary of doctrine that has become the *Summa Theologiae*. "St. Thomas employed his scientific method, inspired as it were

[36] Garrigou-Lagrange, 26.
[37] Chenu, M.-D., OP, *Towards Understanding St. Thomas* (Trans. with corrections and bibliographical additions by A.-M. Landry, OP and D. Hughes, OP, Chicago: Henry Regnery, 1964 of *Introduction a l'etude de Saint Thomas d'Aquin*, Paris: J. Vrin, 1950), 300.
[38] Ibid.
[39] Ibid., 298.
[40] Ibid.

from above, illuminated by the light of vivid faith and the gifts of the Holy [Spirit]; and this light absolutely transcends all systems and all knowledge acquired by human efforts. Thus only by this supernatural light does theology attain its end."[41] One may wonder why this summary of doctrine is so necessarily expansive and complex. To that, James V. Schall, SJ, explains:

> One might say, 'Cannot you simplify this explanation for us?' But that would risk neglecting something vital in the explanation so that it would not explain what it has to explain. Perhaps the point can be understood by recalling the most famous theology book in Catholicism, namely Aquinas' *Summa Theologiae*. This book is over four thousand large pages in length, but it is proposed as a book for 'beginners.' Probably not more than two percent of the human race have ever read that many pages in their lifetimes! Here we have Thomas Aquinas telling us that this enormous series of volumes is pared down to the essentials for beginners. Evidently, the more simple the book the longer it took to explain what needed to be explained simply.[42]

The *Summa* is a masterpiece in part because while it entails the full multiplicity of doctrine, it does so in a unity of order while showing how each truth exists in relation to the other, like the many complex individual parts that make up one simple working machine.

St. Thomas, the Doctor of Humanity,[43] was truly the "ideal teacher, 'the most complete type of the professor of the middle

---

[41] Garrigou-Lagrange, 26-27.

[42] Fr. James V. Schall, S.J., *Catholicism: Simply Complex or Complicated Simplicity?*, June 12, 2005, accessed online at http:// (7/19/05).

[43] John Paul II, *The Method and Doctrine of St. Thomas in Dialogue with Modern Culture* (1980), 3.

ages,' as Mandonnet has typified him."[44] Truly, as Cardinal
Bessarion says of him, "Among the saints, he is the most learned,
and among the learned, the most saintly."[45] After over fifty years
as a Dominican, Benedict Ashley admitted that he thought of St.
Thomas as his brother and himself as still his awe-struck student.[46]
The Church too has consistently invited us to say of St. Thomas,
with Maritain, "I love him."[47] Such things should be able to be
said about every catechist, theologian, and evangelist today.

St. Thomas is the Angelic Doctor of religious doctrine. Fr.
Salaverri, SJ, wrote that "in Theology… the authority of St. Thomas is entirely matchless and greater than that of any other Doctor
or Theologian in the Catholic Church… the authority… of St.
Thomas, which may be called canonical, is greater than the authority of any other Catholic theologian."[48] "By the very fact of
anyone embracing the doctrine of St. Thomas," J. de Guibert,
SJ, concludes, "he embraces the doctrine most commonly accepted in the Church, safe and approved by the Church itself."[49]

The originality and contribution of St. Thomas' work, particularly his *Summa*, "consists less in having sought to solve problems of his time than in trying to find, by placing human reason
at the service of faith in order to found a theological science, a
method of research which could be applied to the problems of
all times."[50] His teaching was not a fashion, not timely, but timeless. As Josef Pieper asserts in *The Silence of St. Thomas*, "timeli-

[44] Van der Ploeg, "The Place of Holy Scripture," 407, quoting Mandonnet, *Revue Thomiste*, 1928, 214.

[45] Bessarion, *Adversus calumniatorem Platonis*, lib. II, cap. 3.

[46] Benedict Ashley, OP, "Introduction," *The Common Things*, ed. by Daniel McInerny (Washington, DC: Catholic University, 1999), 1.

[47] Jaques Maritain, *The Peasant of the Garonne* (New York: Holt, Rinehart, and Win-ston, 1968), 129.

[48] Joachim Salaverri, SJ, *De Ecclesia Christi*, no. 872, 874; p. 757, 758. (Madrid, 1950).

[49] J. de Guibert, SJ, *De Ecclesia Christi*, 386 (Rome, 1928).

[50] Stanislaus M. Gillet, OP, *A Study of Saint Thomas*, Trans. Gerald Christian, OP (Washington DC: Dominican House of Studies Library, n.d.), 134.

ness, in itself, is no criterion for truth."[51] Truth is instead divine, eternal, transcendent, universal, immutable, objective, and absolute. "It is important to make clear, however, that what is being advocated here," as Shanley puts it, "is not some kind of naïve or triumphalistic return to or repetition of premodern theology, but rather a genuine retrieval (*Wiederholung*) of premodern theology in the light of the contemporary problematic."[52] Even writing in 1952, Van Ackeren felt that an understanding of this point would restore Catholic wisdom to all of Catholic evangelization, saying: "I am confident that with the true appreciation of sacred theology as Christian wisdom, theology will be restored to its position of eminence in *all* our Catholic Universities… in this wisdom is found the order of *all things whatsoever* to their final end, and through this wisdom is achieved that peace and tranquility of order which is about all understanding."[53] Such a day of restoration has yet to occur, but the new springtime of the Faith will indeed come, and it is already dawning through our Catholic universities and the faithful exposition of sacred doctrine in our times.

Still needed is a universal critique of dissident theology, bad catechesis, and watered-down evangelization, which have advocated an approach to the Faith that supports conflicting perspectives of religious truth and competing theological claims at variance with the Magisterium; and instead to establish a balance of faith and reason to evangelization, one that is in turn used to critique the culture of modernity, particularly with its permissiveness of the culture of death and the culture of dissent. Advocating this Augustinian-Thomistic approach to evangelization

---

[51] Josef Pieper, *The Silence of St. Thomas*, trans. John Murray, SJ, and Daniel O'Connor (NY: Pantheon, 1957), 106.

[52] Brian Shanley, OP, "*Sacra Doctrina* and the Theology of Disclosure" (*The Thomist* 61, 1997), 186.

[53] Geraldo Van Ackeren, *Sacra Doctrina: The Subject of the First Question of the Summa Theologiae of St. Thomas* (Rome: Catholic Book Agency, 1952), 120-121.

unites religious doctrine and scholastic truth, including the authority of St. Thomas, with Augustine's way of setting souls on fire through a passion for the transcendentals (truth, goodness, beauty), to strike at the *mind and heart* of the modern man, inspiring and converting him with doctrinal truth, which in turn awakens within him a love for Jesus Christ and His Church, and thus fosters the universal call to holiness of life and sets the world on fire with the truth and love of Christ.[54] This is the New Evangelization, and it has begun.

C. *Sacra Doctrina* IN THE *Summa Theologiae*

To understand the necessary role of sacred doctrine in the New Evangelization, we must first examine the meaning of sacred doctrine itself, which derives from Thomistic foundations. St. Thomas' biographer, Bernard Gui, stated that even at the beginning of his career, St. Thomas became known for his unique manner of teaching, which consisted of "new articles" and "new reasonings."[55] "One such new article, it seems, is the very first article of Thomas' *Summa theologiae*,"[56] even though it came late in his career. The meaning of *sacra doctrina* (Latin for *sacred doctrine*), as articulated by St. Thomas in the first question of his *Summa*, has been a topic of debate and controversy for al-

---

[54] Jesus said, "I came to cast fire upon the earth; and would that it were already kindled!" (Lk 12:49). The last words that St. Ignatius of Loyola spoke to the young St. Francis Xavier before Francis set out to preach the Gospel to the peoples of the Far East were these, "Francis, leave this place and set the world on fire." St. Josemaria invites his readers to set the world on fire saying: "Don't let your life be sterile. Blaze a trail. Shine forth with the light of your faith and of your love." (*The Way*, #1)

[55] Bernard Gui, *Legenda S. Thomae Aquinatis*, cap. 11, in D. Prümmer, ed. *Fontes Vitae S. Thomae Aquinatis* (Toulouse: Bibliopolis, 1911-1934), 178, as quoted by Mark F. Johnson, "The Sapiential Character of the First Article of the *Summa Theologiae*," *Philosophy and the God of Abraham*, edited by R. James Long (Toronto: Pontifical Institute of Medieval Studies, 1991), 93.

[56] Johnson, 93.

most as long as the *Summa* has existed. The debate is indeed a most important undertaking, "For the first question of the *Summa* has been regarded for centuries as the *locus classicus* for *theologia* in investigating the nature of [this] science."[57]

St. Thomas uses the term *sacra doctrina* at least one hundred and two times in his writings, while he uses *haec doctrina* fifty-nine times.[58] Aquinas focuses the first question of his *Summa theologiae* on *sacra doctrina*. According to St. Thomas in the *Summa*'s opening question with ten articles, of all the sciences and knowledge of man, *sacra doctrina* itself is the highest science because it transcends human reason and is derived from the divine knowledge of God Himself, thus guaranteeing greater certitude of religious truth, devoid of all error (article 5). *Sacra doctrina* is one science, both speculative and practical (article 3), that belongs to both God and the blessed (article 2), and which is revealed by God as necessary for our salvation (article 1). With the things of God as its content, the whole science of *sacra doctrina* is contained virtually in the articles of Faith, and thus it treats all things so far as they are ordered to God (article 7).

The work of *sacra doctrina*, according to Aquinas, also entails arguing from the known articles of the Faith to prove something else as previously unknown as being true. This is possible provided those engaged in the argument already have personal theological faith in the truths of Revelation, because the truth rests upon the authority of divine Revelation, making use also of human reason (article 8). God's Revelation is passed on to each generation through instruction (evangelization), using the divine truths of inspired Scripture, using both the literal and the spiritual senses in such a way that even the simple may understand (article 9-10), so as to foster faith, impart wisdom, and

[57] Van Ackeren, *Sacra Doctrina*, 9.
[58] J. Merkt, *Sacra Doctrina and Christian Eschatology*. Diss. (Ann Arbor: UMI, 1983), 31. According to him, *haec doctrina* was used many times in STh I, q. 1, a. 1-10 as a substitute for *sacra doctrina*.

encourage charity unto eternal life. "The end of this science, in so far as it is practical, is eternal happiness" (article 5), according to Aquinas. Thus, sacred doctrine learned, lived, and shared leads to Heaven.

Perhaps the most insightful understanding of *sacra doctrina* comes from St. Thomas' use of two very carefully referenced Scripture verses in article one of the first question of the *Summa*.[59] The first, 2 Timothy 3:16 explains that God has given us a divinely inspired content (*sacra doctrina*) of Revelation and that it has been given to be used for our good and for the good of others — to be shared by methodically teaching the Faith (evangelization). The second Scripture passage that St. Thomas cites is Isaiah 64:4, which further explains that this doctrinal content is indeed ordered to God (as holy wisdom) in a way that surpasses man's natural understanding, and can only be understood by our responding with grace to God's initial act of revelatory love, by loving Him in return (faith and charity are necessary to know, live, and pass on the Faith). Only then will both teacher and student attain the Kingdom of God and His heavenly realm. This is why He gave us His Word, His divine Revelation, which has been faithfully communicated to us through the centuries by His Church's teaching authority by the power of the Spirit via sacred doctrines,[60] and with the assistance of great evangelists like St. Thomas Aquinas.

In a key article in question one of the *Summa*, St. Thomas states that "doctrine is wisdom above all human wisdom (absolutely)" (article 6). For him, *sacra doctrina* is the divine truth of the highest wisdom because it considers God Himself, and

---

[59] The first is 2 Timothy 3:16, "All scripture is inspired by God and profitable for teaching, for reproof, for correction, and for training in righteousness." The second is Isaiah 64:4, "From of old no one has heard or perceived by the ear, no eye has seen a God besides thee, who works for those who wait for him."

[60] The Church transmits to every generation all that she believes by way of doctrine, life and worship (CCC 98).

knowledge pertaining to Him, through His Self-Revelation (article 6). As St. Thomas states, sacred doctrine "is the knowledge of divine things.... Sacred doctrine essentially treats of God viewed as the highest cause, for it treats of Him not only so far as He can be known through creatures... but also so far as He is known to Himself alone and revealed to others" (article 6). Thus, sacred doctrine is the Wisdom, Love, and Mercy of God, as revealed by His Spirit through the teaching authority of His Body, the Church.

D. A New Synthesis of *Sacra Doctrina*

As scholars have noted,[61] St. Thomas seems to use most of these terms — doctrine, truth, Scripture, tradition, theology, teaching, wisdom, science, revelation, and faith — interchangeably in referring to *sacra doctrina* in his first question of the *Summa* and elsewhere in his writings.[62] But just because he uses them within a similar context does not necessarily imply that he thought they meant the same thing, nor should we infer that his readers lacked an understanding of the distinctions between them even in his day. Further, he seems to have taken for granted the distinctions among these terms, especially with regard to his audience, to such an extent that he did not feel the need to make known the distinctions more clearly or expressly.

Unity and distinction taken together within the framework of truth conveyed in words used interchangeably reveals fullness of meaning. As the Father, Son, and Holy Spirit are one Being, each is a distinct Person, for example. St. Thomas seems to have understood this balance, one that goes back to "the biblical unity

---

[61] See Appendix 2 at the end of this book.

[62] According to Congar, in *A History of Theology*, 92-93; see Francisco P. Muniz, OP, *The Work of Theology* (Washington, DC: Thomist Press, 1953), 13, especially footnote 10.

in which practice and doctrine are one, a unity grounded in Christ, who is both the *Logos* and the Shepherd: as the *Logos* he is the Shepherd, and as the Shepherd he is the *Logos*."[63] Just as *Logos* and Shepherd are one in unity of meaning (and Person), they are also distinct in truth. So it is with the various terms used by Aquinas in question one of the *Summa* on sacred doctrine.

The analysis of *sacra doctrina* as used in question one of the *Summa* has gone through at least three stages of development by Thomistic commentators — the initial stage marked by the insight of Cajetan, its second revival by Congar which marks the time of its splendor, and the current period, which is specifically marked by a series of repetitions in thought.

Just as the Fathers are the most revered among all the commentators on the Scriptures, due in part to their close historical proximity to the Source, so too in the case of the *Summa* is Cajetan worthy to be considered the "father" of commentators on Aquinas. For him, St. Thomas uses the term *sacra doctrina* with a double meaning: first, that of the Revelation of the Faith, which is passed on in modern theological terms as "catechesis"; and second, as a "virtual" Revelation of God, which uses the articles of Faith to discover the total science of "theology."[64] Other commentators followed Cajetan's lead, while some abandoned his views for a time. Thomist commentators, Báñez[65] and Billuart,[66] thought question one on *sacra doctrina* was about scholastic theology. Garrigou-Lagrange closes the first period of the

---

[63] Joseph Ratzinger's commentary on the Dogmatic Constitution on the Church in H. Vorgrimler, ed., *Commentary on the Documents of Vatican II*, vol. I (1967), 299.

[64] See Van Ackeren, *Sacra Doctrina*, 19-25; Weisheipl, "The Meaning of *Sacra Doctrina*," 57.

[65] Domingo Báñez, OP, *Scolastica Commentaria in I Partem Summae*, q. 1, ed. Luis Urbano, Biblioteca de Tomistas Españoles, vol. 8 (Madrid, 1934), 7-99, quoted in Weisheipl, "The Meaning of *Sacra Doctrina*," 58.

[66] C. R. Billuart, *Summa Sancti Thomae hodiernis Academicarum moribus accomodata* (Paris, n.d.), 2-20, as cited by Weisheipl, "The Meaning of *Sacra Doctrina*," 59.

debate arguing that *sacra doctrina* is theology, "the science of God proceeding from divine revelation."[67]

Although Chenu[68] is responsible for reviving the debate in the second period, Congar[69] is responsible for making the most significant contribution to it.[70] For Congar, *sacra doctrina* reproduced God's science via discursive reasonings from revealed truths: "By this intellectual effort *sacra doctrina* will produce, as far as it can, God's science, that is to say, the order according to which God, in His wisdom, links all things together, each according to its degree of intelligibility and being, and finally brings all things to Himself."[71] Congar states that the prologue of the *Summa* includes *sacra doctrina* to mean Scripture as well as "catechesis, Christian preaching, and theology in its scientific form."[72] Congar saw *sacra doctrina* as a balance of both Christian instruction (catechesis) and theology in its scientific form, a perspective which has been evaluated and built upon by his

---

[67] Garrigou-Lagrange, 3.

[68] According to Brian Shanley, "*Sacra Doctrina* and the Theology of Disclosure", 179, footnote 55 and Johnson, "The Sapiential Character of the First Article of the *Summa theologiae*," 85. Marie-Dominique Chenu, OP, was a controversial figure in the modern era of Thomism, even having his book on *Le Saulchoir* placed on the Index in 1942, according to Komonchak, "Thomism and the Second Vatican Council," *Continuity and Pluralism in Catholic Theology*, ed. Anthony Cernara (Fairfield: Sacred Heart University, 1998), 64.

[69] Yves M.-J. Congar, OP, "Comptes Rendu," *Bulletin Thomiste* (1937-1939): 490-505; Gerald F. Van Ackeren, "Preface," *Sacra Doctrina: The Subject of the First Question of the Summa Theologica of St. Thomas* (Rome: Catholic Book Agency, 1952); "Le Moment 'economique' et le Moment 'ontologique' dans la *sacra doctrina* (Revelation, theologie, somme theologique)," *Melanges Offert a M.-D. Chenu, OP*, Bibliotheque Thomiste, 37 (Paris: J. Vrin, 1967), 135-187. Note that Congar actually wrote this article in 1964, *A History of Theology*, trans. and ed. Hunter Guthrie (New York: Doubleday, 1968). Similar to Chenu, Congar was censured by the Vatican's Holy Office for several years only to be restored to Church favor in 1960. Later, Pope John XXIII asked him to be an advisor at Vatican II. Finally, Pope John Paul II made him a cardinal in 1994, and he died in 1995. He wrote a journal during the years of scrutiny by the Vatican, called *Journal d'un Theologien*.

[70] According to Merkt, *Sacra Doctrina*, 33.

[71] Congar, *A History of Theology*, 95.

[72] *A History of Theology*, 93.

successors even up to the present time. Such a view of *sacra doctrina* has appeared, with some variation, in Van Ackeren's understanding of sacred doctrine whereby he states: "according to St. Thomas sacred doctrine is a participated form of divine revelation… sacred doctrine is divine revelation"[73] under the modern headings of "sacred instruction" and "Catholic education" (which include all forms of evangelization)[74]; in Persson's "holy teaching and theology"[75]; in White's "holy teaching" which implies evangelization[76]; and in Gilby's two senses of *sacra doctrina* — the content itself and the teaching of the content.[77] The emphasis during this period moved from a balance of content and methodology, as depicted by Congar, to a more exclusive emphasis on methodology, understanding *sacra doctrina* in the broadest sense, represented by the views of more recent commentators.

In the third and current period, Thomistic commentators like Henri Donneaud, for example, argue that for St. Thomas *sacra doctrina* has a much broader reality than some earlier Thomistic commentators admit; namely, the ensemble of Christian teaching based on divine Revelation,[78] or in other words, the whole of Christian teaching whose principal object is God

---

[73] Van Ackeren, *Sacra Doctrina*, 120.

[74] Ibid., 101.

[75] Per Erik Persson, *Sacra Doctrina: Reason and Revelation in Aquinas*, trans. Ross MacKenzie (Philadelphia: Fortress Press, 1970), 71.

[76] White, "Holy Teaching: The Idea of Theology According to St. Thomas," 4. On page 8, footnote 1, he also cites St. Augustine's *De Doctrina Christiana* to demonstrate that, by its contents, it is clear that St. Augustine meant much more than merely doctrine by the use of *doctrina*. Fr. White concludes that Aquinas must have depended much on Augustine's understanding of *doctrina* in his own approach to question one of the *Summa*.

[77] Thomas Gilby, OP "Appendix 5: *Sacra Doctrina*." Blackfriars' *Summa Theologiae* (New York: McGraw-Hill, 1963), 58-59.

[78] Henry Donneaud, OP, "Insaisissable *Sacra Doctrina?*", *Revue Thomiste* (April-June 1998), 224; translated by me with the assistance of Fabian Dubois.

Himself.[79] Beginning with Weisheipl[80] and culminating most recently in Neumayr,[81] the emphasis in recent times has been on re-establishing an association between catechesis and theology, as well on achieving a balance between content and methodology to gain a complete understanding of the meaning of *sacra doctrina*. Recent Thomistic commentators conclude that *sacra doctrina* most primarily means "wisdom," which according to Weisheipl, concerns God, derived from divine Revelation, accepted in faith, and which directs toward the eternal beatitude.[82]

So, according to St. Thomas and his commentators, sacred doctrine may be summarized as the Self-revealed wisdom of God, a genuine though limited participation in divine Wisdom Himself, attained by knowledge of and, at the same time, communion with divine Charity, and only through an active theological faith. Sacred doctrine, necessary for our salvation, is an icon of Truth Himself, the Word made flesh, in our own time perpetually re-presenting Himself (via divine Revelation, handed on by the Magisterium) and subjecting Himself (via divine condescension[83]) to being presented by others (catechists, preachers, theologians) as the Word,[84] the divine *Logos*, primarily by

---

[79] Ibid., 197.

[80] Weisheipl, "The Meaning of *Sacra Doctrina* in ST, q. 1," 71.

[81] John W. Neumayr, "The Science of God and the Blessed," *Return to the Source*, et. al., Vol. 1, No. 1 (Winter 1999), 27-36. For him, *sacra doctrina* is most completely a personal knowledge of God, of Him who reveals, which leads first to divine contemplation and second to contemplative communication, a sharing in the Divine Wisdom of God. As God revealed Himself to us out of love, so too, we can only know His Revelation, *sacra doctrina*, via the return of love for Him through the theological virtue of charity. Our lives will be given over to "divine contemplation," to a comprehension of *sacra doctrina*, only in as much as we carry out the commandment to love God with our whole heart, soul, mind and strength, and communicate this contemplation to others in love and as a spiritual work of mercy, so that our neighbor too may experience His sweetness and eternal bliss.

[82] Ibid., 80.

[83] DV 13.

[84] We know that "the Word is Jesus Christ, the Word made man and that his voice continues to resound in the Church" (GDC 94) through evangelization.

way of evangelization, catechesis, liturgy, and theology. He is handed on to us through a rational language[85] by authentic living witnesses (the baptized faithful) so that we can truly understand Him as He is, His divine truth, and His love and mercy, but even more for us to enter into communion with the Word Himself, in our earthly life through words and deeds of faith, hope, and love, and eventually, in an eternal communion of heavenly glory with the Triune God, together with His Angels and Saints. Sacred doctrine is a gratuitous gift of God and a glimpse of the glory of the beatific vision, when we will truly be face to face with Truth unveiled. Sacred doctrine is the doorway to the Kingdom of God, the gateway to the liturgy of the Eucharist, and as such, leads to the archway of the heavenly banquet. So, it is clear that Jesus Christ, in a certain sense, is Sacred Doctrine personified — the mirror that Catholic sacred doctrine reflects is nothing other than Christ.[86]

Sacred doctrine is the primary source utilized in the science of theology, but for our purposes, it is better not to consider doctrine as theology itself. One does not do sacred doctrine, but one does theology as founded upon sacred doctrine; one theologizes using sacred doctrine. For St. Thomas, theology is discourse about God, *"theologia, quasi sermo de Deo"*,[87] while *sacra doctrina* is the divine truth which has come to us through divine Revelation, *"sacram doctrinam per revelationem haberi,"*[88] and from which theology finds its source and content. Sacred doctrine is to theology what quantities are to mathematics, what natural living beings are to biology. Thus, sacred doctrine is no more theology itself than a plant is biology.

---

[85] "And so without ceasing to be the word of God, [the Deposit of faith] is expressed in human words" (GDC 94).
[86] See CCC 231, 97.
[87] STh I, q. 1, a. 7.
[88] STh I, q. 1, a. 1.

Sacred doctrine is, however, the content of and the means by which to evangelize and share the Faith. In a similar way, one could not do biology without or apart from the usage of living organisms, and one could not do math without or apart from the already established notion of numbers and a respect for their already determined interrelationship — one must first be familiar with numbers sufficiently before one can do mathematics, and one could never make it up as one went along or deny what is already established as the foundational and objective principles of a given science. So it is similarly with handing on the Faith — one must first have a sufficient and in-depth grasp of the whole of sacred doctrine, and have a faithful respect for it and obedience to its principles (the articles of faith),[89] before one can witness and herald the Good News to others, before one can apply what is known to what is unknown in the work of theology.

---

[89] STh I, 1, 7.

CHAPTER THREE

Sacred Doctrine in Recent Church Teaching

Aware of the current crisis of faith and of teaching doctrine, since Vatican II the Church has promulgated several documents on the nature of evangelization, which emphasize the central role of sacred doctrine. As well in these times, "throughout his entire pontificate, John Paul II... continually proposed a constant magisterium of the highest catechetical value."[1]

These documents have addressed a wide range of issues and topics within the ministry of handing on the Faith — like the need to clarify the relation and distinction between catechesis and theology, the need to re-assess the role of sacred doctrine within evangelization, and the need to re-establish the necessary congruency between sacred doctrine and the faith of those who pass it on (between what is taught and who is teaching). These Church documents continue to acknowledge that a departure from Thomistic teaching with its emphasis on doctrine, together with the growth of dissent, have led to a global crisis of faith.

A. SACRED DOCTRINE IN CATECHESIS AND THEOLOGY

1. Relation

The Church teaches that catechesis and theology are both parts of the Ministry of the Word and thus are closely bound

---

[1] GDC 5.

together.[2] Sacred theology and catechesis are both authentic means of evangelization.[3] John Paul II as well emphasized: "The connection between catechesis and theology should be well understood."[4]

In some ways, theology is an advanced form of catechesis and catechesis is, in relation to theology, its embryonic counterpart. Throughout Catholic history, catechesis and theology have been closely related. St. Thomas Aquinas defined *theologia* in brief as *discourse about God*,[5] one which utilizes sacred doctrine. But, he did not foresee the many various and distinct types of theology and catechesis that would evolve in later centuries. Catechesis is also *teaching the truths of God*. Catechesis is really a part of theology, and catechetics has been referred to as a "pastoral theology," as by Paul VI in his General Catechetical Directory.[6]

Both seek to foster or encourage a living and maturing faith on the part of those being taught.[7] Catechesis "is intended to make men's faith become living, conscious, and active, through the light of instruction,"[8] while similarly the work of theology is intended to *increase* men's faith, making it more living, conscious, and active, and to increase their knowledge and devotion to the Faith as well.

Pope John Paul II states that the connection between the-

---

[2] GCD 17.

[3] Paul VI, *Evangelization in the Modern World* [*Evangelii Nuntiandi*] (1975), 44.

[4] CT 61.

[5] STh I, q. 1, a. 7.

[6] See John A. Hardon, SJ, "General Catechetical Directory," *Pocket Catholic Dictionary* (New York: Image, 1985), 160. Also, John Paul I, as Cardinal Luciani, used to speak about a "catechetical theology," considering it a serious branch of theology, following the thought of Antonio Rosmini-Serbati, a famous nineteenth century Italian theologian who stressed catechetics. The term "catechetics" became a common discipline in theology in the 1950s. The new General Directory of Catechetics states that catechetics is based on "theologico-pastoral principles" (9).

[7] GCD 15.

[8] GCD 17, quoting *Christus Dominus* 14.

ology and catechesis is profound and vital because both draw from the true Source, in the light of the Magisterium.[9] The primary task of both catechesis and theology is to teach the meaning of the Word of God in divine Revelation as transmitted through inspired Sacred Scriptures and handed on by the living Sacred Tradition of the Church, in communion with the Church's Magisterium.[10]

There are other similarities as well. Both theology and catechesis must be taught systematically. Both entail "the systematic treatment and the scientific investigation of the truths of faith."[11] Both utilize sacred doctrine, the unified summation of all the divine truths of Revelation, to systematically pass on the Faith. The Faith must be taught systematically because, as Paul VI explains in *Evangelii Nuntiandi*, "the intelligence needs to learn through systematic religious instruction the fundamental teachings, the living content of the truth which God has wished to convey to us and which the Church has sought to express."[12]

The object of both theology and catechesis is the same: the living, divine Truth Himself.[13] Both concern themselves principally with the Mystery of Christ. Both study the divine truths of the Faith, in the form of doctrine, which is "wisdom above all

---

[9] CT 61.

[10] For a Magisterial discussion on the definition of these terms, their close relation and role within catechesis, see CCC 50-100; for their central place in theology, see ECE 29, FR 93, and *Donum Veritatis* 6. Concerning the relation between Scripture, Tradition, and the Magisterium, DV 10 (and CCC 95) states: "It is clear, therefore, that in the supremely wise arrangement of God, sacred Tradition, Sacred Scripture, and the Magisterium of the Church are so connected and associated that one of them cannot stand without the others." (The word "Sacred" is capitalized when used as an adjective with "Tradition" in more recent Magisterial documents; for example, GDC 95. The word "Apostolic" is also used as an adjective with "Tradition" and is also capitalized; for example, FD 3.)

[11] GCD 17.

[12] Ibid., 44.

[13] For catechesis, see CT 5-8; for theology, see *Donum Veritatis* 8.

human wisdom,"[14] and only attained through a profound and authentic "fear of the Lord" (Pr 1:7).

Both theology and catechesis have the task of passing on the Revelation of God brought to completion in Christ, while they are both also called to apply the light of His Revelation to human life in every age and situation.[15] Both teach and explain the sacred doctrines of the Deposit of Faith, though each according to its audience's level of intelligence. Their primary content is the one Faith of Christian Revelation.[16] Theology and catechesis both ponder "what God has said and thought before us,"[17] and which we now come to know primarily through doctrine — the errorless means the Church uses to preserve God's Revelation to man. Theology and catechesis both entail "the quest to understand the Word,"[18] which is given by God, organized into doctrine by the Church's teaching authority, and transmitted via sacred doctrine by faithful living witnesses of Christ. Thus, those involved in these two sciences must be faithful to their content of truth. Concerning theology in particular, Ratzinger (Benedict XVI), in *The Nature and Mission of Theology*, warns that if theology abandons the secure ground of Revelation, it annuls its own constitution. And if a theology rejects the teachings of doctrine and disavows the Magisterium, he continues, it "forfeits the firm ground under its feet and, by stepping out of the realm of thought into the play of power, it also falsifies its scientific character. It thus loses the two foundations

---

[14] STh I, q. 1, a. 6.

[15] See GCD 11.

[16] See Pius XII, Encyclical *Humani Generis* (1950). He states: "It is true, again, that a theologian must constantly have recourse to the fountains of divine revelation. It is for him to show how the doctrine of the teaching authority of the Church is contained in Scripture and in the sacred Tradition, whether explicitly or implicitly… [though] the task of interpreting the deposit authentically was entrusted by our divine Redeemer not to the individual Christian, nor even to the theologian, but only to the Church's teaching authority" (ND 859).

[17] Ratzinger, *The Nature and Mission of Theology*, 104.

[18] Ibid., 105.

of its existence."[19] Elsewhere he continues: "When you are studying theology, your intention is not to learn a trade but to understand the faith, and this presupposes, as we said a while ago, using
the words of Augustine, that the faith is true, that, in other
words, it opens the door to a correct understanding of your own
life, of the world and of men."[20]

Thus, Catholic theologians[21] and catechists, with all evan-

---

[19] Ibid., 107. See also *Donum Veritatis* 12.

[20] *Salt of the Earth: Christianity and the Catholic Church at the End of the Millennium: An Interview With Peter Seewald* (San Francisco: Ignatius Press, 1997), 59.

[21] Catholic theologians are required to obtain a *mandatum*, which obliges them to teach in union with the Magisterium and the doctrines of the Catholic Faith. The *mandatum* is a written commission from the local Bishop to teach Catholic theology at a Catholic college. This calls for theologians to sign and adhere to a creed and oath of fidelity to the Magisterium as outlined in the *Profession of Faith and the Oath of Fidelity on Assuming an Office to be Exercised in the Name of the Church* found in John Paul I's Apostolic Letter *Ad Tuendam Fidem* (1998) as *Appendix* A and B, which were originally issued by the Congregation for the Doctrine of the Faith in 1989. The *mandatum* was first called for by CIC, Can. 812 (1983): "It is necessary that those who teach theological disciplines in any institute of higher studies have a mandate from the competent ecclesiastical authority," and Can. 833: "The following persons are obliged to make a profession of faith in accord with a formula approved by the Apostolic See... professors of theology and philosophy in seminaries... teachers in any university whatsoever who teach disciplines which deal with faith and morals." The *mandatum* is mentioned in the Code of Canons of the Eastern Churches (1990) as follows: "Those who teach subjects regarding faith and morals in Catholic universities must possess a mandate of the ecclesiastical authority [patriarchs]... the same authority can remove this mandate for a serious reason especially if the teachers lack scientific or pedagogical suitability, probity, or integrity of doctrine" (CCEO Can. 644). John Paul II in *Ex Corde Ecclesiae* (1990) states: "In ways appropriate to the different academic disciplines, all Catholic teachers are to be faithful to, and all other teachers are to respect, Catholic doctrine and morals in their research and teaching. In particular, Catholic theologians, aware that they fulfill a mandate received from the Church, are to be faithful to the Magisterium of the Church as the authentic interpreter of Sacred Scripture and Sacred Tradition" (General Norms 4, 3). In the United States, *The Application of Ex Corde Ecclesiae for the United States* (2000) states: "Catholics who teach the theological disciplines in a Catholic university are required to have a *mandatum* granted by competent ecclesiastical authority" (4, 4, e). and *Guidelines Concerning the Academic Mandatum in Catholic Universities* (2001) states, "A professor already hired by the effective date (May 3, 2001) of the *Application* is required to obtain the *mandatum* by June 1, 2002" (4d); and "If all the conditions for granting the *mandatum* are fulfilled, the professor has a right to receive it and ecclesiastical authority has an obligation in justice to grant it" (5a).

gelists, must faithfully teach in accordance with every doctrine[22] of the Church — or they themselves risk losing the theological virtue of faith that secures their union with Christ, while at the same time exposing their students to the same risk. Not only must they believe with theological faith the whole of sacred doctrine, but teachers of the Faith must also be authentic living witnesses of the doctrine they teach.

It is imperative to clarify that sacred doctrine and a lively faith in it, are central to the success of evangelization. Vatican II explains: These "subjects [the doctrines] should be taught in the light of faith, under the guidance of the magisterium of the Church, [so] that students will draw pure Catholic teaching from divine revelation, will enter deeply into its meaning, make it the nourishment of their spiritual life, and learn to proclaim, explain, and defend it"[23] in their encounters with the world. Students deserve to receive the whole of sacred doctrine given to them from the vantage point of a grace-filled, faith-filled witness.

Theology and catechesis also share the same primary two-fold Source of the Faith. First, theology and catechesis must always be impregnated with Sacred Scripture. Discussing the primacy of Scripture not only for catechesis, but also for all of theology, the Congregation for Catholic Education states that "Scripture is the starting point, the *permanent foundation*, and the life-

---

[22] With regard to a member of the Church who obstinately disbelieves even one article of the Faith, St. Thomas Aquinas teaches that they lose all the grace of theological faith: "Neither living nor lifeless faith remains in a heretic who disbelieves one article of faith.... Therefore it is clear that such a heretic with regard to one article has no faith in the other articles, but only a kind of opinion in accordance with his own will" (STh II-II, 5, 3; see also Jm 2:10). As to the meaning of the term "article," the term "has a long history and designates whatever a Catholic must believe, whether defined by the Church as revealed or commonly held by the Church's ordinary and universal magisterium as revealed in Scripture or sacred tradition" (John A. Hardon, SJ, *Modern Catholic Dictionary*, Bardstown, Kentucky: Eternal Life, 2001, 42-43).

[23] *Optatam Totius* 16.

giving and animating principle"[24] of all evangelization. Vatican II adds, "Therefore, the study of the sacred page is, as it were, the very soul of sacred theology,"[25] and of all of evangelization as well.

The second primary Source of evangelization is Sacred Tradition, as summarized in the *Catechism of the Catholic Church*. Confirming this, Ratzinger (Benedict XVI) and Schönborn stated that the *Catechism* is an essential "aid to comprehending and communicating the faith as a living, organic whole."[26]

All those involved in teaching the Faith must be careful that their teaching "in no way does harm to the doctrine of the faith... [but maintains a] very disinterested service" involving Christian charity from a faith-filled perspective.[27] After all, we are dealing with "the science of the things of faith,"[28] states Pope Leo XIII.

Sacred doctrine is as important to sacred theology as it is

---

[24] Congregation for Catholic Education, *The Theological Formation of Future Priests* (2/22/76), 79.

[25] DV 24; see also *Optatam Totius* 16.

[26] Ratzinger and Schönborn, *Introduction to the Catechism*, 7.

[27] *Donum Veritatis* 11. Bernard Lonergan discusses the interconnectedness of theology and catechetics in *Method in Theology* (New York: Seabury Press, 1979), wherein he categorizes theology into eight functional specialties (research, interpretation, history, dialectic, foundations, doctrines, systematics, and communications) in which catechetics is classified under the specialty of communications (125). According to Lonergan, every functional specialty of theology should have a catechetical concern, since, as he insists, there must be a "dynamic unity" between all the subspecialties in the service of God's truth (138ff). About the importance of communications, with catechetics contained as one of its parts, Lonergan writes: "It is in this final stage [or specialty] that theological reflection bears fruit.... But without the last [specialty] the first seven are in vain, for they fail to mature" (355). He continues, "At their service, then, are the seven previous functional specialties. Next, those that would communicate the constitutive meaning of the Christian message, first of all, must live it. For without living the Christian message one does not possess its constitutive meaning, and one cannot lead another to share what one oneself does not possess. Finally, those that communicate the effective meaning of the Christian message, must practice it. For actions speak louder than words, while preaching what one does not practice recalls sounding brass and tinkling cymbal" (362).

[28] Leo XIII, Encyclical *Depuis Le Jour* [*On the Education of the Clergy*] (1899), 19.

to catechesis. The Church teaches that the work of theology, like catechesis, must be grounded in sacred doctrine. The Congregation for the Doctrine of the Faith (whose documents pertain to the ordinary Magisterium[29] and thus require religious submission of will and intellect[30]) states: "The object of theology is the Truth which is the living God and His plan for salvation revealed in Jesus Christ"[31]; and according to Pope John Paul II, the ultimate truth which Revelation provides is always theology's prime concern.[32] He adds, "The chief purpose of theology is to provide an understanding of revelation and the content of faith (sacred doctrine). The very heart of theological inquiry will thus be the contemplation of the mystery of the triune God."[33] Such a theological inquiry necessarily requires that the theologian himself have theological faith, according to Cardinal Francis George, who speaking to the Chicago theologians about the nature of theology, said: "Catholic theology is a science of faith in which the faith itself, as interpreted by the magisterium, is the final criterion of what is true."[34]

There are certain things to keep in mind when considering the relation between these two side-by-side modes of evangelization. As John Paul II stated, "Theological work in the church is first of all at the service of the proclamation of the faith and of catechesis."[35] Theologians must also be mindful that the content of their theology courses have implications in catechesis. John Paul II warns that if theologians wish to express their in-

---

[29] *Donum Veritatis* 18.
[30] Congregation for the Doctrine of the Faith, *Commentary on the Concluding Formula of the 'Professio Fidei,'* 10, publisahed with John Paul II, Apostolic Letter *Motu Proprio Ad Tuendam Fidem* (1998).
[31] *Donum Veritatis* 8.
[32] John Paul II, Encyclical *Fides et Ratio* (1998), 92.
[33] Ibid., 93.
[34] Lieblich, "Catholic colleges mum on teacher 'loyalty oath,'" 11.
[35] FR 99.

vestigative inquiries with their students, then they "have a duty to take great care that people do not take for certainty what on the contrary belongs to the area of questions of opinion or of discussion among experts."[36] This is important not only for the sake of clarity within theology but also to prevent such opinions from being filtered down and re-presented to those in catechesis as if they were doctrine. The point is that there is a close connection between theology and catechesis and that "every stirring in the field of theology also has repercussions in that of catechesis."[37]

Not only do theologians have to take care in not misleading their students, who might in turn mislead others, but catechists themselves must also exercise prudence. While catechists may choose to "pick from the field of theological research those points that can provide light for their own reflection and teaching,"[38] they must do so with caution and wisdom. Ultimately, truth, faithfulness to Revelation, and consideration of their audiences' maturity and level of faith are factors for all such considerations and legitimate interchanges between theology and catechesis.

2. Distinctions

There are also some distinctions that exist within the various modes of evangelization, particularly between catechesis and theology. Catechesis basically focuses on imparting the essentials of the Faith, respecting genuine inculturation, while theology further incorporates the dimensions of a scientific investigation which strives to develop further understanding of the mysteries of the doctrines of the Faith through reasoning and research.

---

[36] CT 61.

[37] Ibid.

[38] Ibid.

Theology is also distinguished from catechesis in that it is called to investigate and further develop the ways in which the Faith can shed light on new questions raised by contemporary culture.[39] While both catechesis and theology must utilize reason illumined by faith and prayerful contemplation, theology tends to presuppose that theological faith already exists with its students while catechesis focuses more on fostering personal faith as one of its more direct goals. Theology, building upon a solid catechesis, then tends to strive further to engage in scientific inquiry, one that ensures a liberty of principles within an authentic theological method. In their scientific endeavors, theologians "may, according to the case, [even] raise questions regarding the timeliness, the form, or even the contents of magisterial interventions."[40] "Nevertheless," John Paul II explains in *Veritatis Splendor*, "in order to 'reverently preserve and faithfully expound' the word of God, the Magisterium has the duty to state that some trends of theological thinking and certain philosophical affirmations are incompatible with revealed truth."[41]

Theology certainly goes beyond catechesis in its investigative and scientific dimension. While in speculative theology, "doctrinal and moral teaching must be presented in harmony with the best theological insights which have received ecclesial approbation," on the other hand, according to Francis D. Kelly, in catechesis and catechetics, "it would be irresponsible for publishers or catechists to propagate the themes of individual theologians or scholars which have not been subject to critical examination and review by other theologians and by the official and authentic Magisterium of the Church. Catechetics is not an exercise in speculative theology but a faithful transmission and fostering of the Church's accepted faith."[42]

---

[39] ECE 29.
[40] *Donum Veritatis* 24.
[41] John Paul II, *Veritatis Splendor* (1993), 29.
[42] Francis D. Kelly, 122-123.

B. The Role of Sacred Doctrine Today

To assist us in understanding the necessity of using sound doctrinal resources in catechesis to hand on the Faith and to foster conversion, let's examine the Church's definition of catechesis,[43] as the foundation of the Church's ministry of evangelization, more closely and then proceed to discuss the contemporary role of sacred doctrine in spreading the Good News.

Catechesis means 'to echo the Word of God,' by faithfully transmitting and passing it on. This word, which the ancient Greeks used in reference to the theatre and appears neither in the Old Testament nor in the Gospels, was taken up by the nascent Church to indicate their primordial duty to make disciples,[44] to provoke an "echo" in the mind and heart of those being evangelized, to bring about conversion to Christ and transformation in Christ. This entails a teaching about the things of God, "so that [those taught] may learn to fear [Him] all the days that they live upon the earth, and that they may teach their children so" (Dt 4:10). "The content of catechesis is found in God's word, written and handed down."[45] Catechesis is simply the effective communication of divine Revelation[46] in "the school of the word of God."[47] It is "the transmission of God's Word to invite people to personal faith."[48] To echo the Word of God, catechists must impart the sacred doctrines of God's Revelation

---

[43] According to one catechetical expert, the term "catechesis" is preferred to other terms such as religious education, religious socialization, and Christian religious education, "because it is a term the Church has historically used for this essential ministry of instruction in the faith" (Kelly, *Mystery*, 43).

[44] Editorial Commission of the *Catechism of the Catholic Church, Informative Dossier* (6/25/92), accessed online at http://usccb.org/catechism/general/dossier.htm # limits (7/22/05).

[45] GCD 45.

[46] GDC 143.

[47] GDC 142.

[48] Francis D. Kelly, *Mystery*, 44.

so that their students receive a "'divine education'... [both] by means of catechesis and by means of knowledge and experience."[49] Thus in a very real sense, the contents of catechesis do not originate in the teacher, but are derived from one true Source.

Ultimately, catechesis points beyond doctrine itself to a Person, such that "what is communicated in catechesis is not (simply) a body of conceptual truths, but the mystery of the living God."[50] "This involves making known the true face of God and his loving plan of salvation for man, as it has been revealed in Jesus Christ"[51] and handed down through the Christian ages through sacred doctrine. It is Christ Who reveals and is Himself discovered *through* doctrinal truth by way of doctrinal teaching. Thus, "the fundamental task of catechesis is to present Christ and everything in relation to him,"[52] namely, "the teaching of Jesus Christ, the truth that he communicates, or more precisely, the Truth that he is."[53] Every endeavor to present an "exposition of doctrine" in catechesis, according to the *Catechism*, must "seek to help deepen understanding of faith, its putting down roots in personal life and its shining forth in personal conduct"[54] in relation to Christ and His Church.

In his *General Catechetical Directory*, Paul VI states that the nature and purpose of catechesis is precisely to impart doctrine so as "to make men's faith become living, conscious, and active, through the light of instruction."[55] Cardinal Ratzinger (Benedict XVI) summarized the task of catechesis in his book, *Gospel, Catechesis and Catechism*, by stating: "Catechesis aims at com-

---

[49] Ibid.
[50] FR 99.
[51] GDC 23.
[52] GDC 98.
[53] CT 6.
[54] CCC 23.
[55] GCD 17.

ing to know Jesus concretely"[56] through the sources of His Revelation. The goal of catechesis is to foster in every student a constant deepening of grace in their soul so that their mind may be enlightened with divine truth, with the *lumen fidei*, so as to motivate their will to love and so as to have their being transformed into another image and likeness of Love Himself, Christ, thereby causing an ever closer union of each with Christ and with one other. "Christ enables us to live in him all that he himself lived, and he lives it in us."[57]

The goals of catechesis are summarized in "Specific Aims of Catechesis," a subsection of John Paul II's catechetical reference guide, *Catechesi Tradendae*, wherein he states:

> Catechesis aims, therefore, at developing understanding of the mystery of Christ in the light of God's Word, so that the whole of a person's humanity is impregnated by that Word. Changed by the working of grace into a new creature, the Christian thus sets himself to follow Christ and learns more and more within the Church to think like Him, to judge like Him, to act in conformity with His commandments....
>
> To put it more precisely: ... the aim of catechesis is to be the teaching and maturation stage, that is to say, the period in which the Christian, having accepted by faith the Person of Jesus Christ as the one Lord and having given Him complete adherence by sincere conversion of heart, endeavors to know better this Jesus to whom he has entrusted himself.[58]

John Paul continues, "the definitive aim [or end] of catechesis is to put people not only in touch but in communion, in intimacy,

---

[56] Joseph Cardinal Ratzinger, *Gospel, Catechesis, Catechism* (San Francisco: Ignatius Press, 1997), 56.
[57] CCC 521.
[58] CT 20.

with Jesus Christ,"[59] yes, *intimacy*. Thus, authentic catechesis fosters conversion and seeks to complete the "integral Christian initiation"[60] of every person taught. At its core, catechesis is simply the passing on of the Person and Message of Jesus Christ as found in the Sacred Scriptures, the Sacred Tradition as summarized in the catechisms, and in the history, laws, prayers, writings of the Magisterium, Saints, Fathers, and Doctors, and liturgical rites of His Church.

Sacred Scripture and the *Catechism* have a particularly important role in bringing those evangelized into intimate relation with Jesus. Evangelization "should contribute to the gradual grasping of the whole truth about the divine plan by preparing the faithful for the reading of the Sacred Scripture and the learning of tradition."[61] It must continually maintain assiduous contact with the source texts themselves, as John Paul II confirms in *Catechesi Tradendae*: "Catechesis will always draw its content from the living source of the Word of God transmitted in Tradition and the Scriptures."[62]

The Scriptures have special importance in evangelization. To get to know the Lord, the *National Catechetical Directory* (United States) recommends that every student have his or her own copy of Scripture.[63] According to the Holy See's catechetical directory, students should also be taught to pray the Scriptures and to see their connection to the Sacraments.[64]

The Scriptures must be regarded and handed on as the inspired Word of God,[65] "the speech of God put into writing under the breath of the Holy Spirit."[66] To assist with this, the *Cat-*

[59] Ibid., 5; GDC 116.
[60] CT 21.
[61] GCD 24.
[62] See CT 27.
[63] NCD 60.
[64] GCD 43.
[65] See DV 11.
[66] CCC 81.

echism and Ratzinger (Benedict XVI) have advocated utilizing the *lectio divina* approach so as to foster among students a deeper understanding of Scripture.[67] Cardinal Ratzinger added that even in the classroom, the Scriptures should not be read as purely a theoretical reading or seen with only an intellectual curiosity (similar to how in the science of anatomy one looks at and examines a cadaver), but must be listened to with true and profound attention of heart, for it is God Who speaks to us through His Word.[68] This is always a spiritual experience, more than an academic one.

This is how the Faith has been transmitted from the time of Christ. As famed catechist theologian Msgr. Kevane points out: "The Word of Jesus is the Gospel which the Apostles preached and taught to their converts. The Word of Jesus is the Word of God placed in their hands as a divine deposit, a teaching of Faith to be guarded by them (1 Tm 6:20), indeed infallibly, in their own evangelization and teaching."[69] For most of Christian history, and more formally since the development of a systematic presentation of sacred doctrine as first masterfully organized in Aquinas' *Summa* and later in the Church's catechisms, the foundations of the Faith have been taught in these ways, utilizing Scripture and Tradition to assist those evangelized in coming to know and love Christ.

Though there is a crisis of faith today on many local and academic levels, the Church herself has consistently upheld the necessity of teaching sacred doctrine in the work of evangelization. This crisis of faith stems back several decades. But, back in

---

[67] *Lectio divina* is a way of reading Scripture, which is open to responding to God's active and living Word with all our heart. It traditionally includes several aspects: *lectio, meditatio, oratio, contemplatio, consolatio, discretio, deliberatio*, and *actio*. This method of praying Scripture is recommended in the *Catechism* (1177, 2708).

[68] Joseph Cardinal Ratzinger, *Address to the Council of the European Bishops* (Sept. 14-18, 1992), quoted in *The Catholic World Report* (Nov. 1992), 49.

[69] Eugene Kevane, *Jesus the Divine Teacher* (Steubenville: Franciscan University, 1991), 303.

1965, when the *Declaration on Christian Education* (*Gravissimum Educationis*) was issued by the Fathers of Vatican II, the catechetical crisis to come was not yet underway in full force. In fact, some in catechetical work were rightly stating that catechesis was in certain ways suffering not from the negation of doctrine, but from the other extreme, namely a dry overemphasis on the rote memorization of the doctrines of the Faith, one that lacked emphasis on an internalization that fostered a relationship with Christ and adapted to His new way of life. In a certain sense, this situation gave impetus to a new catechetical renewal, with good changes proposed at first, but one that eventually swung to the other extreme, which almost exclusively focused on subjective experience and relativism. Instead of solving a real problem within pre-Vatican II catechesis, these proponents of the new catechesis caused worse problems.

The teaching authority of the Church has not remained idle while watching this crisis grow. Already trying to exhort teachers of the Faith to balance both the emphasis on the doctrines of the Faith with the lived faith experience of the teacher and students, Vatican II's *Gravissimum Educationis* defined the goal of Christian education as follows:

- That the baptized, while they are gradually introduced to the knowledge of the mystery of salvation become ever more aware of the gift they have received;
- That they learn in addition how to worship God the Father in spirit and truth (see John 4:23) especially in liturgical action;
- That they be conformed in their personal lives according to the new man created in justice and holiness of truth (Eph 4:22-24);
- That they develop into perfect manhood, to the mature measure of the fullness of Christ (see Eph 4:13);
- That they strive for the growth of the Mystical Body;

- That they become aware of their calling, learning how to bear witness to the hope that is in them (see Peter 3:15); and
- That they learn how to help in the Christian formation of the world that takes place when natural powers viewed in full consideration of man redeemed by Christ contribute to the good of the whole of society.[70]

With all this stated, it is evident that the first order of teaching the Faith is still clearly to teach "the knowledge of the mystery of salvation" so as to form holy and perfect Saints in Christ. Catechesis is thus the imparting of the content of the Catholic Faith so as to foster conversion and personal holiness so that the students may become witnesses themselves of the love of Christ to the world to both attain eternal life and to save other souls.

Thus, evangelizers are given the task of forming other teachers from the students they catechize. Such would likely have been the enduring successes of the modern catechetical movement that has reigned since Vatican II if the doctrines of the Faith had remained the primary content of their teaching. Imagine if students had more regularly been 'introduced' to the *truths* of the Faith, instead of facing situations where these truths were neglected or set aside for more modern approaches or for one-sided subjective, overly experiential 'content.'

The Church at Vatican II did not re-define the meaning of doctrine or its role in evangelization. The Council Fathers were aware of their responsibility to safeguard doctrinal truth, and thus confirmed that teaching the Faith in our day "has the responsibility of announcing the way of salvation to all men, of communicating the life of Christ to those who believe... and of assist-

---

[70] GE 7. See also Msgr. Francis D. Kelly in *The Mystery We Proclaim*, Part Three: The Goals of Catechesis (67-88), lists the five C's of catechesis, which are similar to those of Vatican II: they are: conversion, community, content, contemplation, and commitment.

ing men to be able to come to the fullness of this life."[71] This ministry of "communicating the life of Christ" entails passing on the truths of His life and message and of His sacramental and liturgical institutions. In other words, the content of catechesis is objective; it is nothing other than the deposit of sacred truths.[72] The primary goal of "all catechetical instruction," *Gravissimum Educationis* states, "is to enlighten and strengthen [students'] faith, nourish their life according to the spirit of Christ, lead them to intelligent and active participation in the liturgical mystery, and give them motivation for apostolic activity."[73] However it occurred, what later ensued in catechetical practice in the United States and elsewhere was the result of an improper reading of Vatican II.

All authentic evangelization is biblical-doctrinal. The Church's documents since Vatican II have also consistently and clearly confirmed that her sacred doctrine is to be utilized in the work in teaching the Faith. The Church has reiterated that the primary Source for catechetical teaching is always and has always been the Word of God.[74] In this endeavor, besides utilizing Sacred Scriptures, the Church has also explained that the sources for teaching the Faith should be derived from the wellspring of Church documents themselves. According to the Congregation for Catholic Education, in *The Religious Dimension of Education in Catholic Schools*, teachers are encouraged to use the documents of Vatican II in religion classes to answer questions raised.[75] The Congregation for Catholic Education also states that

---

[71] GE 9.

[72] This does not omit the fact of a hierarchy of truths and an ever-growing understanding of the Faith throughout the development of doctrine in Tradition and Magisterial teaching. See CCC 90-95.

[73] GE 9.

[74] See CT 27; CCC 2688.

[75] Congregation for Catholic Education, *The Religious Dimension of Education in Catholic Schools* (1988), 44 (hereafter cited as RDE).

authentic religious education necessarily entails "generous and humble communion with the Holy Father."[76]

The *General Directory of Catechesis* (GDC) goes further to instruct teachers to actively use Sacred Scripture and the *Catechism of the Catholic Church* in developing their course syllabus, and to use them as the primary twofold Source "for all catechetical activity in our time."[77] John Paul II, in his post-synodal document *Ecclesia in America*, also recommended the use of the *Catechism* together with the GDC itself in the primary and secondary levels of religious education, stating: "I heartily recommend the use of these two resources, of universal value, to everyone involved in catechesis in America."[78] Finally, the *Code of Canon Law* confirms that doctrine is the essential content of catechesis: "It is necessary that the formation and education given in a Catholic school be based upon the principles of Catholic doctrine."[79]

The fact that the Church has even had to clarify such otherwise obvious principles regarding doctrine in evangelization, and the active utilization of Church documents in the work of catechesis, points to the fact that such sources of content have not been thought by some to be necessary in teaching the Faith today. But, by so strongly advocating the use of these principles in evangelization, the Church is sending out a clear message — namely that first *obeying* and then *faithfully teaching* Catholic doctrine (for detail on the threefold order and requirements of obedience regarding the doctrines of the Deposit of Faith, see Table 1) is central to all authentic evangelization.

We may ask ourselves what is the answer to the crisis of Faith. Given all that has been said, I think the answer is three-

---

[76] Ibid., 72.

[77] GDC 128.

[78] John Paul II, Post-Synodal Apostolic Exhortation *Ecclesia in America* (1999), 69. The GDC itself also states that these two texts "are two distinct but complementary instruments at the service of the Church's catechetical activity" (120).

[79] CIC, can. 803.

fold: obedience, obedience, obedience.[80] As the Saints demonstrate, to be obedient to the will of God is not stubbornness or fanaticism, it is true love. Obedience is the key to doing God's will — obedience to God and obedience to the Body of Jesus, His Church. Obedience of faith (free assent/submission of the will with the assistance of the supernatural virtue of faith infused by God as a gift), to the whole truth of sacred doctrine is the responsibility of all the faithful. Concerning doctrine and obedience, in the past decade, the Magisterium has shown a development of doctrine in regards to understanding the threefold order of religious truth and the corresponding levels of obedience of faith required regarding the doctrines of the Deposit of Faith, as outlined in Table 1 as follows.

---

[80] See Rm 1:5, which speaks of the "obedience of faith."

The Blessed Virgin Mary is the Model of holy obedience, as demonstrated in the most heroic way through her *fiat*: "Let it be done to me according to your Word," and as she advocated in her last recorded words in the Scriptures: "Do whatever He tells you" (Jn 2:5).

Every person has the obligation to properly form *and obey* his conscience according to the objective truths concerning good and evil that have been determined by God through reason and divine Revelation (CCC 1799), so as to protect human dignity and attain true happiness. The Magisterium is the most certain guide of true conscience. "Christians have a great help for the formation of conscience in the Church and her Magisterium. As the Council affirms: 'In forming their consciences the Christian faithful must give careful attention to the sacred and certain teaching of the Church...' (DH 14). It follows that the authority of the Church... in no way undermines the freedom of conscience of Christians. This is so not only because freedom of conscience is never freedom 'from' the truth but *always and only* freedom 'in' truth." (VS 64)

On the other hand, disobedience typically originates from lack of formation and/or wrong decisions. Sources of such malady often stem from the following: "Ignorance of Christ and his Gospel, bad example given by others, enslavement to one's passions, assertion of a mistaken notion of autonomy of conscience, rejection of the Church's authority and her teaching, lack of conversion and of charity" (CCC 1792).

[81] Chart organized from information provided from the following — *Ad Tuendam Fidem*: the CDF's *Commentary* (1998) 5-11; the CDF's *Donum Veritatis* (1990) 15-17, 23; CCC 882-3, 891-2; LG 25. The examples used in levels I and II of the *Examples* column come directly from these magisterial documents. All of these doctrines are specifically stated and classified by level in the CDF's *Commentary* to *Ad Tuendam Fidem* (#11), though they are not meant to give the impression of completeness or exhaustiveness. The Magisterial documents do not give specific examples for level III. The three levels of doctrinal truth may be categorized as (I) dogmatic doctrine, (II) definitive doctrine, and (III) authoritative, non-definitive doctrine.

TABLE 1

The Threefold Order of Religious Truth and the Requirements of an Obedience of Faith Regarding the Sacred Doctrines of the Deposit of the Faith[81]

Order of Truths	Level of Doctrine Proposed	How Proposed	Level of Obedience Required	Examples
I.	All divinely revealed truths; infallibly pronounced and solemnly declared (defined) to be found in Revelation (necessary for eternal salvation); dogmas of the Faith; as truths per se revealed[82]	1. By the Roman Pontiff speaking *ex cathedra*[83] 2. By the College of Bishops gathered in ecumenical council, in union with the Pope[84] (teaching infallibly) 3. By infallible proposal for belief by the ordinary and universal Magisterium	Requires the firm and definitive (loyal and obedient) assent of theological faith (and "whoever obstinately places them in doubt or denies them falls under the censure of *heresy*"[85]) and is based directly on faith in the authority of the Word of God as found in Scripture and Tradition (doctrines *de fide credenda* — to be *believed* with faith)	1. The articles of faith of the Creed 2. The Christological & Marian dogmas 3. The institution of the sacraments by Christ; the Real Presence of Christ in the Eucharist 4. The foundation of the Church by the will of Christ 5. The primacy & infallibility of the Roman Pontiff 6. The doctrines on original sin and on the immortality of the spiritual soul 7. The absence of error in the inspired sacred texts 8. The voluntary killing of an innocent human being
II.	Everything definitively proposed by the Church (to be held definitively and absolutely) regarding faith and morals; though not necessarily proposed as formally and divinely	1. By the Roman Pontiff speaking *ex cathedra* 2. By the College of Bishops gathered in (ecumenical) council, in union with the Pope 3. By an infallible teaching of the	Requires firm and definitive (loyal and obedient) assent (or would be no longer in full communion with the Catholic Church); based on 1) faith in the Holy Spirit's assistance to the Magisterium, and	1. The development in the understanding of the doctrine connected with the definition of papal infallibility, prior to Vatican I, whereby it was held to be definitive but not yet defined as a divinely revealed truth 2. The reaffirmation of the priestly ordination of men only

---

[82] Pertaining to all doctrine, the Christian faithful must believe as true "the *whole* truth that God has revealed" and "*all* 'that which is contained in the word of God, written or handed down, and which the Church proposes for belief as divinely revealed'" (CCC 150, 182, quoting Paul VI, CPG, 20; see also canon 750). This "faith is necessary for salvation" (CCC 183). The faithful are obliged to obey, with assent or submission, *all* of the doctrines of the Faith; and disobedience (with an informed conscience and free will) of *any* doctrine (on all three levels) may lead to mortal sin.

revealed truth, nonetheless are intimately and intrinsically connected with them and some of which are to be affirmed as deriving from Revelation itself (necessary for eternal salvation) while also including truths necessary to safeguard the truths per se revealed	ordinary and universal Magisterium as a *sententia definitive tenenda*	2) on the Catholic doctrine of the infallibility of the Magisterium (doctrines *de fide tenenda* — to be *held* with faith)	3. The illicitness of euthanasia, prostitution, & fornication 4. The legitimacy of the election of the Supreme Pontiff or of the celebration of an ecumenical council 5. The canonization of Saints (papal canonizations of Saints are infallible teachings; and are dogmatic facts, though not dogmas of the Faith) 6. The invalidity of Anglican ordinations
III. All of the Church's teachings regarding faith and morals which have been presented as true or at least as sure, even if they have not been defined with a solemn judgment or proposed as definitive by the ordinary and universal Magisterium[86]	Expressions of the ordinary Magisterium of the Roman Pontiff or of the College of Bishops in union with him, who set forth doctrines in a non-definitive way	Requires religious submission of will and intellect, understood within the logic of faith and under the impulse of obedience to the Faith (and a proposition contrary to these doctrines can be qualified as erroneous, or as rash or dangerous – *tuto doceri non potest*)[87]	In general, the teachings set forth by the authentic ordinary Magisterium in a non-definitive way (Many think that the development in the understanding of the doctrine of Mary as Co-Redemptrix is currently in this category.[88] The doctrines of monogenism, contraception, and capital punishment may currently be in this category.)

---

83 "The Roman Pontiff, by reason of his office as Vicar of Christ, and as pastor of the entire Church has full, supreme, and universal power over the whole Church, a power which he can always exercise unhindered" (LG 22; CCC 882).

84 "The college or body of bishops has no authority unless united with the Roman Pontiff, Peter's successor, as its head. [Its] supreme and full authority over the universal Church... cannot be exercised without the agreement of the Roman Pontiff" (LG 22, 25; CCC 883).

85 ATF: the CDF's *Commentary* 5; CIC canon 750-751, 1364.

86 These doctrines in the third order of truths are proposed for three reasons: (1) to aid a better and deeper understanding of Revelation and explain its contents; (2) to recall how some teaching is in conformity with the truths of faith; or (3) to guard or warn against ideas that are incompatible with these truths or against dan-

It is also important here to note that all the doctrines of the Church are true and require a certain level of obedience of faith, although in varying degrees as delineated by Magisterial sources and discussed in column four of Table 1.[89] This required belief is based on grace and free will in the light of truth and obedience to Christ.

gerous opinions which can lead to error (see ATF: CDF's *Commentary* 10, *Donum Veritatis* 23). Such doctrines are part of the Deposit of Faith and passed on through Tradition and the *sensus fidelium* (sense of the Faithful), that which is a recognition that the Holy Spirit keeps the truth alive in the hearts of God's faithful people, in general and throughout the Church's history. In this, the hierarchy and the laity of the Church are united in the one Body of Christ. This does not exclude the possibility that the bishops of a whole country (England in the 16th century with Anglicanism) or a large group of theologians in a given period, like in today's culture of dissent, could not be wrong as to doctrinal truth.

[87] These doctrines "require degrees of adherence according to the mind and the will manifested [by the Church]; this is shown especially (1) by the nature of the documents, (2) by the frequent repetition of the same doctrine, or (3) by the tenor of the verbal expression" (ATF: CDF's *Commentary* 11; LG 25).

[88] See Mark Miravalle, STD, *Mary: Coredemptrix, Mediatrix, Advocate* (Santa Barbara: Queenship Publishing, 1993), 1-24. By the mid-1990's, the movement for this dogma had received nearly 7 million petitions and the endorsements of 43 cardinals and over 550 bishops worldwide from the Universal Church.
  In June of 1997, a theological commission issued a negative opinion on the possibility of defining a dogma on Mary's maternal mediation. Though this is the case, it is also evident from recent Church history that other theological advisory commissions organized by the Holy See have come to conclusions which ultimately were not adopted by the Holy See. A recent example was the theological commission requested by the Holy See to examine the question of artificial birth control, the conclusion of which was overridden by Pope Paul VI when he reaffirmed the constant Church teaching against artificial birth control in his 1968 Encyclical, *Humanae Vitae*. The only statement from the Holy See to date on the possibility of defining the fifth Marian dogma, by Dr. Joaquin Navarro-Valls, director of the Holy See Press Office, stated: "There is no study underway at this moment in time by the Holy Father Pope John Paul II or the Congregation for the Doctrine of the Faith on the subject of the possibility of a papal definition on this theme" (1997). However, it in no way implies there may not be one in the future. See also http://www.voxpopuli.org/.

[89] As to carefully pronounced teachings proposed in encyclicals, Pius XII states in *Humani Generis*, an encyclical which condemned the theory of polygenism: "It is not to be supposed that a position advanced in an encyclical does not, *ipso facto*, claim assent.... And when the Roman Pontiffs carefully pronounce on some subject which has hitherto been controverted, it must be clear to everybody that, in the mind and intention of the Pontiffs concerned, this subject can no longer be regarded as a matter of free debate among theologians" (ND 858). Examples of this also include the doctrine on contraception by Paul VI in *Humanae Vitae* (14) and the illicitness of euthanasia taught by Pope John Paul II in *Evangelium Vitae* (65).

C. The *Catechism* is the Source of Sacred Doctrine

The Church's fundamental source text for all three levels of sacred doctrine is the *Catechism of the Catholic Church*. The purpose of the *Catechism* is to provide a systematic exposition of God's Revelation in the form of sacred doctrine for evangelization, sharing the Good News of Christ. John Paul II explains in his Apostolic Constitution, *Fidei Depositum*, that the *Catechism* is "a statement of the Church's faith and of Catholic doctrine," which is "attested to or illumined by Sacred Scripture, the Apostolic Tradition, and the Church's Magisterium."[90] In other words, the *Catechism*, the Church's most official text of sacred doctrine, must be actively utilized as the basic systematic Source for all of evangelization. So too, the primary content of catechesis must be the content of the *Catechism* itself, namely objective doctrinal truths of faith and morals that derive from Sacred Scripture and Apostolic Tradition as authentically interpreted by the Church's Magisterium.

Teaching the Faith *is* teaching sacred doctrine faithfully. Thus, as the Constitution states, the *Catechism*, which is comprised of doctrine, is "a sure norm for teaching the faith" because it is "a sure and authentic reference text for teaching catholic doctrine."[91] This is the primary and almost exclusive task of authentic Catholic evangelization. The Prologue of the *Catechism* continues this line of thinking, stating:

> This catechism aims at presenting an organic synthesis of the essential and fundamental contents of Catholic doctrine, as regards both faith and morals, in the light of the Second Vatican Council and the whole of the Church's Tradition. Its principal sources are the

---

[90] John Paul II, Apostolic Constitution *Fidei Depositum* (1992), 3.
[91] Ibid.

Sacred Scriptures, the Fathers of the Church, the liturgy, and the Church's Magisterium.... This work is intended primarily for those responsible for catechesis... [and] will also be useful reading for all other Christian faithful.[92]

The GDC reiterates the importance of the *Catechism* as the premier source of doctrine, calling it "an act [an 'instrument,' a 'document,' and 'an official text'] of the Magisterium of the Pope, by which, in our times, in virtue of Apostolic Authority, he synthesizes normatively the totality of the Catholic faith."[93] The *Catechism* is "an official text of the Church's Magisterium, which authoritatively gathers in a *precise* form, and in an organic synthesis, the events and fundamental *salvific truths*"[94] of the Faith, "without 'presenting as doctrines of the faith special interpretations which are only private opinions or the views of some theological school.'"[95] In other words, the *Catechism* is a "comprehensive synthesis of the faith of universal value,"[96] which is "a doctrinal point of reference"[97] and "a particularly authentic act of interpretation of [the Word of God, proclaiming and transmitting it] *in all its truth* and purity."[98] Just as glass and steel and wood are combined to make a building, as the analogy goes, so the doctrines of the Faith have been organized into one unified cathedral of truth in the *Catechism*.

By its nature, the *Catechism* does not itself advance the development of doctrine, but only authoritatively communicates it. "The individual doctrines which the *Catechism* presents," ac-

---

[92] CCC 11-12.
[93] GDC 120.
[94] GDC 124 (italics added).
[95] Ibid.
[96] GDC 121.
[97] GDC 122.
[98] GDC 125 (italics added).

cording to Ratzinger (Benedict XVI), "receive no other weight than that which they already possess."[99] Thus, the *Catechism* contains the threefold level of doctrines: (1) divinely revealed truths, (2) truths definitively taught but not as divinely revealed,[100] and (3) other propositions which are not contained among the revealed truths of faith but are nonetheless intimately connected with them.[101]

While not all the doctrines in the *Catechism* are infallibly defined[102] as such, the *Catechism* is the best expression to date of the Catholic Faith and of her sacred doctrines; thus it is without error. The *Catechism*, as "a significant contemporary expression of the living Tradition of the Church and a sure norm for teaching the faith,"[103] is a uniquely authoritative and precise composite of the Church's doctrine, the truths of faith and morals, and the Deposit of Faith. This being so, nonetheless, there will continue to be a development of doctrine[104] such that some of the expressions and language used in the *Catechism* will as time progresses likely be more clearly, and perhaps even more definitively, formulated, communicated, expressed, and elaborated on by the Magisterium. Doctrine itself will not change, but

---

[99] Ratzinger and Schönborn, *Introduction to the Catechism*, 26.

[100] "By its nature, the task of religiously guarding and loyally expounding the deposit of Revelation (in all its integrity and purity), implies that the Magisterium can make a pronouncement 'in a definitive way' on propositions which, even if not contained among the truths of faith, are nonetheless intimately connected with them, in such a way, that the definitive character of such affirmations derives in the final analysis from revelation itself" (CDF, *Donum Veritatis*, 16).

[101] The *Catechism* also contains teachings that are *not* infallible definitions and have *not* been officially pronounced in a defined manner, but are proposed in the exercise of the ordinary Magisterium, and thus lead "to better understanding of Revelation in matters of faith and morals" (CCC 892).

[102] When a Pope infallibly defines a doctrine, he proclaims "in an absolute decision a doctrine pertaining to faith and morals... [whereby] his definitions are rightly said to be irreformable by their very nature" (LG 25). Otherwise, "No doctrine is understood to be infallibly defined unless it is clearly established as such" (Can. 749.3).

[103] GDC 128.

[104] CCC 94.

succeeding generations will continue to build on the insights of
earlier ones, and doctrinal truth will become better understood
and its meaning and beauty become more apparent over time,
as certain doctrines may be declared more definitively with the
guidance of the Holy Spirit. So shall it continue until Christ re-
turns.

The *Catechism*, because it teaches Church doctrine, teaches
truth. The *Catechism* is truth. The assurance that all the teachings contained in the *Catechism* are true is presupposed on the
authority of the Magisterium[105] and is nonetheless an extension
of the Magisterium's charism of infallibility, guaranteed by the
promised assistance of the Holy Spirit.[106] For, "[a]longside this
infallibility of *ex cathedra* definitions, there is the charism of the
Holy Spirit's assistance, granted to Peter and his Successors so
that they would not err in matters of faith and morals... [which]
is not limited to exceptional cases, but embraces in varying degrees the *whole exercise* of the Magisterium."[107] Even when magisterial teaching concerns discipline and practice, and not doctrine, such teaching is also guided by God's Hand, and thus the
faithful must give adherence. For, according to the CDF, "*All*
acts of the Magisterium derive from the same source, that is, from
Christ... [and] are not without divine assistance and [thus] call
for the adherence of the faithful."[108]

---

[105] See LG 25.

[106] Concerning the direct extent of the Magisterium's infallibility, the CCC states:
"This infallibility extends as far as does the deposit of divine Revelation; it also
extends to all those elements of doctrine, including morals, without which the
saving truths of the faith cannot be preserved, explained, or observed" (2035).

[107] John Paul II, General Audience (3/24/93).

[108] *Donum Veritatis* 17 (italics added). This includes decisions in matters of discipline, though "a theologian may, according to the case, raise questions regarding
the timeliness, the form, or even the contents of [some] magisterial interventions
[or judgments]" because some magisterial pronouncements may contain asser-
tions which are true and others which are not sure, though both are inextricably
connected at the time they are made (*Donum Veritatis* 24). In regards to "interventions" and "judgments" of the Magisterium as mentioned above, as well as
"elaborations" (Vatican II, *Unitatis Redintegratio* Decree on Ecumenism [1964],

It is important to note that the confidence the faithful must place in the *Catechism* is *not* to be based on whether its teachings are subjectively convincing to them or not, *but* as previously stated, on the authority of the Magisterium that promulgated it, and on the language used by John Paul II in the Apostolic Constitution *Fidei Depositum* on the publication of the *Catechism*.[109] All the propositions in the *Catechism* require either the assent of faith or at least religious submission.[110] Adherence

---

7), "expressions" (UR 17), and even the language used to "formulate" doctrine (GS 62), there may exist *deficiencies* (though *not errors* per say), and thus "theologians are invited to seek continually for more suitable ways of communicating doctrine to the men of their times. For the deposit of faith or revealed truth are one thing; the manner in which they are formulated *without violence to their meaning and significance* is another" (GS 62) (italics added for emphasis).

We must distinguish between doctrine, that which is truth, and the manner in which it is expressed. The doctrines of the Church are without "error or need of adaptation; but in the manner of expressing them there can be deficiencies (cf. UR 6b) and new and more suitable ways of communicating them must be found (cf. GS 62c)," states Bonaventura Kloppenburg, OFM, in *The Ecclesiology of Vatican II*, trans. Matthew J. O'Connell (Chicago: Franciscan Herald Press, 1974), 146. Thus, the Church's doctrines may not be subject to the interplay of differing opinions as to their content, which is otherwise permitted and common among theologians on issues not understood to be doctrines or at least not yet clearly presented by the Church as such.

[109] For a discussion on the weight of Magisterial teachings, see LG 25.1; *Donum Veritatis* 24.

[110] "In the new formula of the Profession of Faith recently approved (cf. AAS 81 [1989]: 105, 1169), a distinction was made between divinely revealed truths and truths definitively taught but not as divinely revealed, [the latter of] which therefore require a definitive assent that nevertheless is not an assent of faith" (John Paul II, General Audience [3/24/93]). Further, with regard to the non-definitive teachings of the ordinary Magisterium found in the *Catechism*, "the faithful 'are to adhere to [them] with religious assent' which, though distinct from the assent of faith, is nonetheless an extension of it" (CCC 892). See also Table 1 above.

and assent are based upon theological faith[111] and upon reason,[112] the latter which prepares for faith and explores it, together motivated by trusting love, in what is called "the obedience of faith."[113]

In essence, the *Catechism*, according to Schönborn, was promulgated "to serve the guardianship and the transmission of the deposit of faith... the 'faith that was once for all entrusted to the saints (Jude 3; cf. CCC 171).'"[114]

Even the *Compendium of the Catechism of the Catholic Church* (2005), a 200-page synthesis of the voluminous 1992 *Catechism*, draws its source from the *Catechism* itself and uses the same phraseology as the *Catechism*, with specific reference numbers to the *Catechism* as well. Assuring the completeness and integrity of Catholic doctrine, like the *Catechism*, the *Compendium* is "an authoritative, certain and complete text regarding the essential aspects of the faith of the Church... in harmony with the *Catechism*... [and] which faithfully reflects the *Catechism*... [the *Compendium* is] a harmonious and authentic explanation of Catholic faith and morals."[115] While remaining faith-

---

[111] St. Thomas stated, "what you neither see nor grasp, faith confirms for you, leaving nature far behind; a sign it is that now appears, hiding in mystery realities sublime" (quoted in FR 13, from the Sequence for the Solemnity of the Body and Blood of the Lord). And although the truths of Faith are not contrary to reason, it is very important to understand that we do *not* believe them simply because they are reasonable; for arguments from reason alone do not convert people. God in His grace does, and living faith is only possible with grace. Instead, we believe *because* God who can neither deceive nor be deceived has revealed His truths and *not* because His truths appear as true and intelligible to our reason (see CCC 156). This is not to advocate a blind fideism, one that uses doctrine as a substitute for rational thinking, but the necessity of faith *with* reason as its handmaid.

[112] Reason prepares for faith, for a man "would not believe unless he saw that truths should be believed" (STh II-II 1, 4). John Paul II discusses the unity of faith and reason, saying, "Both the light of reason and the light of faith come from God, [St. Thomas] argued; hence there can be no contradiction between them" (FR 43).

[113] CCC 143, quoting Rm 1:5.

[114] Ratzinger and Schönborn, *Introduction to the Catechism*, 56-57.

[115] Pope Benedict XVI, *Introduction to the Compendium*.

ful to the structure of the *Catechism* (using the 4-pillars of the Faith), the *Compendium* follows a question-and-answer format (598 questions), which is similar to the format of the *Baltimore Catechism* of the early twentieth century in the United States. To summarize, there exists a twofold Source of evangelization. The GDC notes that although "Sacred Scripture should have a pre-eminent position... Sacred Scripture and the *Catechism of the Catholic Church* are presented as two basic sources of inspiration for all catechetical activity in our time."[116] The GDC concludes with a definition of catechesis in relation to its sources, stating, "Catechesis, [in particular] by definition, is nothing other than the living and meaningful transmission of these [two] 'documents of faith.'"[117] After all, the Church "does not derive her certainty about all revealed truths from holy Scriptures alone. Both Scripture and Tradition must be accepted and honored with *equal sentiments* of devotion and reverence."[118]

Another misconception of evangelization that has occurred in recent times has been the notion that the work of teaching the Faith is not meant to be a discipline with the same academic rigor as the other academic sciences, nor should it strive to foster critical assimilation and rigorous academic discipline. However, the GDC unambiguously states that all religious instruction must make "present the Gospel in a personal process of cultural, systematic and critical assimilation... [and that it] appear as a scholastic discipline with the same systematic demands and the same rigor as other disciplines... with the same seriousness and the same depth with which other disciplines present their knowledge."[119] This being said, and though each area of evangelization should include a "critical" dimension, this form of critical thinking must not entail "a critical thinking focused

---

[116] GDC 127.
[117] GDC 128.
[118] DV 9; CCC 82.
[119] GDC 73.

on the Church [her]self as an institution — her organization, discipline, and practices…. Indeed [such an approach] can have a subtly corrosive effect on the whole catechetical mission of the Church,"[120] according to respected catechist theologian, Francis D. Kelly. The role of religious truth in the realm of general education as a whole is an important ancillary issue to that of the crisis of faith today. Even within overall Catholic education itself the *Catechism* should be utilized actively in all the sciences being taught within the schools and colleges (namely, utilizing faith and reason across the academic spectrum). Unfortunately, this has been usurped in favor of secularity and an over-compartmentalization of the sciences, with each area of academia existing segregated from the others. This too has added to the crisis of faith and a breakdown of religious truth, even truth in general.

Instead of adapting to current trends in secular teaching, Catholic education is called to be the model for all authentic education, such that every discipline is challenged to adopt a religious dimension so as to be open to all truth, from both reason and faith, combining both secular and religious truth. After all, faith is more certain than reason could ever be, and there could never be a contradiction between them.[121] This is what in prin-

---

[120] Francis D. Kelly, 124-125.

[121] "By natural reason man can know God with certainty. But there is another order of knowledge, which man cannot possibly arrive at by his own powers: the order of divine Revelation" (CCC 50). "Faith cannot contradict reason. Both the light of reason and the light of faith come from God; hence there can be no contradiction between them" (FR 43). "But the human capacity to know the truth is impaired by sin… human reasoning, if left to itself, is inclined to falsehood" (FR 19, 22). "Faith is certain. It is more certain than all human knowledge because it is founded on the very word of God…. Though faith is above reason, there can never be any real discrepancy between faith and reason… [because] the same God who reveals mysteries and infuses faith has bestowed the light of reason on the human mind…. Consequently, methodical research in all branches of knowledge, provided it is carried out in a truly scientific manner and does not override moral laws, can never conflict with the faith, because the things of the world and the things of faith derive from the same God" (CCC 157-159).

ciple makes a Catholic school unique: it is open to all truth, including both secular and religious truth. About this, the Apostolic See teaches: "Teachers dealing with areas such as science, history, literature, art, anthropology, biology, psychology, sociology, and philosophy all have the opportunity to present a complete picture of the human person, including the religious dimension,"[122] especially within the environment of a complete Catholic education.

A complete education should not exclude the reality of Revelation, but should include the moral, spiritual and religious dimensions of man and of reality in evaluating the attainments of science and technology so as to maintain a perspective that respects the dignity of the human person. As John Paul II puts it, a Catholic education is *"more* capable of conducting an *impartial* search for truth, a search that is neither subordinated to nor conditioned by particular interests of any kind,"[123] which often are the underlying agendas of modern secular educational endeavors.

One goal of Catholic education is for the Church to influence the sciences and cultures of our age,[124] so that they may attain true certainty, wisdom and a "higher synthesis of knowledge... enlightened by the Gospel... [and] therefore by a faith in Christ."[125] This unity of all truth is *precisely* what allows science, with its proper methodologies, to be *truly scientific* — taking into account faith, moral norms, Catholic religious doctrine (religious truth) and reason to attain an total vision of reality. The *Catechism* offers the wisdom of God's truths for the salvation of all, while it also provides the most relevant knowledge of religious truth for all areas of academia.

---

[122] RDE 71.
[123] ECE 7.
[124] ECE 10.
[125] ECE 16.

D. TEACHING SACRED DOCTRINE FOR CONVERSION TO CHRIST

Should the Catholic Faith ever be taught without a call to conversion? Should evangelizers teach without themselves having, and at the same time fostering in their students, theological faith (in catechesis) or refrain from teaching with the expectation of a pretext of theological faith (in theology)? The answer to these questions is a negative. The emphasis on both theological faith and the call to conversion is fundamental to the pedagogy of teaching sacred doctrine within all areas of the ministry of evangelization. But some teachers have sought to present the Faith in such a way that the content being presented lacks the invitation to conversion and is engaged in without any indication of the need for conversion or, instead, with the false assumption that students are already permanently and completely converted. These teachers claim that such a conversion-oriented approach would harm the necessary "objective" (as they call it) nature of the teaching environment, the disinterested teacher-student relationship, and the scientific (i.e., faithless) realm of the classroom.[126] But how can sacred doctrine,

---

[126] Dietrich von Hildebrand, *Trojan Horse in the City of God* (Manchester: Sophia Institute, 1967) discusses how "a neutral attitude cripples catechesis." He explains:
  Religion has often been taught to children in the same way as history or spelling. Instead of presenting the mysteries of Christian faith in a way proper to their unique and extraordinary character, teachers of religion have often taught them with a kind of neutral objectivity suitable to any purely academic matter.
  The real teacher of religion, on the contrary, communicates the realization that religion is something completely different from any other topic. He appeals to the entire person. He creates a truly religious atmosphere which evokes feelings of wonder and awe in the child and at the same time corresponds to the longing for God that lives in every human soul. The real teacher of religion attempts to awaken and develop a sense of mystery and reverence in his pupil.
  Religious truth, which appeals to faith, cannot be taught in the manner of secular subjects which appeal either to a mere apprehension or to a rational understanding. To teach religion as just one topic of learning among others (as is currently being recommended to the public schools of the United States) is one example of the neutralization of religion which renders it dull and inert and incapable of penetrating our entire life (52).

derived from Truth Himself and deduced by the teaching authority of His Church, be presented as if it were a mathematical equation or a philosophical theory, lifeless in nature? Unlike in the situations of other academic disciplines, such an approach within the ministry of teaching the Faith actually may undermine the need for conversion. Even when some of these teachers remain true to the doctrines of the Faith in their teaching, they stifle the life of faith within their students by such an 'impartial' methodology. If such teachers of the Faith neglect to teach from a life of personal holiness coupled with docility to the Holy Spirit, their effectiveness will be greatly diminished, even damaging. Their fruits will be barren and bitter. Saint Pius X in speaking about such teachers, declares: "For, unaccustomed to speak with God [themselves], they lack the divine fire when they speak to men about him, or impart the principles of Christian living, so that the gospel message seems to be lifeless in them."[127] Oh, what harm such teachers have done in our day.[128]

---

[127] Pius X, Encyclical *Haerent animo* (August 4, 1908), as quoted in Francis Fernandez, *In Conversation with God*, vol. 3 (New York: Scepter, 1994), 661.

[128] The ramifications of this problem have been catastrophic. How many have lost the Faith due to such bad theology? I know firsthand these consequences. A close friend of mine suffered a collapse of faith after receiving damaging theological teaching and methodology. Years ago, both of us had an "awakening" experience about the same time while in college; we soon became roommates and spiritual friends, and began living for the love of God and to share the Catholic Faith. We went to daily Mass, participated in prayer groups, held Bible studies, and would give retreats for youth and college peers. After college, we went into full time youth ministry at nearby parishes, and began our families. Then we went back to college to get a Master's Degree in Theology. I went to an orthodox Catholic university, and he went to a nearby seminary and then to a well-known Catholic university, though one that has been openly critiqued by George Weigel for neglecting its Catholic identity ["What Makes a University 'Great'?" *The Catholic Difference* (June 22, 2005)].

About my friend's experience in the seminary and in the doctorate program, he says:

"My shock came as I began a Master's program in Theology at the local Catholic seminary. I took classes during the day with all the seminarians, so I got to see what life might have been like. The classes themselves shocked the narrow-minded belief system that had sustained me in college... I got my MA in Theology and then my PhD from a large Catholic university in the Midwest. By the end of gradu-

Instead, evangelizers are called to encourage the conversion of their students to Christ and His Church, to be missionaries of the New Evangelization. Thus, the GDC calls them to "adopt a *missionary dimension* rather than a strictly *catechumenal* dimension."[129] As John Paul II states, "Let us first of all recall that there is no separation or opposition between catechesis and evangelization,"[130] as both call for conversion.

Fostering conversion should be seen as central to religious doctrinal teaching, and more than ever in today's Catholic primary and secondary schools, parishes, and colleges. While avoiding (sectarian) 'indoctrination' or 'proselytism' in the negative sense of these terms, and while always respecting students' in-

---

ate school, I had naturally become more liberal in my theological thinking (it is impossible not to without some serious mental gymnastics and/or self-delusion." After college studies, my friend and I took theology positions at Catholic universities. I am still a professor, and am thankful to God for the grace of faith. But, my friend is now an agnostic, and has since resigned from his position as a theologian and taken up a secular career. He says about this:

"I was finally freed from the pressure and stress of youth ministry when I landed a professor job at a small Catholic college... By the time I resigned from there three years later, I had let go of nearly all of the beliefs of Christianity. Instead of pretending for the rest of my life (as I'm sure many theologians do), I opted out and started a whole new career unrelated to religion.'"

My friend has listed 10 areas that he says led him to agnosticism, certainly due to the bad theological foundations and faith-impairing methodologies he received from his professors:

#1 Evolution is undeniably true and has negative consequences for Christianity.

#2 The "problem of evil" has no satisfactory answer in Christianity.

#3 The doctrine of Divine Providence does not seem to apply to this world.

#4 Religious phenomena and experience are nearly indistinguishable in religions.

#5 The Bible and its formation make calling it "the Word of God" meaningless.

#6 It is very possible that "Jesus Christ," as we know him, never even lived on earth.

#7 It is probable that Christianity, like Judaism beforehand, drew its main language, doctrines, and structure from so-called "pagan" religions and cultures.

#8 Christian history does not look how it should if the Church were truly the work of the Holy Spirit.

#9 The Sacraments do not seem to work as they should if they were real.

#10 Christian soteriology is full of contradictions and exceptions.

129 GDC 185.

130 CT 18.

dividual right to freedom, teaching the truths of the Catholic Faith while fostering conversion is vital within every work of evangelization, even in regard to the various personal faith perspectives of students. The *General Directory of Catechesis* presents this as follows:

- For believers — religious instruction assists them to understand better the Christian message;
- For students who are searching or who have religious doubts — religious instruction assists them to discover what exactly faith in Jesus Christ is, what response the Church makes to their questions, and gives them the opportunity to examine their own choice more deeply;
- For nonbelievers — religious instruction assumes the character of a missionary proclamation of the Gospel and is ordered to a decision of faith.[131]

John Paul II echoes the call to conversion necessary in teaching the Faith in *Catechesi Tradendae*. He states that all initial Faith teaching must concern itself with four conversion-oriented tasks:

- Nourishing and teaching the Faith, and arousing it with the help of grace;
- Opening the hearts of the students;
- Fostering the conversion of each student;
- Preparing the students for total adherence to Jesus Christ.[132]

These tasks are also supported by the Second Vatican Council's Declaration on Christian Education, *Gravissimum Educationis*.[133] Thus, as the Church's teaching explains, every enterprise where

---

[131] GDC 74.

[132] CT 21. John Paul II also discusses four characteristics of authentic catechesis. They are as follows: (1) It must be systematic (See also *Evangelii Nuntiandi*, 44); (2) It must deal with essentials; (3) It must nevertheless be sufficiently complete; and (4) It must be integral Christian initiation.

[133] Paragraph 4.

the Faith is being taught necessarily entails teaching the sacred doctrines of the Faith while fostering conversion in those being taught, or "teaching for conversion," as master catechist Barbara Morgan expresses it.[134]

Every person is to be called to an ever-deepening relationship with Christ — child, catechumen, non-Catholic, non-Christian, college student, adult, catechist and theologian alike, and thus teaching for conversion should be the goal of the methodology of every type of evangelization.

Simply put, those who present the teachings of the Faith will be successful in accomplishing their task only to the degree that they first contemplate the Lord with faith and then faithfully present His sacred doctrines of the Faith, and second, do so while teaching for conversion both from the perspective of a personal lively theological faith and with at least a hope of fostering an increase of faith among their students. Even the college theology professor, to some degree, should engage in his or her science, unique as it is, with the mindset of teaching for conversion and with the hope of imparting an ever-deeper understanding of the Mystery of Christ's love and wisdom; for it is Christ Himself who is the one Teacher and it is Christ Himself who is what is being taught within this science as well.

One of the central themes of the Sacred Scriptures is that every person is in need of conversion and that those who are called to teach the Faith must teach for conversion. When Christ commanded His disciples to "Go therefore and make disciples of all nations," He indicated that the way to do this was by "teaching them to observe *all* that [He had] commanded [them]" (Mt 28:19-20). Jesus gave His followers His Spirit and commissioned them to teach with the assurance that, if they remained faithful, then Christ would speak through them. He said, "He who

---

[134] Barbara Morgan was Director of Catechetics at Franciscan University of Steubenville from the mid-1990s to 2005.

hears you, hears Me" (Lk 10:16). By 'teaching,' He meant faithfully passing on His Spirit and His Word; and in actuality, Christ intended for His followers to allow Him to be the Teacher teaching through them. To succeed, this requires that evangelizers themselves be wise in the doctrines of the Faith and remain personally faithful to all the teachings of Christ and His Church.[135]

A great evil is spiritual or doctrinal indifference (Rv 3:15-16), so is it a greater evil if a teacher of the Faith is lukewarm in faith, even if disguised as 'objectivity,' as St. John of Avila warns,

> If the simple folk live in a lukewarm state, the situation is regrettable. They hurt themselves, but a remedy is possible. If, however, it is the teachers who are lukewarm, then the Lord's warning must needs be considered: 'Woe to him by whom they come!' Great harm can come from their lukewarmness, because it will easily spread to others and dampen their spiritual fervour.[136]

---

[135] We are not here speaking of Donatism, the heresy that claimed that for Sacraments to be valid, priests had to be holy. But in regards to teaching, holy teachers commonly produce holy students. Throughout Christian ages, Saints often produced Saints, and heretics produced more heretics. Some examples of this can be seen in the effects of the witness and teaching of the following: the Blessed Mother in the Upper Room with her spiritual children, St. John the Evangelist whose disciple was St. Polycarp who in turn taught St. Irenaeus, St. Anthony who caused the Egyptian deserts to become filled with monks, St. Bernard and the 31 friends he induced to join him in religious life, St. Maximilian M. Kolbe who gathered 800 religious at his *Niepokalanów* in Poland, St. Francis Xavier with the masses of converts he baptized in the east, the conversions won over by the preaching of saints like St. Francis de Sales and St. Louis M. de Montfort, the witness of the simple poor peasant priests St. John M. Vianney and St. Pio of Pietrelcina and their eighteen hour days of hearing scores of confessions, and of course, the Saints who were influenced by teachers like St. Ambrose and St. Albert the Great; and on the other hand, the teaching of Arius, Nestorius, Luther, Zwingli, and Calvin and the many who thus followed their erroneous teachings.

[136] St. John of Avila, *Sermon* 55.

Christ wants us to pass on the Faith by being living witnesses of His Good News, in the same way that we received it from the true living Witness Himself and from other faithful teachers who handed it to us in His Name. The Deposit of Faith, the whole message of Jesus as guarded, taught, and handed on by His Apostles and His Church, has been uniquely entrusted by Christ to the Magisterium, which in turn has commissioned teachers to faithfully teach this deposit (1 Tm 6:20). The Magisterium's goal is not only to impart a knowledge of religious propositions or abstract truths understood reasonably, as vital as this is, but through religious truth to put people into contact with Jesus Christ, and even into communion and intimacy with Him, and precisely by their personal living witness of the authentic doctrines of the Catholic Faith,[137] which reproduces in them and those they evangelize a mirror of Christ Himself. As the *Catechism* states: "What makes us believe is not the fact that revealed truths appear as true and intelligible in the light of our natural reason: we believe 'because of the authority of God himself who reveals them, who can neither deceive nor be deceived'"[138] and through evangelists who live this belief.

The Church's post-Vatican II catechetical documents propose solid guidance concerning sacred doctrine and its role in evangelization today. As cited above, the Source of all evangelization is the Sacred Deposit of the Word of God, which has been organized into the sacred doctrines of the Faith, as found in Sacred Scripture and Tradition (or at least directly connected to it), the latter of which includes the teachings in the *Catechism of the Catholic Church* and the *General Directory of Catechesis*, and at least indirectly, Aquinas' *Summa Theologiae* — evidenced by its having been utilized by the teaching authority of the

---

[137] See CT 5-7.
[138] CCC 156; STh I, q. 1, art. 5.

Church in her Magisterial documents over the past seven hundred years.[139]

Taken together, Church documents such as *Gravissimum Educationis*, the *Code of Canon Law*, the *General Catechetical Directory*, *Evangelii Nuntiandi*, *Catechesi Tradendae*, *The Religious Dimension of Education in a Catholic School*, *Fidei Depositum*, the *Catechism of the Catholic Church* and its *Compendium*, the *General Directory for Catechesis*, and the *Compendium of the Social Doctrine of the Church*, together demonstrate that the Church has been working enthusiastically to re-establish sound and sacred doctrine to the science and art of passing on the Faith, forming authentic living witnesses who in turn become true heralds of God's Good News.

---

[139] According to Pope Leo XIII, "the chief and special glory of Thomas, one which he has shared with none of the Catholic Doctors, is that the Fathers of Trent made it part of the order of conclave to lay upon the altar, together with Sacred Scripture and the decrees of the supreme Pontiffs, the *Summa* of St. Thomas, whence to seek counsel, reason, and inspiration." Cited in Leo XIII's *Aeterni Patris* #22. As Pope Pius XI confirms, "the Fathers of Trent resolved that two volumes only, Holy Scripture and the *Summa Theologica*, should be reverently laid open on the altar during their deliberations." Cited in Pius XI's *Studium Docem* #11. See Appendix 1 at the end of this book for more detail.

CHAPTER FOUR

A Hermeneutic of Sacred Doctrine
for All Times

A. A Theology of Sacred Doctrine:
The 'Hermeneutic of the Whole'[1]

To speak of the *hermeneutic of the whole* of sacred doctrine does not intend to imply that the branches in which theology is divided are necessarily detrimental to the theological endeavor itself, for St. Thomas structures his *Summa* into main subsections, and so too do the catechisms which later follow his inspiration.

It must be maintained however that sacred doctrine is to be understood and imparted as a comprehensive whole, as a *hermeneutic of the whole*.[2] Pius XI, in his Encyclical, *Studiorum Ducem*, attributes the wisdom of systemizing theology into various branches — fundamental, dogmatic, moral, spiritual, biblical, and sacramental — to St. Thomas himself, and then says of

---

[1] A term borrowed from Shanley, *"Sacra Doctrina,"* 186.

[2] The term "whole" is defined by Muniz to have three possible meanings: a universal whole, an integral whole, and a *totum potestativum* or potential whole. A universal whole is present to each part in its complete essence and power. An integral whole is that which is found in any one of its parts, neither in its full essence nor by virtue of its total power. A potential whole is a mean between the other two, for it is present to each of its parts in its complete essence, but not in all its power (Muniz, *The Work of Theology*, 1, footnote 1). According to Muniz, theology is an integral whole and a potential whole, but not a universal whole (cf. 5-7).

him, "There is no branch of theology in which he did not exercise the incredible fecundity of his genius."[3] Theology necessarily deals with numerous branches or tracts because, by its very nature, it discusses divine Revelation, which is itself multifaceted to say the least. Francisco P. Muniz, OP, states, "Theology [and I would add, all evangelization as well] is concerned with an almost infinite number of material objects constituting one total or adequate object, namely, all of revelation. Thus it includes numerous tracts, of the widest variety, wherein the diverse material objects are examined, e.g., tracts on the One God, the Triune God, the Creator, the angels, man, etc."[4]

Despite its parts, a holistic and systematic approach to evangelization is necessary for those we evangelize to learn the Faith properly, so as to live it heroically. This approach has been maintained throughout most of the past seven hundred years, even since the foundations of the Church. Once again in our time, the holistic approach is being restored as normative to evangelization, greatly due to the new *Catechism* and a call for reunification of doctrine by the Magisterium, and from a rediscovery of the genius of Aquinas.

1. Authentic Plurality, Catholic Pluriformity

In Scripture, Genesis has two creation accounts, and there are four Gospels. Authentic pluralism, as the Scriptures demonstrate, is legitimate and is part of the divine pedagogy. A certain plurality — or a "unity-in-diversity," from whence the term "university" derives its name[5] — allows theology and religious education to be authentically "catholic." As the Congregation for the Doctrine of the Faith states, "Essential bonds link the dis-

---

[3] Pope Pius XI, Encyclical *Studiorum Ducem*, 17-23.
[4] Muniz, *The Work of Theology*, 6.
[5] Fr. Benedict Ashley, "Introduction," 3.

tinct levels of unity of faith, unity-plurality of expressions of the faith, and plurality of theologies." About the necessity for maintaining a healthy plurality, the CDF also declares, "The ultimate reason for plurality is found in the unfathomable mystery of Christ who transcends every objective systematization."[6] On the other hand, to be pluralistic in regard to the content of the truths of the Faith themselves or of the objective value of truth itself, which involves a contempt for the teaching authority of the Church and her doctrines — leading to dissent — is a different matter altogether.[7] At the crux of the issue of plurality is the distinction between a doctrinal truth, which is unchanging, and the ways it is taught which can be adapted and varied. One may ask whether genuine plurality allows for a moving away from the formulations of the Faith toward opening the door to the vast potential discoveries of a New Theology which allows for altogether new doctrines, or actual changes to doctrines, or the negation of "old" doctrines. The answer is negative.

To understand this situation further, it is important to understand the relation between an article of Faith and the truth it reveals. Aquinas describes an article of Faith as "a perception of truth aiming at the truth itself."[8] About this, Congar goes so far as to state "no [doctrinal] expression is ever totally adequate to what it expresses or its final outcome... and we must not confuse the faith [exclusively with] its historical formulations."[9] But, while "faith terminates not in its own formulae, but in God Him-

---

6   *Donum Veritatis*, 34.

7   See ibid. About this dissenting plurality, Fr. J.A. DiNoia, OP, states: "The vastly pluralized postmodern contexts in which theology is practiced today accentuate the challenge [of dissent]," in "American Catholic Theology at Century's End: Postconciliar, Postmodern, Post-Thomistic," 518.

8   *Perceptio veritatis tendens in ipsam*. STh II-II, 1, 6; III Sent 25, 1, 1.

9   Yves Congar, OP, *Diversity and Communion* (Mystic, CT: Twenty-Third Publications, 1982), 40.

self,"[10] this does not mean that we are able to abandon formulations of the truths of the Faith, which themselves can be known with certainty as truths. And while "indeed it can be a real duty for the Church not simply to repeat monotonously its ancient dogma but to rephrase it in such a way that earlier and possibly misleading overtones or outdated forms [i.e. expressions] of thought may be excluded,"[11] as Karl Rahner points out, it however may not be supposed that the Church has ever erred in one of her doctrines.[12] Even "St. Thomas was absolutely certain," according to the CDF's *Donum Veritatis*, "that the right to judge in matters of doctrine [is] the sole responsibility of the *officium praelationis*."[13] Evangelizers must be mindful of these distinctions, and thus keep in mind their legitimate parameters of presentation and debate.

Some of the advocates of the 'new theology' have tried to replace the old notion of a healthy pluralism concerning various viable methods of handing on the Faith with a new form of pluralism concerning the content of the Faith itself, claiming there is no unity of truth.[14] Such advocates see faithfulness to Tradition as "the 'old hat,' [that which is] unenlightened, preconciliar, obsolete, naive, closed-minded, unecumenical, obscurantist, ul-

---

[10] Aidan Nichols, OP, *From Newman to Congar: The Idea of Doctrinal Development from the Victorians to the Second Vatican Council* (Edinburgh: T & T Clark, 1990), 256, commenting on Congar's "*La Tradition et la vie de l' Eglise*" (Paris: 1984), 71.

[11] *Sacramentum Mundi*, 1969 ed., s.v. "Magisterium," by Karl Rahner.

[12] While all of the Church's doctrines are true, not all are "irreformable" in how they are formulated. Rahner thinks that "we may expect a greater 'reformability' in Church doctrine than was counted on in modern times, before Vatican II" (Rahner, 356).

[13] *Donum Veritatis* footnote 27, citing *Contra impugnantes*, 2; *Quodlib*. III, q. 4, a. 1 (9); *In IV Sent.* 19, 2, 2, q. 3 sol. 2 ad 4.

[14] John Paul speaks about this distinction in *Fides et Ratio*: "Recent times have seen the rise to prominence of various (false) doctrines which tend to devalue even the truths which had been judged certain. A legitimate plurality of positions has yielded to an undifferentiated pluralism based upon the assumption that all positions are equally valid, which is one of today's most widespread symptoms of a lack of confidence in truth... assuming that truth reveals itself equally in different doctrines even if they contradict one another" (5).

tramontane, and, in general, obstructive."[15] This new form of teaching the Faith has been a main factor in causing the catechetical crisis of faith since the 1960s. The problem with this new approach is exposed by Dietrich von Hildebrand when he says: "A theology [and, by extension, all of evangelization] that denied any article of faith — or even gave it a different interpretation from the traditional one — would necessarily be false... the facts revealed to us, which find their expression in dogma, can never be replaced with a 'new theology.'"[16] Concerning those notions of a plurality that undermine the unity of Faith, the CDF summarizes: "As far as theological pluralism is concerned, this is only legitimate to the extent that the unity of the faith in its objective meaning is not jeopardized."[17]

Thus, part of the solution to this crisis of Faith is to restore a Catholic pluriformity to evangelization that allows for a variety of expressions and approaches concerning the teaching of divine truth while safeguarding the Deposit of Faith itself. In the final analysis, all genuine plurality must maintain a unity and faithfulness to the doctrines of the Faith.[18]

2. Comprehensive, Systematic, Integral, Synthesized and Faithful

In organizing and presenting a comprehensive body of theological content, like that exemplified in the *Summa* or the *Catechism*, the necessity of maintaining a comprehensive perspective of the Deposit of Faith is essential.[19] Expounding upon what

---

[15] John McCarthy, *The Task of Living Tradition*, Living Tradition No. (Jan. 1987), accessed online at http:// (7/28/05).

[16] D. von Hildebrand, *Trojan Horse in the City of God*, 67.

[17] *Donum Veritatis* 34, quoting Paul VI, Apostolic Exhortation *Paterna Cum Benevolentia*, n. 4: AAS 67 (1975), 14-15.

[18] Ratzinger and Schönborn, *Introduction to the Catechism*, 20. About the limitations of plurality in theology, they state, "unity in fundamentals is the indispensable condition of a vital plurality."

[19] GDC 97.

this implies, one might say that authentic evangelization today, as in previous centuries, necessarily requires passing on the Faith in a doctrinal, ecclesial, inculturated, holistic, theocentric, Trinitarian, and Christocentric way, one that is also comprehensive, systematic, scientific, and a unified synthesis, and in a way that incorporates faith and reason to impart wisdom with love; in a way that is "challenging, thought-provocative, coherent, timely, forward-looking, inviting and suitably sophisticated."[20] As Benedict Ashley, OP, aptly states, "a holistic education must aim at wisdom in the sense of a unified vision of reality."[21] Stressing the need for organic and comprehensive Christian instruction, John Paul II warns, "the rigid compartmentalization of knowledge within individual academic disciplines makes the task increasingly difficult," while further stating that in the search for truth, "[i]t is necessary to work toward a higher synthesis of knowledge."[22] As Weisheipl confirms, the training of teachers of the Faith "requires that beginners in the 'science' [must] be aided by a systematic view of the whole of 'sacred doctrine.'"[23]

Charles Boyer, SJ, unabashedly critiques the position of the New Theology, as proposed by Rahner and others, stating that such gibberish is not the work of *theology* at all, but instead, is only a philosophy of opinion or at best a *philosophy* or *sociology of religion*. Boyer says about this:

> It is clear that all theology, being by definition based on the principles of faith, must remain consistent with these principles. If it contradicts them, it excludes itself from the field of theology. A theology deserves this name only on the condition that it proves, with

---

[20] McCarthy, *The Task*.
[21] Fr. Benedict Ashley, OP, "Introduction," *The Common Things: Essays on Thomism and Education*, 3.
[22] ECE 16.
[23] Weisheipl, *Friar Thomas D'Aquino*, 219.

arguments that are at least probable, that it is in harmony with the principles of faith. This condition limits theological pluralism.[24]

Commenting on how the methodologies of Faith teaching need to be re-centralized and balanced, J.A. Di Noia, OP, states: "In an effort aimed at *riaccentramento,* the Extraordinary Synod of 1985, under the leadership of Pope John Paul II and Cardinal Ratzinger (now Benedict XVI), sought to resolve this question by balancing tradition-mindedness with modernization... only to be accused of being retrogressive and anti-conciliar.[25] Now, decades later, such an accusation has proven to be altogether false.

B. The Hermeneutic of God

The intent to establish the hermeneutic of the whole regarding the handing on of sacred doctrine is really an attempt to unite the best in scholastic theology, with particular emphasis on its content, with the authentic modern advances in methods of evangelization, and together, to present the Faith authentically by living witnesses who become heralds of the Good News in the light of the Holy Spirit, all in the context of the New Evangelization.[26] What is needed to address the current crisis of faith is the implementation of the *divine hermeneutic of sacred*

---

[24] Charles Boyer, SJ, "Theological Pluralism," *L'Osservatore Romano* - English Edition (Aug. 12, 1971), 6, quoted in Kevane, *Creed and Catechetics,* 52, footnote 38.

[25] DiNoia, "American Catholic Theology at Century's End," 501.

[26] John Paul II provided Catholics with a new spirit of identity and mission in his Encyclical *Veritatis Splendor:* "The present time is... marked by a formidable challenge to undertake a 'new evangelization,' a proclamation of the Gospel which is always new and always the bearer of new things, an evangelization which must be new in its ardor, methods, and expression" (VS 106).

doctrine, which would replace the superficial and imbalanced underpinnings of the type of *new theology* (doctrine-less, doctrine-critical, and overly experientially based) that has been so prevalent in contemporary Catholic evangelical activity in recent decades.

What needs to be emphasized is both the primacy of sacred doctrine together with the congruent faith life of the evangelizer. The purpose of the divine hermeneutic of sacred doctrine (the art and science of interpreting and proclaiming the meaning of sacred doctrine from God's perspective) is a sharing in the Truth, Jesus Christ, and in the mystery of His Revelation as contained in the doctrines of faith. This encompasses the condescension of God (via Revelation) to man's capacity of understanding throughout salvation history, and today through the Church, with the divine intent of elevating man to the life of the divine. In various ways (e.g., catechesis, theology, preaching, prayer), the Word Incarnate also places His truth in the mind of each member of the faithful through the use of words, experiences, and grace, as John Paul II states, "...the Logos, [with His] Spirit of intelligence and love, enables the human person with his or her own intelligence to find the ultimate reality of which He is the source and end."[27] The divine hermeneutic of doctrine allows God to teach each of the faithful through His Church, through her doctrinal truths and through every man's heart.

---

[27] John Paul II, Apostolic Constitution *Ex Corde Ecclesiae* (1990), 4.

CHAPTER FIVE

Doctrine and the Evangelist

In the midst of this sacred activity of handing on the Faith, there are several components working together: the content (what is being taught), the methodology (how the content is taught), the student (who is being taught), and the evangelist (who is doing the teaching).[1] In addressing the crisis of faith, the role of the evangelizer, together with the methodology he or she utilizes to transmit the Faith to those being evangelized, must be re-evaluated.

A. CHRIST AS THE SOLE TEACHER OF SACRED DOCTRINE

The content of the Catholic Faith is a specific and universal message — the Message Who is Christ. At the heart of the Good News, as the Scriptures explain, is Jesus Christ Who is Lord, Savior, Mediator, and Source of eternal life. He is the Way, the Truth and the Life (Jn 14:6). He is the One Who was, Who is, and Who is to come (Rv 4:8), "the key, the focal point, and the goal of human history."[2] St. Peter discusses the centrality of

---

[1] About the relation between the evangelist and the student, John Paul II says: "The educator is a person who 'begets' in a spiritual sense... [There is] a profound relationship between the educator and the one being educated." He speaks of a "mutual influence" they have as being "both sharers in truth and love." He says that education is "a reciprocal 'offering.'" (Letter to Families 16)

[2] Vatican II, Pastoral Constitution *Gaudium et Spes* (1965), 10.

all things in Christ when he states: "There is no salvation through anyone else, nor is there any other name under heaven given to the human race by which we are to be saved" (Ac 4:12). In evangelization, Christ must be taught centrally, with emphasis on the revelational truth that He alone liberates and saves mankind[3]; this is the core of His life and teaching and the central message of the Sacred Scriptures. Through Jesus Christ we discover ourselves and our life's meaning. John Paul II, in his Encyclical, *Redemptor Hominis*, makes clear that the only way for persons to truly know themselves is through Christ:

> The man who wishes to understand himself thoroughly — and not just in accordance with immediate, partial, often superficial, and even illusory standards and measures of his being — must come to Christ with his unrest and uncertainty, and even his weakness and sinfulness, his life and death. He must so to speak enter into Christ with all his own self... in order to find himself.[4]

Besides helping us to discover who we are in Christ, Catholic evangelization must declare the truth that Jesus Christ, the God-Man, knows and loves each of us as if there were only one of us (St. Augustine), and that He also knew each of us "all during His life, His agony, and His Passion, and gave Himself up for each one of us."[5] All evangelizing is Christ-evangelizing. Evangelization must be Christocentric, as well as Trinitarian.[6]

Jesus Christ is the fullness and fulfillment of all Revelation.[7]

---

[3] See Joseph Cardinal Ratzinger, *The Ratzinger Report* (San Francisco: Ignatius Press, 1985), Ch. 13 passim.

[4] John Paul II, Encyclical *Redemptor Hominis* (*Redeemer of Man*) (1979), 10.

[5] CCC 478; See also Gal 2:20: "The Son of God... loved me and gave Himself [up] for me."

[6] See CT 5-8.

[7] DV 2, 4.

The *Catechism* confirms that Christ is the heart of all evangeli-zation[8]; He is its first and last point of reference[9]; and the *General Catechetical Directory* states that Jesus is the central Truth, Who holds first place, and that from Him the other truths of the Catholic Faith derive their order and hierarchy.[10] Jesus is Wisdom Incarnate, and what He reveals is true wisdom.

The goal of teaching the Faith is thus nothing less than the insertion of those evangelized into Christ — "Christ in you, the hope of glory" (Col 1:27) — also called the Trinitarian Life (through Christ, to the Father, in the Holy Spirit),[11] and also expressed as going to Jesus through Mary with Peter. Like St. Paul, the great Evangelist to the Gentiles, teachers must know their goal well: it is a total insertion of each and every man into Christ, such that teachers may then "present every man mature in Christ" (Col 1:28) to the Lord. Success in teaching the Faith implies, in addition to knowledge of truth and docility to the Spirit, the assistance of grace and an active sacramental life, union with the Eucharistic Christ as the source, summit and font of our lives and apostolate of evangelization. For the evangelist must never forget Who causes conversions, as St. Paul stated, "Neither the one who plants nor the one who waters is anything, but only God, who causes the growth" (1 Cor 3:7).

The only way to immerse those evangelized into Christ and the Trinitarian Life is for Christ to do so Himself, which He often chooses to do through the evangelizer who is docile to the Holy Spirit. John Paul II explains: "It is Christ alone who teaches — anyone else teaches to the extent that he is Christ's spokes-man, enabling Christ to speak with his lips."[12] Jesus is "the one

---

[8] CCC 426-429.
[9] CCC 1698.
[10] GCD 16.
[11] See GCD 40-42, GDC 100.
[12] CT 6; see also CT 5-9.

genuine 'Teacher'" of God's Truth, of sacred doctrine,[13] and He is both the Teacher as well as what is Taught.[14]

Thus, the doctrine we teach is Christ, and Christ teaches it through us. Teaching doctrine faithfully, teachers must be able to exclaim like Christ in St. John's Gospel: "I have not spoken on My own authority.... The things, therefore, I speak I speak as the Father has bidden Me" (Jn 12:44-50), and "the things that I heard from Him (the Father), these I speak in the world... of Myself I do nothing: but I preach only what the Father has taught Me" (Jn 8:26-29), and also, "I have given them the words which You gave Me, and they have received them and know truth" (Jn 17:8).

The task of the teacher of the Faith is clearly modeled by Christ Himself. Like Christ, evangelizers are called to pass on the Word of God while themselves remaining ever faithful to the Truth. "As instruments of Christ," teachers should desire "naturally to teach only what He would teach these real students in these concrete circumstances."[15] Teachers therefore must not tamper with God's Word in their teaching (see 2 Cor 4:1-2). To teach the Faith as Christ taught it to His disciples, evangelists must themselves be in continuous contemplative communion with Christ Himself while remaining impregnated with the wisdom of sacred doctrine and the love of God.

The *Catechism* is our guide to understanding the Mystery of Christ as the content of teaching the Faith. It illustrates the centrality of Christ and states that Jesus is the glory of God, the Divine Teacher, and the First Truth.[16] Even the structure of the *Catechism* illustrates Christ's centrality: the four pillars of the *Catechism* are subdivided into two parts, the first being that

---

[13] RDE 25.

[14] CT 6.

[15] J. Hofinger, SJ, and Francis Buckley SJ, *The Good News and Its Proclamation* (Notre Dame: U of ND Press, 1968), 13.

[16] CCC 241.

whereby Christ reaches out to us, revealing Himself to us in the Creed and giving us His grace and life in the Sacraments, and the second being the invitation to respond to Him in love by living moral lives in obedience to the Decalogue and by living lives of prayer in communion with God modeled by the Our Father Prayer.

No matter how good the catechetical sources are, the necessity of having a teacher who is an authentic living witness of Christ and of holy wisdom is most vital to passing on the Faith. About this in relation to the *Catechism*, Cardinal Ratzinger (Benedict XVI) states that though "the Catechism appeals to the 'interior teacher' (as Augustine calls it) present in every man, the Catechism needs the exterior teacher... to mediate it... to be a living voice"[17] of Christ. To summarize this using the words of Christ, teachers of the Faith are commissioned by Him to "make disciples of all nations... teaching them to observe all that [He has] commanded" (Mt 28:19-20), not more and not less.

B. CATHOLIC EVANGELISTS
MUST BE LIVING WITNESSES OF CHRIST

"Do you really believe what you are proclaiming? Do you live what you believe?"[18]

1. Living Lives of Prayer and Virtue

These two penetrating questions of Paul VI ask evangelizers if they truly model what they propose to believe and teach. He explains: "The witness of life has become more than ever an

---

[17] Ratzinger, *Gospel, Catechesis, Catechism*, 59.
[18] EN 76.

essential condition for real effectiveness in [teaching the Faith]."[19] Paul VI is saying that teachers themselves have to be in communion with Christ and His Church, constantly at prayer and actively participating in the Sacraments, essentially living holy lives in pursuit of Christian perfection, if they hope to have success in their teaching.[20] John Paul II proposes that "the proclamation of truth, especially when it is of a moral-spiritual order, is much more credible when the one who proclaims it is not only a doctor from the academic point of view, but above all an existential witness" who consciously strives to live evangelically, especially with a "humility of virtues practiced and not displayed."[21] Among the four means of how to teach effectively as discussed by St. Augustine in *De Doctrina Christiana* (*On Christian Doctrine*), a most important aspect of evangelizing is prayer.[22] According to him, evangelizers must be in communion with Christ through ongoing daily prayer, together with regular fasting. They must pray as Jesus prayed, for both themselves and those they are about to teach, because "so far as he succeeds, he will succeed more by piety in prayer than by gifts of oratory," according to St. Augustine.[23] In *De Catechizandis Rudibus* (*On Catechetical Instruction*), Augustine also clarifies that from out of the abundance of the heart the mouth speaks (Lk 6:45), and thus, with the help of personal prayer, evangelists, filled with charity, must

---

[19] Ibid.

[20] This reflects the teaching of Vatican II's *Gaudium et Spes*, which states: "One of the gravest errors of our time is the dichotomy between the faith which many profess and the practice of their daily lives" (43).

[21] Reported in ZENIT News Service from Vatican City on April 3, 2000. See also Mt 23:1f.

[22] St. Augustine, *On Christian Doctrine* [*De Doctrina Christiana*], Book IV, chs. 13, 15, and 17. In summary, the four goals of teaching are: (1) to teach so as to give instruction with intelligence; (2) to give pleasure by your teaching so as to keep the students' attention; (3) to pray so as to be heard with ready compliance; and (4) to sway the mind so as to subdue the will to obedience (of faith).

[23] Ibid., Ch. 15.

proclaim the Good News of Christ cheerfully.[24] Besides being educated in knowledge and truth, students must see in the evangelist a life of virtues, including faith and love, or simply, a life that is another Christ. Hans Urs von Balthasar, while speaking of St. Thérèse, Doctor of the Church, exemplified this point in saying of her: "*It is not so much her writings as her life itself which is her doctrine.*"[25] So should it be with every Christian, and especially those who evangelize.

2. Imitating the Pedagogy of Christ and of the Apostles

When Christ teaches, He proclaims, undiluted, the Kingdom of God as the good news of the truth. As a good teacher, He does this by utilizing all the forms of communication proper to man. So that they may attain true happiness and peace, He invites His hearers to total conversion.[26] He is not influenced by ideological considerations or by purely human interests, but by the love of God and neighbor. He intentionally and conscientiously desires to communicate the truth of the Revelation of God. He seeks to liberate man from the bonds of sin, evil, and slavery and attract him to the embrace of freedom, love, and life. He exemplifies God's mercy. This too is the work of every teacher of the Faith. "For this reason there cannot be teachers of the faith other than those who are convinced and faithful disciples of Christ and his Church."[27]

The Apostles first had to learn the Sacred Deposit of Faith themselves, both through being taught and through personal experience, before they could live it and pass it on. They had to

---

[24] St. Augustine, *On Catechetical Instruction* [*De Catechizandis Rudibus*] (Westminster: Newman Press, 1962), 34-37.

[25] *St. Thérèse: The Contemplative Life and Carmel* (Philadelphia: Carmelite Monastery, 1993).

[26] See GDC 139-144.

[27] GDC 142.

hear and see Christ teach, and they had to grow in theological faith with grace before they could understand and imitate Him. They came to understand through contact with the Perfect Man that the goal of life is to live the truth of the Faith, which He Himself is and gives to all who seek Him with a sincere heart. The Apostles had to come into contact with the living God through methods of the divine pedagogy. The GDC explains:

> Jesus gave careful attention to the formation [of His students].... [He] presented himself to them as the only teacher and, at the same time, a patient and faithful friend. He exercised real teaching 'by means of his whole life.' He stimulated them with opportune questions.... He introduced them to prayer. He sent them out on a missionary apprenticeship.... Jesus Christ is 'the Teacher who reveals God to Man and Man to himself,' the Teacher who saves, sanctifies, and guides. He is the Teacher who lives, speaks, rouses, moves, redresses, judges, forgives, and walks with [His students].[28]

Christ tells His followers that they must first hear and accept before they can blossom and bear fruit, and that when they do cleave to the Truth and share Him with others, their fruit will blossom a hundredfold (see Mk 4:20).

And so it must be with Catholic evangelizers today. To learn the Faith and not to strive to live it faithfully is to betray having learned it at all. And students will not be able to understand the Faith without a model to exemplify it. The witness of a faith-filled teacher is vital. As authentic witnesses of the Faith, evangelizers must in a certain sense be able to testify with St. John the Evangelist: "That which was from the beginning, which

---

[28] GDC 137.

we have heard, which *we have seen* with our eyes, which *we have looked upon and touched* with our hands, concerning the word of life — the life was made manifest, and *we saw* it, and *testify* to it, and *proclaim* to you the eternal life which was with the Father and was *made manifest to us* — that which *we have seen and heard* we proclaim also to you" (1 Jn 1:1-4).

As teachers of the Word, we are called, like the first Apostles, to imitate the Divine Teacher, by our teaching in word and deed. But, in order to grow in the grace of faith, we must first hear and take to heart the Word of God (Rm 10:13-17). This Word entails the whole Deposit of Faith as handed down from Jesus and His Apostles to every generation.

Scripture itself admonishes teachers of the Faith to adhere to the 'standard' of the Faith (see Rm 6:17), to "guard what has been entrusted to [them]" (1 Tm 6:20) and to "stand firm and hold on to the traditions [they] were taught" (2 Th 2:15), namely the teachings of Christ, the doctrines of the Faith, as found in the Bible and the *Catechism*.

Teachers of the Faith must not only teach the Word of God, they must be immersed in it themselves. Teachers themselves must become "born anew, not of perishable seed, but of imperishable, through the living and abiding Word of God" (1 P 1:23). Only after immersion in the Word can authentic evangelizers exclaim with St. Paul: "For we are not peddlers of God's Word, but as men of sincerity, as commissioned by God, in the sight of God we speak in Christ" (2 Cor 2:17). In this, St. John Chrysostom advocates imitating St. John the Evangelist as the model for evangelizing and says of him: "See the great boldness and power of the words, how he speaks nothing doubting or conjecturing, but declares all things plainly."[29] This is due to his

---

[29] St. John Chrysostom, *Homily 2 on John's Gospel*, par. 7, quoted in Msgr. Kelly's *The Mystery We Proclaim*, 2nd edition, 38.

personal union with the Savior. This is the task of every evangelizer.

Thus, to come to faith in the Word of God, the Deposit of Faith must also be *seen, touched, and made manifest* to the believer, as St. John the Apostle explains in his first epistle. In short, it must be experienced through the witness of believers, through those who are Christ-like teachers. Thus, the imparting of the Faith must include teaching the Word within the dynamism of the living witness of the teacher. The first principle of teaching Christ is the witness of an authentically Christian life.[30]

Evangelizers must draw those they teach into the life of Christ, first and always by example, so that those evangelized then too may experience the life and grace of the Holy Spirit. Seeking to balance doctrine with witness, the Church recognizes that witness alone is not enough. Paul VI explains, "Nevertheless, this [witnessing] always remains insufficient... if it is not explained, justified... by a clear and unequivocal proclamation of the Lord Jesus,"[31] by utilizing the sacred doctrines of the Faith.

Both doctrine and witness are equally vital to all authentic evangelization. The psychological dimension of man necessitates this twofold approach — first, the authentic Christ-like witness of the evangelizer, and second, the faithful and complete proclamation of Christ and His Revelation — in transmitting the Faith. Paul VI clarified best this necessary relation between the teacher and the sacred doctrine which is handed on when he declared: "Modern man listens more willingly to witnesses than teachers and if he listens to teachers, it is because they are witnesses."[32]

As representatives of the one true Teacher, evangelizers are called to not only teach His content but also to utilize His pedagogy. The word *martyr* means witness, and evangelizers must be

---

[30] EN 41.
[31] EN 22.
[32] EN 41.

witnesses, even to the point of martyrdom,[33] if called. It should be evident by their life and faithful teaching that they would give their life for Christ and the truth of His Word; and if those who hand on the Faith are to be willing to die for the truth (Si 4:28), they must then at least live for it, handing it on completely and intact with a living faith.

Catholic evangelizers must realize that their calling is *to be Christ*, such that they will eventually say: "I live, no longer I, but Christ lives in me" (Gal 2:20). Thus, evangelizers must first know and live the Faith, and at least be on the lifelong journey toward Christian perfection, before they are capable of passing it on effectively. Like Christ, they must endeavor to achieve the virtue of maintaining cohesiveness between what they teach and what they do, forming who they are,[34] such that the whole of their lives is a continual and faithful teaching of sacred doctrine in the

---

[33] Archbishop J. Michael Miller, CSB, Secretary for the Vatican's Congregation for Catholic Education, speaks about the need to find evangelists who are willing to risk or endure the martyrdom that teaching the Faith entails in today's climate: "We need teachers with a clear and precise understanding of the specific nature and role of Catholic education. The careful hiring of men and women who enthusiastically endorse a Catholic ethos is, I would maintain, the primary way to foster a school's catholicity. The reason for such concern about teachers is straightforward. Catholic education is strengthened by its 'martyrs.' Like the early Church, it is built up through the shedding of their blood. Those of us who are, or have been, teachers know all about that." (*The Holy See's Teaching on Catholic Schools*. The Catholic University of America, Sept. 14, 2005). Such heroic evangelizers as St. Charles Lwanga are again needed today. In 1886 St. Lwanga was martyred by the king of Buganda, Uganda, a pedophile and alcoholic. St. Lwanga taught the doctrines of the Faith to the king's pages, to these boys who were victims of the king's abuses. They in turn stood up to the king, objecting to his immoral conduct. The king responded by martyring thirteen Catholics, and other Christians, for their witness to the Faith. St. Lwanga, a captain of the pages, was slowly roasted over fire to his death. His last words were of encouragement to his fellow pages, a call to his executioners to repent, and finally to Jesus saying with great devotion, "My God." He is a patron saint of catechists. St. Paul also testifies to this kind of witness, saying: "Who shall separate us from the love of Christ? Shall tribulation, or distress, or persecution, or famine, or nakedness, or peril, or the sword?" (Rm 8:35-39)

[34] See CT 7.

work of evangelization.[35] Then the world will indeed experience the New Evangelization and springtime of Catholic renewal!

A lived faith is a pre-requisite to an understanding of the Faith, and teachers must understand the Faith before they can effectively engage in the art of teaching it. St. Anselm's "faith seeking understanding" (*fides quaerens intellectum*) comes to mind here. About this, St. Thomas Aquinas believed that with growth in faith, the gift of understanding inevitably increases; and St. Augustine thought that understanding is a reward of faith, as he says: "I believe in order to understand; and I understand, the better to believe."[36]

Teachers must live what they teach, as Christ the Teacher lived, and later as His Apostles lived — hearing, seeing, believing, converting, understanding — because only then will they become effective teachers of the living Faith themselves. Then their teaching, because they are faithful to their doctrinal and apostolic apprenticeship to Christ with holy audacity, will cause an increase in their joy (see Lk 10: 17-20). Evangelizers are called to sanctity. They must understand that they participate through Baptism and Confirmation in Christ's prophetic, priestly, and kingly office, and as well, they must be mindful that they have certain moral and professional obligations to the Church, in whose name they teach, or at least are in juridical relation with.

An ever-increasing growth in the knowledge and life of faith, together with the love and mercy it encourages, is not just about completing courses or finishing a process; instead, it is the central goal of life — both for the teacher and for those being evangelized. Bishop Edward K. Braxton explains: "Those who

----

[35] See CT 9.

[36] CCC 158. St. Anselm, St. Augustine, and St. Thomas essentially agree. As Gilson sums up, "the safest way to reach truth is not the one that starts from reason and then goes on from rational certitude to faith, but, on the contrary, the way whose starting point is faith and then goes on from revelation to reason." Étienne Gilson, *Reason and Revelation in the Middle Ages* (New York: Charles Scribner's Sons, 1938), 17.

successfully complete their 'life course' in the Catholic Faith do not graduate by receiving a diploma. They graduate by being raised from the dead!"[37] The task of the teacher is now made manifest, namely to live in charity and teach with wisdom the Catholic Faith in such a way as to guide students along the path to eternal life via the way of the Saints and the glory of the Cross.

For holy wisdom to be imparted with divine charity, the teacher must first internalize the doctrines of Faith. He must begin with faith and then move to charity. It is not enough for the teacher to have a grasp of the content to be taught, seeing it as merely a subject of information, facts, and data. Instead, the evangelizer must understand it as something he himself first internalizes and grasps as true.[38] For this to take place, a personal encounter between the teacher and Jesus must precede all effective instruction, and a personal encounter between the student and Jesus must also be encouraged, because as Fulton J. Sheen explains, "Neither theological knowledge nor social action alone is enough to keep us in love with Christ unless both are preceded by a personal encounter with Him."[39] And according to Josef Pieper, "Teaching in the real sense takes place only when the hearer is reached when the truth of what is said reaches the hearer as truth."[40] Students learn not only by memorizing truth, but also by seeing the truths of doctrine lived by their teacher. Students experience doctrine via their teacher's teach-

---

[37] Bishop Edward K. Braxton, NCEA/CACE Conference (10/20/98).

[38] Dom Chautard states about this, "The professor who has no interior [spiritual] life imagines [falsely] he has done all that is required of him if he [intellectually] keeps within the program of his examination. But if he is a man of prayer some word will now and again slip out, not only from his lips but from his heart… [which] may have a more profound influence on his students than a whole sermon." Dom Jean-Baptiste Chautard, OCSO, *The Soul of the Apostolate* (Rockford, IL: TAN, 1946), 116.

[39] Fulton J. Sheen, *Mornings with Fulton Sheen*, ed. Beverly Coney Heirich (Ann Arbor, MI: Servant Publications, 2000), 15.

[40] Josef Pieper, *Guide to St. Thomas*, trans. Richard and Clara Winston (San Francisco: Ignatius Press, 1986), 32.

ing *and* life. In this way, the truth reaches the student as actualized, lived truth.

In every science, teaching begins with what is known to be true and proceeds toward what might be true to see if it is indeed true. Objective principles and criteria are utilized, and the teacher has an understanding of where he is taking his student, of what he hopes to get across to the student, that is, the objective truth that he has discovered and desires for the student to discover as well, all based on previously discovered and mutually internalized truths and principles. Learning itself "means to perceive that what the teacher has said is true and valid, and to perceive why this is so," according to Pieper.[41] Teaching is not simply about imparting ideas, but about faith formation in truth as well. Thus, the Fathers of Vatican II declare, "doctrinal training should not have the mere communication of ideas as its objective, but a genuine and profound formation of the students,"[42] calling them to become like Christ.

One only needs to recall the teacher-student relationship between Sts. Ambrose and Augustine. Ambrose lived and taught with a lively faith, and Augustine found faith through Ambrose's teaching. Christopher Rengers, OFM Cap, explains:

> St. Ambrose was not a scholar interested in the abstract. He was a bishop interested in stirring his [students] to piety and a good life. This method, strangely enough, helped the demanding mind of St. Augustine, the great shining light among the converts of St. Ambrose. When he listened to St. Ambrose, the many difficulties of the literal explanations of the Bible vanished for him, and he saw that obscure passages could teach valuable truths. St. Augustine says, "I was

---

[41] Ibid.
[42] Vatican II, Decree on the Training of Priests [*Optatam Totius*] (1965), 15.

pleased to hear Ambrose keep on repeating in his public instructions: 'The letter kills, it is the spirit which gives life.'...." St. Augustine would be baptized by St. Ambrose in 387.[43]

St. Augustine came to a living faith in Christ after many failed attempts only through the teaching of a living witness of the Gospel, who in turn brought him to a personal experiential encounter with the Lord. As his moment of conversion arrived, first inspired by the teachings of Ambrose, Augustine heard the heavenly voices of children inviting him to "take and read" the Sacred Scriptures. In his autobiography, he describes the moment of his conversion not as simply a hearing, but as one of a profound, personal encounter with the living Christ. He writes to the Lord years later about this event, saying:

> You called, you shouted, and you broke through my deafness. You flashed, you shone, and you dispelled my blindness. You breathed your fragrance on me. I drew in breath and now I pant for you. I have tasted you, now I hunger and thirst for more. You touched me and now I burn for peace.[44]

St. Augustine came to the point of this life-changing personal conversion to Christ through the teaching *and* life witness of his teacher, St. Ambrose.

Thus, teachers of the Faith must realize their vocation is to teach the Faith solely in relation to and in the Name of Jesus Christ, in the same way that Ambrose taught Augustine. Today's evangelizers are called to cooperate with the Lord in producing

---

[43] Christopher Rengers, OFM Cap, *The 33 Doctors of the Church* (Rockford, IL: TAN, 2000), 76.

[44] St. Augustine, *The Confessions*, Book Tenth, Chapter XXVII.

Saints too. That is the power of the Word faithfully handed on by a living witness of Christ. As John Paul II reminds us, Christ is the Model of all evangelization, such that anyone else who teaches the Faith authentically, does so only "to the extent that he is Christ's spokesman, enabling Christ to speak with his lips."[45]

3. Loving with the Love of Christ

The renewal of faith in the New Evangelization depends upon faithful and holy teachers. Living witnesses, those who are true believers living just and holy lives truly in love with Christ, are needed more than ever today in order to communicate Christ's message authentically and effectively to this un-catechized generation. To be most effective, these evangelizers of the New Evangelization must love their students.[46] Commenting on the love of teachers for their students, John Paul I, during his brief pontificate, insightfully stated, "To teach John Latin, it is not enough to know Latin — one must also know and love John."[47] But, it takes a just man to teach true wisdom[48] with love. John Paul II exhorts, "Only in deep communion with [Christ] will catechists find light and strength for an authentic, desirable renewal of catechesis."[49] The goal of teaching the Faith is nothing less than to produce Saints, to achieve a *summa* in the mind and a fire for *divine love* in the heart of every student.

Teachers must learn to imitate the holy zeal of the Saints, some of whom were known for their lifelong love-cry, "Give me souls and away with the rest."[50] Paul VI exhorted teachers of the Word to be "servants of the Truth... animated by Love... with

---

[45] CT 6.

[46] "Teachers, love your students" (RDE 110).

[47] John Paul I, *Angelus* (9/17/78).

[48] As the psalmist says: "The mouth of the just man utters wisdom, and his tongue speaks what is right; the law of God is in his heart" (Ps 36:30-31; see also Ps 51:6).

[49] CT 9.

[50] Sts. Francis de Sales and John Bosco were known to use this approach.

the fervor of the Saints!"[51] This is not to be understood as simply a pious ideal, but it must be understood as the fundamental prerequisite of all contact with the Sacred Deposit and with those who are being evangelized. St. Pius X, in his *Exhortation on Catechetics to Catholic Parents and Teachers*, put it succinctly when he reminded teachers of the Faith: "It is the salvation of souls which is at stake" in their students, as well "as their own eternal salvation"[52] as evangelizers. After all, Jesus explained, "Truly, I say to you, as you did it to one of the least of these my brethren, you did it to me" (Mt 25:40). In considering the mystical Body of Christ, teachers must remember that they are to be Christ to their students, while at the same time, considering that each of their students is another Christ.

To fail culpably to teach the whole Deposit of Faith or to teach it erroneously would be greatly detrimental to a teacher's own salvation. As Jesus warns, "It would be better for him if a millstone were hung round his neck and he were cast into the sea, than that he should cause one of these little ones to sin" (Lk 17:2). Teachers of the Faith cannot separate themselves from the Christian message they impart, which is a message of love. Perhaps Vatican II sums it up most clearly: "Intimately linked in charity to one another and to their students and endowed with an apostolic spirit, may teachers by their life as much as by their instruction bear witness to Christ, the unique Teacher."[53]

Finally, Catholic teachers must have special devotion to Mary, Seat of Wisdom. She who is the "living catechism" is also the "mother and model" of all Catholic evangelists.[54] They should find themselves often, like the Apostles, close to Mary, the

---

[51] EN 78-80.

[52] Pope St. Pius X, "An Exhortation on Catechetics to Catholic Parents and Teachers," 3, quoted in Kevane, *Catechism on Christian Doctrine*, Ch. 6.

[53] GE 13.

[54] Congregation for the Evangelization of Peoples, *Guide for Catechists* (1993), 10.

Mother of God, listening, learning and experiencing the love of Christ, in her school of holy wisdom, divine love, and unfathomable mercy. For as one Saint testifies: "The master, before ascending to the right hand of the Father, told the disciples, 'Go and preach to all nations', and they had remained full of peace. But they still had doubts: they did not know what to do, and [so] they gathered around Mary, Queen of Apostles, so as to become zealous preachers of the Truth which will save the world."[55] And so we gather around her as well, to then go forth as they did to save the world.

C. The Vocation of the Catholic Evangelist

The primary function of the evangelist is to pass on the Word of God through genuine example and the faithful teaching of sacred doctrine. The *Guide for Catechists* states, "The office of the catechist is basically that of communicating God's word."[56] The GCD reiterates, "the summit and center of catechetical formation lies in an aptitude and ability to communicate the Gospel message."[57] As I have been saying, there is a direct correlation between the faith life of the evangelist and the fruitfulness of handing on the Faith effectively. So in order "to give witness to the gospel, the catechist must establish a living, ever-deepening relationship with the Lord... [and] frequently reflect on the scriptures."[58] This work involves their whole being, as they first make their own the Word of God before they even begin to teach it, so that when they speak, they are reflecting upon He Whom they know and Whom they love.[59]

[55] St. J. Escrivá, *Furrow*, 232.
[56] Ibid., 7.
[57] GCD 111.
[58] NCD 207.
[59] *Guide for Catechists*, 8.

1. The Formation of the Evangelist

The solid formation of evangelizers is of utmost importance in evangelization. "It is indispensable to ensure a teacher's continuing formation aimed to animate them as witnesses of Christ," states the Sacred Congregation for Catholic Education.[60] Elsewhere, the SCCE defines the role of the religion teacher as that of imparting the Church's teachings, stating: "What is asked for is not that one impart one's own doctrine, or that of some other teacher, but the teaching of Jesus Christ Himself (see CT 6)" while also reminding educators that "they should remember that life witness and an intensely lived spirituality have an especially great importance."[61] For them to be effective, they must first receive solid catechetical formation and ongoing spiritual enrichment.

Concerning teachers of religion, the Code of Canon Law states: "Teachers are to be outstanding for their correct doctrine *and* integrity of life... those who are assigned as religion teachers in schools [must] be outstanding for their correct doctrine, their witness of Christian living and their pedagogical skill."[62] To ensure "correct doctrine," John Paul II discusses the need for evangelizers to be faithful to the teachings of the Church:

Every catechist must constantly endeavor to transmit by his teaching and behavior the teaching and life of Jesus. He will not seek to keep directed toward himself and his personal opinions and attitudes the attention and consent of the mind and heart of the person he is catechizing. Above all, he will not try to incul-

---

[60] S. Congregation for Catholic Education, *The Catholic School* (1977), 78.
[61] Congregation for Catholic Education, *Lay Catholics in Schools: Witness to Faith* (1982), 59.
[62] CIC, Can. 803 & 804.

cate his personal opinions and options as if they expressed Christ's teaching and the lessons of His life.[63]

The Fathers of Vatican II insisted that evangelists take their role seriously, saying: "This vocation demands special qualities of mind and heart, very careful preparation, and continuing readiness to renew and adapt!"[64] Elsewhere, the Church explains why this is so important, stating: "Unprepared teachers can do a great deal of harm."[65]

Evangelizers, in particular among the laity, are called to be Christians par excellence, to be "teachers, educators, and witnesses of the faith."[66] The Fathers of Vatican II were concerned with the kind of teachers who would teach sacred doctrine to the children of future generations. They exhorted teachers of the Faith to have specific characteristics and to foster particular skills, as follows:

- To be prepared.
- To have appropriate qualifications and knowledge of the art of education.
- To possess charity both toward one another and toward their pupils.
- To be inspired by an apostolic spirit in order to inspire their students.
- To bear testimony by their lives and teaching to the one Teacher.
- To work with the parents.
- To continue to help the students after they leave school.[67]

---

[63] CT 6.
[64] GE 10.
[65] RDE 97.
[66] GDC 237.
[67] GE 8.

2. *Experiencing the Triumph of the Cross*

The dynamic witness of the evangelizer is an essential element of teaching the Faith. The Apostolic See invites teachers to be personal and genuine, by saying to them: "Teachers should share their spiritual lives and pray for the students entrusted to them,"[68] and as well, by stating that "the teacher's personal witness is what brings the content of the lessons to life."[69] According to the Bishops of New York in their catechetical document, *The Catechist in the Third Millennium*, evangelizers should also possess the Christian virtues, such as compassion, common sense, a sense of humor, a real vital Christian faith, and a personal relationship with Jesus nourished in and through the Church.[70]

Evangelizers, like all the baptized faithful, are called to the perfection of charity. They are to love what is good and true, cleaving to God and heroically enduring mortifications and the daily crosses of the Christian life and of their service as a teacher of Faith. Comparing the theologian who carries his cross to the one who allows mediocrity to reign and thus easily falls prey to dissent, Fr. Thomas Dubay states:

> To my knowledge no one in the theological community denies that theology should be done in a prayerful manner. But in actual fact there is only the slimmest evidence that the theological enterprise is animated to any appreciable extent by deep prayer. I can think of no moral theologian who both approves of masturbation, contraception, homosexuality and premarital sexual relations and who discusses his position in the context of the great biblical prayer themes or

---

[68] RDE 71.

[69] RDE 96.

[70] The GDC (156, 231ff) also refers to various virtues that catechists should foster and pray for so as to be good teachers.

the writings of the mystics. Seldom, if ever, do we find him even slightly touching on the New Testament hard and narrow road that leads to life, on the necessity to carry the Cross every day, on the seeking of God alone, on the unimportance of earthly pleasure and comfort in comparison with the overriding necessity of an enthralling immersion in God.[71]

Essential to evangelizers is growth in grace through active participation in the Sacraments, while habitually giving their whole hearts to God. With the Eucharist as the true source and summit of their lives, they are called to model a life of knowing, loving and serving God. In short, they are to strive to be perfect (Mt 5:48) and to become Saints (1 Cor 1:2), despite all hardships[72] and sufferings[73] remembering that "Christ also has suffered for [them], leaving [them] an example that [they] may follow in His steps" (1 P 2:21). As Dom Jean-Baptiste Chautard, OCSO, explains in *The Soul of the Apostolate*, "The best way to get men to listen to you is to hold out to them the secret of carrying the cross, which is the lot of every mortal, with joy."[74] In the cross are victory and the salvation of souls.

Thus, evangelizers are called to be Saints. The teacher of faith must have "[t]he charism given to him by the Spirit, a solid spirituality and transparent witness of life."[75] Summarizing the saintly qualities needed to be a good evangelist, John Paul II exclaims: "What assiduous study of the Word of God transmitted by the Church's Magisterium, what profound familiarity with

---

[71] Thomas Dubay, *Faith and Certitude* (San Francisco: Ignatius Press, 1985), 200-201.

[72] See CT 40.

[73] As Scripture attests, Teachers of the Faith are to "make up what is lacking in the suffering of Christ" (Col 1:24). "Unto this indeed, (to do right and suffer evil) you have been called" (1 P 2:20).

[74] Chautard, *The Soul of the Apostolate*, 124.

[75] GDC 156.

Christ and with the Father, what a spirit of prayer, what detachment from self must a catechist have in order that he can say (with St. Paul): 'My teaching is not mine!'"[76]

The Lord has chosen us to go and bear fruit as witnesses of the Gospel. To do this, "we must be inspired by a holy restlessness: restlessness to bring to everyone the gift of faith, of friendship with Christ... [because] we have received the faith to give it to others."[77] Yes, every evangelizer is called to be a Saint, which "is nothing other than to speak with God as a friend speaks with a friend. This is holiness.... To be holy does not mean being superior to others; the saint can be very weak, with many mistakes in his life. Holiness is this profound contact with God, becoming a friend of God: it is letting the Other work, the Only One who can really make the world both good and happy.... Truly we are all capable, we are all called to open ourselves up to this friendship with God."[78]

In essence, the necessity that teachers of the Faith uphold the integrity of the doctrine of the Faith in their teaching and life cannot be overstated. John Paul II makes it clear that students of sacred doctrine have "the right to receive 'the word of faith' not in mutilated, falsified or diminished form but whole and entire, in all its rigor and vigor.... Thus, no true [evangelist or] catechist can lawfully, on his own initiative, make a selection of what he considers important in the deposit of faith as opposed to what he considers unimportant, so as to teach the one and reject the other."[79] John Paul II's biographer, George Weigel, reminds us that "Doctrine is not excess baggage weighing down the Christian journey. Doctrine is the vehicle that

---

[76] CT 6.

[77] Cardinal Ratzinger (Benedict XVI), *Homily at the Mass for the Election of the Roman Pontiff* (April 18, 2005).

[78] Cardinal Ratzinger (Benedict XVI), *Letting God Work*, Talk on the occasion of the canonization of Josemaría Escrivá (October 6, 2002).

[79] CT 30.

enables the journey to take place at all."[80] To the General Council of the Dominicans, John Paul II confirmed the necessary connection between sacred doctrine and holiness: "The men of our time, perhaps not always in a conscious way, ask today's believers [who are evangelizers] not only to talk about Christ, but in a certain sense to have seen Him... *to give to others what has been contemplated*.... Only the one who has experienced God can speak about Him in a convincing way... [we] are called to be teachers of truth and holiness."[81]

Holiness is essential to discovering truth, for "wisdom will not enter a deceitful soul, nor dwell in a body enslaved to sin" (Ws 1:4). The study and handing on of sacred doctrine is not simply "the fusion of what is true [to] the exclusion of what is false... [but] the self-oblation in love of the creature to the Creator... the contemplation by the creature of the Creator... [which thus leads as well to] holy contemplation overflowing into action"[82] and teaching. St. Thomas assures us that then we will "Taste and see that the Lord is sweet."[83] For, as it was for the author of the *Wisdom of Solomon*, each evangelizer who contemplates wisdom and remains faithful to doctrinal truth will be able to say: "Therefore I prayed, and understanding was given me; I called upon God, and the spirit of wisdom came to me.... I learned without guile and I impart without grudging" (7:7, 13). In the New Evangelization, we evangelizers must seek to become Saints, to pass on sacred doctrine, the Holy Wisdom of God, with the grace of divine self-giving love, to form the Saints of tomorrow.

[80] George Weigel, *Witness to Hope* (New York: HarperCollins, 1999), 853. See also Hans Urs von Balthasar, *In the Fullness of Faith*, trans. Graham Harrison (San Francisco: Ignatius Press, 1988; originally published in 1975 as *Katholisch*, Einsiedeln, Switzerland), 55-57.

[81] John Paul II, Address (Feb 15, 2002), from ZENIT News Service (ZE02021507).

[82] Gerald Vann, OP, *The Aquinas Prescription* (Manchester, NH: Sophia Press, 1939), 163.

[83] STh I, q. 180, a. 7, quoted in Vann, 176.

Teaching Holy Wisdom with Divine Love and Mercy

Teaching the Faith requires an understanding of the meaning of sacred doctrine (*sacra doctrina*) itself. To summarize — sacred doctrine is sacred, revealed and reasoned, divine truth, which taken as a whole makes up the one, comprehensive and unified propositional summation of the Deposit of Faith given to the Church by Jesus Christ and His Apostles. Sacred doctrine is known through natural law and divine Revelation, containing the twofold Source of the Word of God — contained in Sacred Tradition[1] and the inspired Sacred Scriptures — both of which have the Magisterium, with its charism of infallibility, as their sole official interpreter, thus safeguarding the truths of faith and morals without error.[2] Sacred doctrine includes three levels of religious truth: (1) dogmatic doctrine, all divinely revealed truths infallibly pronounced and solemnly declared to be part of Revelation; (2) definitive doctrine, everything definitively proposed by the Church regarding faith and morals (as revealed doctrine or at least as intimately and intrinsically connected with formally and divinely revealed truth); and (3) authoritative, non-definitive doctrine, including all of the Church's teachings regarding faith

---

[1] GDC 95. For details on how St. Thomas includes Tradition, though not by name, in his *Summa*, as a primary source of *sacra doctrina*, see G. Geenan, OP "The Place of Tradition in the Theology of St. Thomas," *Thomist* XV (Jan. 1952), 110-135.

[2] CCC 100.

and morals which have been presented as true or at least as sure. Sacred doctrine is transmitted by holy teaching (with a pedagogy which respects the natural order of learning and utilizes a genuine inculturation) via evangelization, which includes Christian catechesis[3] (the service of charitably handing on the Faith whole and entire in all its rigor and vigor) and sacred theology (the queen of the sciences whose task is to penetrate to a deeper understanding of the mysteries of the Catholic Faith and apply them accurately to the other sciences and modern culture) by baptized faithful who are authentic, living witnesses of Christ, through reasoning, prayer, contemplation, and love-inspired exposition. Sacred doctrine is only received (as acquired or infused knowledge) and imparted to others faithfully, as such, if the evangelist and the one being evangelized attain holy wisdom, in accordance with a living theological faith in Christ and His Church, the hope of eternal life, and communion with divine love. Sacred doctrine is a share in the very Knowledge of God in Himself, Who became incarnate in the Word made flesh. In His humanity Christ is the personification of sacred doctrine, and now through the Church sacred doctrine is the "icon" of Jesus Christ. Thus, Jesus Christ, in a certain sense, is Sacred Doctrine personified; the mirror that Catholic sacred doctrine reflects is nothing other than Christ. The truth of the meaning of sacred doctrine is itself a doctrine, and as part of divine Revelation (or at least directly connected with it), it is incontestable.

To deny a doctrine of the Catholic Church is to deny Christ Himself. As St. Thomas teaches, to obstinately disbelieve even one doctrine of the Faith (with an informed conscience and free

---

[3] Congar states that the prologue of the *Summa* includes *sacra doctrina* to mean Scripture as well as "catechesis, Christian preaching, and theology in its scientific form" (*A History of Theology* 93); Fr. Robert Bradley also remarks that their meanings are similar in the *Summa*, "where 'sacred doctrine' and 'sacred Scripture' are practically synonyms, that for him (Aquinas) too catechesis and the Bible are intimately intertwined," cited in *The Roman Catechism in the Catechetical Tradition of the Church*, page 55.

will) places oneself outside of communion with Christ and His Church,[4] and is a mortal sin. On the other hand, to embrace the doctrines of the Faith is to embrace Christ.

Authentic evangelization is a ministry that engages in the divine hermeneutic of the whole of sacred doctrine. The task of evangelizers is to faithfully hand on Christ's Word, via sacred doctrine, in the form of a logical, systematic, scientific, and comprehensive exposition. Those engaged in this ministry must let Christ teach through them, and they can only do this in as much as they are living witnesses in communion with Wisdom and Love Incarnate Himself.

Holy wisdom must be passed on with divine love by authentic living witnesses of the Faith. As the *Roman Catechism* states, "The whole concern of doctrine and its teaching must be directed to the love that never ends."[5] St. Augustine noted that at the source of every Christian teaching must be the love of Christ: "With this love set before you as an end to which you may refer all that you say, so give all your instructions that he to whom you speak by hearing may believe, and by believing may hope and by hoping may love."[6] St. Francis too was known to say, "Love, and cause to be loved, Love Who is not loved." This is the vocation of the teacher of Faith, of all the baptized faithful.

The ministry of handing on the Faith is also not just about memorizing or spouting doctrine. Both teacher and student must move, *through* the knowledge of the doctrines of Revelation, toward Him Who reveals Himself. "Faith without propositions is

---

[4] STh II-II, 5, 3. This whole book has established this truth. But while having *difficulties* with a doctrine is one thing, as John Henry Cardinal Newman wrote, "Ten thousand difficulties do not make one doubt" (CCC 157), it is an altogether different matter, regarding a doctrine as a doctrine, to be *obstinately opposed to it with doubt or disbelief.*

[5] *Roman Catechism*, Preface, 10.

[6] St. Augustine, *De Catechizandis Rudibus*, 24.

faith without facts,"[7] according to Schönborn, and for St. Thomas, faith terminates not in propositions but in realities (*Fides non terminatur ad enuntiabile sed ad rem*). In a general audience on catechesis, John Paul II stated, "Catechesis cannot be limited simply to the communication of religious information. It must help to set alight in souls that light which is Christ."[8]

Evangelists themselves must be immersed in the reality and light of Christ through contemplation in order to then share Him effectively. To understand doctrinal truth, they must first love Truth, spend time immersed in Truth. As faith precedes understanding, so love precedes wisdom. St. Thomas explains, "For just as a lamp is not able to illuminate unless a fire is enkindled, so also the spiritual lamp does not illuminate unless he first burn and be inflamed with the fire of charity. Hence, ardor precedes illumination, for a knowledge of truth is bestowed by the ardor of charity."[9]

Evangelists must first be holy and prayerful to attain the full perception of truth. They must seek wisdom in prayer-filled study and personal piety. They must have theological faith, which is absolutely necessary as a prerequisite to penetrate and attain unto deeper knowledge of the divine mysteries. Once attained, they must convert every truth into a prayer, and teach their students to do so as well. By enlightening their own intellect with doctrine and grace first, evangelizers will be able to further elevate their hearts to God in love, so that their increased knowledge will in turn increase their religious fervor and devotion, instead of decreasing it due to pride. Then, they shall become evangelizers in the truest sense and bear fruit a hundredfold.

---

[7] Ratzinger and Schönborn, *An Introduction to the Catechism of the Catholic Church*, 55; see also CCC 170.

[8] John Paul II, General Audience (August 29, 1979).

[9] St. Thomas Aquinas, *Commentary on the Gospel of St. John*, as quoted in Christopher Rengers, OFM Cap, *The 33 Doctors of the Church* (Rockford: TAN, 2000), 373.

To be able to engage in good evangelization, teachers must spend regular times in prayerful contemplation of the Faith with a lively theological faith. Gerald Vann, OP, writes that contemplation is to be understood here in a broad sense. For him, as for St. Thomas, there is a threefold approach to contemplation — "(1) contemplation in the strict sense of prayer, mysticism; (2) rational investigation of the things of God, theology, philosophy [as well as catechesis]; and (3) rational investigation of the problems agitating the contemporary world, so as, if possible, to find the right answer to them in the light of eternal truth."[10] Contemplation is to gaze upon Truth with love and to look at the world around us in the Light of Truth.

Evangelizers will then be motivated and ready to share the truths and joys of their contemplation with their students. For just as it is better to illuminate than to shine, according to St. Thomas, so it is better to pass on the fruits of contemplation to others than just to contemplate.[11] With this approach to the ministry of evangelization, teachers will lead both themselves and their students into ever-deeper union with the Triune God, while also preparing both for eternal life.

But St. Thomas also teaches (or I might say, witnesses), not in what he writes in his *Summa*, but in what he does *not* write by not finishing it — that knowledge must lead to adoration. St. Thomas never finished writing his *Summa*, because after receiving a vision of God, he saw his writing as nothing but straw compared to what he had personally experienced of God, through what it taught him. Pieper comments that the genius of Thomas is found not only in what he wrote, but in what it led him, and later others, to do and see: doctrine, rooted in faith, leads to a "veneration toward everything that is"; and as St. Thomas demonstrates, this "veneration is revealed above all in [Thomas'] fall-

---

[10] Vann, *The Aquinas Prescription*, 9.
[11] STh II-II 186, 6.

ing silent before the ineffability and incomprehensibility of Being."[12] Faith in sacred doctrine leads to union with Truth, as Thomas shows us.

Teachers must hold fast to the Sacred Deposit (Mt 28:20; 1 Tm 6:20; 2 Tm 1:4) of God's revelatory truth. They must allow it to lead them to experience Christ, and then to share Him with their students through the transmission of doctrine.

Our intelligent grasp of the Faith depends to a great extent not only on a study of the doctrines of the Faith, but on a growth in the theological virtue of faith, as well as wisdom, knowledge, understanding, together with love and mercy; and this is acquired or infused only in conjunction with prayer, in what has been called a "kneeling and sitting" evangelization.[13]

"What is truth?" Pontius Pilate's question to the Suffering Servant demonstrates that even in a face-to-face encounter with the incarnated first Truth and highest Good, one may still be blind, deaf, and dumb, without the proper dispositions of grace, faith, and love. So it is with the evangelist and those evangelized today.

Evangelizers must also be willing and ready to die for Christ (see Si 4:28), to "suffer 'the loss of all things...' in order to 'gain Christ and be found in him,' and... [to] share his sufferings, becoming like him in his death, that if possible [they] may attain the resurrection from the dead.'"[14]

This is the hour of the New Evangelization for the Church; and this is the time for evangelizers to unite its two essential components — the one with a focus on sacred doctrine and orthodoxy, the other on faithful living witness, personal relationship with Jesus Christ and commitment — as a united synthesis for the authentic renewal of evangelization. This book has ad-

---

[12] Pieper, *Guide to St. Thomas*, 159.

[13] The concept of a "kneeling and sitting theology" is discussed by Robert A. Stackpole, *Jesus, Mercy Incarnate* (Stockbridge, MA: Marian Press, 2000), 14, as being related to H.U. von Balthasar, but without a citation.

[14] CCC 428, quoting Ph 3:8-11.

dressed the modern issues of evangelization, especially those which have led to the deep-rooted crisis of faith, and has proposed a series of related syntheses for evangelists to utilize as the solution to this crisis — the synthesis of uniting emphasis on sacred doctrine together with focus on the authentic living witness of the evangelizer in fostering personal conversion and new life in the community of faith, which is an application within evangelization of Vatican II's *aggiornamento* together with the *Communio* movement's call for a return to *resourcement*. Ratzinger (Benedict XVI) proposed a similar synthesis in his book, *Principles of Catholic Theology*. He spoke of the need in theology for the synthesis of Aquinas' focus on orthodoxy and objective doctrinal content with its self-subsistent primacy of truth (*scientia speculativa*) together with Bonaventure's emphasis on orthopraxis and the proper methodology (*scientia practica*)[15] of the faithful witness as teacher, while also acknowledging the delicate balance of maintaining "the primacy of *logos* over *pragma*."[16] This balance of the spiritual praxis in which we are *and* act, we learn *and* live the Faith in an integral unity will bring about a true spiritual reform,[17] and in doing so, will form new Saints in the renewal of evangelization that has already begun.

---

[15] The relationship between these two is discussed further by Joseph Cardinal Ratzinger (Benedict XVI) in *Principles of Catholic Theology: Building Stones for a Fundamental Theology* (San Francisco: Ignatius Press, 1987), 315-331.

[16] Ratzinger (Benedict XVI), *Principles of Catholic Theology*, 322.

[17] Catherine de Hueck Doherty, foundress of Madonna House, in her book, *The Gospel Without Compromise*, discusses exactly what is missing today from the work of authentic and effective evangelization, and in turn, what is needed to form Saints in the renewal of evangelization, stating:
"Let's face it. If the world is atheistic, if much of it has not yet heard the Good News, or if it has heard but not accepted it, then *the main fault lies with us Christians who have not lived the Gospel....*
"My impression from traveling was that the world is crying for the Bread of Life, for the Living Waters that Christ promised — in fact, for God Himself. But Christians who possess the bread and the water *do not know how to share* the bread they eat. They forget that whoever eats the bread of the Lord must be truly 'eaten up' by others. Having received Love, the Christian should give love....
"We should stop [just] talking about God and start living out the Gospel in our

One of the outcomes of this book has been to urge the re-establishing of the teachings in Aquinas' *Summa Theologiae* to pre-eminence and to confirm that it still remains one of the benchmark sources of *sacra doctrina*, as Aquinas defined it, for evangelization.[18] The consistent and overwhelming evidence of Church teaching discussed herein have clearly established that St. Thomas Aquinas is still the Angelic and Common Doctor, the Apostle of truth, the perfect theologian, the Prince of teachers, and, as patron saint of Catholic schools and students, the heavenly patron of the highest studies.

What has not been proposed herein is that all catechists and theologians must become Thomists, and to think so would,

---

lives, manifesting the image of the Lord so clearly in our hearts that no one can possibly say that He is dead. We should stop worrying about theological theory and begin building among ourselves communities of love.

"We live in pentecostal times. Once again the invincible love of the Holy Spirit is among us. We have only to open our hearts to it and *we shall change the world*.

"Then our own hearts will contain the fire and flame that Jesus sent to renew the earth...

"Why can't we modern Christians adopt the techniques of the apostles and of the early Christians? True, we may wind up in some prisons, prisons of rejection, ridicule and maybe even physical prisons. We may be crucified in a thousand ways, maybe even locked up in psychiatric wards as St. Francis of Assisi might be if he were alive today. But so what? The Gospel would be preached to the poor and the kingdom of God would begin at least to have a toehold in our modern world. Yes, Jesus came to cast fire on the earth. Would that this fire were enkindled in our hearts today....

"Whatever label we want to put on these times, we of the West who have heard the Gospel have certainly not INCARNATED the teaching of Christ in Whom we profess to believe....

"We stand on a very narrow ledge today. Which way are we going to move? Along the ledge of faith, hope and love? This is the path God gives us when we listen. On either side is an abyss. Which are we going to choose? It's up to us. This is the hour of choosing."

Accessed on-line at http://www.madonnahouse.org/doherty/without.html (August 10, 2005).

[18] According to Pope John XXIII in his address to the Fifth International Thomistic Congress (Sept. 16, 1960), St. Thomas' "teaching was, more than any other, fully in keeping with the truths that God has revealed, with the writings of the Holy Fathers, and with the principles of right reason, and therefore Holy Church has adopted it as her own, and has given the name of common or universal teacher to its author."

in actuality, be to promote a closed system of theology, one that would then deserve great criticism.[19] What has, in fact, been proposed is first, that all evangelizers be anchored to the Church and be rooted in sacred doctrine, as found in Magisterial documents (like the Sacred Scriptures and the *Catechism*), as well as in the writings of the Church Fathers *and* in great theological works like Aquinas' *Summa Theologiae*; and second, that all evangelizers seek wholeheartedly to fashion their own lives after Christ and model their approach to teaching the Faith after Jesus Himself and such masters as St. Thomas Aquinas. This book has sought to advocate such an approach to teaching the Faith; it has also sought to demonstrate this approach in method throughout its pages.

Church evangelizers should look with an anagogical sense to the reward for those of them who remain faithful to the Sacred Deposit of Faith to the end. Sacred Scripture gives us a hint about this, stating that those who faithfully remain "beyond all reproach in the midst of a twisted and depraved generation... [will] shine like stars in the sky while holding fast to the word of life" (Ph 2:15-16). "Those who are wise shall shine like the brightness of the firmament, and those who turn many to righteousness [will sparkle] like the stars for ever and ever" (Dn

---

[19] Having said this, Reginald Masterson, OP, does however make a solid argument for Thomism as a good, if not the best, method in teaching theology in his article, "The Nature of Sacred Theology," in *Theology in the Catholic College*; and in the same book, James M. Egan, OP, in his article, "Preparation of Theology Teachers" argues that "No apology is needed for using the *Summa Theologiae* of St. Thomas... [because it] is a work of continual analysis, of pulling apart and carefully scrutinizing all the elements of divine revelation... and in the reiterated judgment of the Church, [it is] the supreme achievement of the human mind in the realm of theology... [and, together with the since developed doctrinal teaching of the Magisterium,] the overall order and the theological formulations of the great truths of divine revelation as found in the *Summa* retain their validity and timeliness and are as necessary today for the formation of a theologian or a teacher of theology according to the mind of the Church as they have been since St. Thomas first produced his magnificent synthesis." See Reginald Masterson, OP, ed., *Theology in the Catholic College* (Dubuque, Iowa: The Priory Press, 1961), 39-66.

12:3). This is the reward of the faithful teacher of sacred doctrine. This is their sacred vocation, which will continue until the day when the Lord Himself will bring to full fruition His Word: "I will put my Law within them, and I will write it upon their hearts; and I will be their God, and they shall be my people. And no longer shall each man teach his neighbor and each his brother, saying 'Know the LORD,' for they shall all know me, from the least of them to the greatest, says the LORD" (Jr 31:33-34). May the Lord give us His wisdom, love, and mercy so that we can bring others to see Him face to face, and He may say of us as He said to St. Thomas Aquinas: "Well done, good and faithful servant!" (Mt 25:21); "Well have *you* written (and taught) of Me."

We know the Lord as He Who is both Teacher and Taught. Since Christ alone is the Teacher, teachers who accept the vocation to teach in His Name, will be effective only to the degree they are living witnesses of Christ and faithful communicators of His doctrine, while utilizing Scripture, Church documents, and sound theological works and catechetical texts as their content of teaching.

This is how we will combat the evils of our times and usher in the springtime of the Faith. A century ago, St. Pius X, who originally organized the Confraternity of Christian Doctrine, exclaimed, "Most of the evils which beset the Church and most of the problems with which the Catholic Church is plagued, are not due to bad will," he says, "no, they are mainly due to ignorance of Christ's revealed truth."[20] And so it is today perhaps

---

[20] St. Pius X, *Acerbo Nimus*, 1. Similarly on the topic of religious illiteracy and how it has caused great misfortune, particularly among non-Catholics, Archbishop Fulton J. Sheen, host of the popular Catholic primetime television show, "Life Is Worth Living", was well known to have said, "Not one hundred in the United States hate the Roman Catholic Church, but millions hate what they mistakenly think that the Roman Catholic Church is." Three decades of new approaches to handing on the Faith have not improved these matters, both among Catholics themselves and in their witness to non-Catholics. Catechists and theologians have their work cut out for them and, as this book discusses, the plan for the New Evangelization is clear.

more than ever. Ignorance of doctrine is our greatest evil and modern crisis. The solution remains as clear as ever, as St. Pius X elsewhere declares: "Nothing is needed more to promote the kingdom of Jesus Christ in the world than the holiness of churchmen, who should stand out above the faithful by their example, their words and their teaching."[21] These are the true evangelizers of the New Evangelization.

For man does not live by bread alone, but by the words of eternal life![22] We must join the Church in venerating sacred doctrine in some ways as we venerate the Scriptures and the Lord's Body.[23] Thus, the role of every believer of the Catholic Faith is to maintain enthusiastically, with the episcopacy, a *holy keeping and faithful exposition* of the Deposit of Faith, in the form of the Church's sacred doctrines, which taken as a whole make up an icon of the Incarnate Word, Truth Himself.

---

[21] Letter, "La ristorazione," Acta Pius X, I, p. 257.

[22] See Mt 4:4; Jn 10:10.

[23] See CCC 103. *Dei Verbum* states: "The Church has always venerated the divine Scriptures just as she venerates the body of the Lord, since, especially in the sacred liturgy, she unceasingly receives and offers to the faithful the bread of life from the table both of God's word and of Christ's body. She has always maintained them, and continues to do so, *together with sacred tradition*, as the supreme rule of faith" (21, italics added).

A Survey of Magisterial Support for St. Thomas Aquinas

The following text is meant to be a survey of significant magisterial references concerning St. Thomas Aquinas, the "Apostle of truth," and his writings. The magisterial citations were organized in chronological order from the thirteenth to the twenty-first century to demonstrate the Church's accumulative and consistent affirmation of his work. The Church calls St. Thomas Aquinas the "perfect theologian" and the "Prince of teachers." As one Pontiff directed, "Go to Thomas," so thus we begin our journey by tracing the love and admiration of the Church for this "heavenly patron of the highest studies."

1254 **Alexander IV**
"To Our beloved son, Thomas Aquinas, distinguished alike for nobility of blood and integrity of character, who has acquired by the grace of God the treasure of divine and human learning."[1]

1318 **John XXII**
Consistorial Address
Pope John XXII declares Aquinas' doctrine miraculous: "He alone enlightened the Church more than all other doctors;

---

[1] Alexander IV was Pope during Aquinas' lifetime; he was the first pope to speak about Aquinas according to Pius XI in *Studiorum Ducem* #10.

a man can derive more profit in a year from his books than from pondering all his life the teaching of others."[2] "Why should we seek more miracles? He has performed as many miracles as he wrote articles. Truly this glorious Doctor, after the Apostles and the early Doctors, has greatly enlightened the Church."[3]

1323   **Redemptionem misit Dominus**
        In this Bull, Pope John XXII canonizes Thomas Aquinas.[4]

1344-   **Clement VI**
1346   **Bull *In Ordine Fratrum, Praedicatorum***
        Pope Clement VI orders the Friars Preachers not to deviate from the doctrine of St. Thomas.[5]
        "That famous and fruitful branch, the blessed Thomas of Aquin, outstanding doctor and confessor. The whole Church, gathering many fruits of his spiritual maturity from the writing and teaching of his wisdom and doctrine, is continually refreshed by their aroma."[6]

1350s   **Innocent VI**
        Serm. De St. Thoma
        "His teaching above that of others, the canonical writings alone excepted, enjoys such a precision of language, an order of matters, a truth of conclusions, that those who hold to it are never found swerving from the path of truth, and he who dare assail it will always be suspected of error."[7]

---

[2] As quoted by Pius XI in *Stud. Ducem* #10; St. Pius X also quotes this emphatic statement of John XXII in *Doctoris Angelici.*
[3] P. Percin, *Monumenta Conventus Tolosani Ord. Praed.*, cf. J. Berthier, op. cit., 50.
[4] Cf. Maritain, Append. II, page 219.
[5] Cf. Maritain, Append. II, page 219.
[6] Cf. Berthier, op. cit., 55.
[7] *Serm. De S. Thoma.*; quoted by Leo XIII in *Aeterni Patris* #21.

1368   **Urban V**
        Address to the University of Toulouse
        "It is our will, which we hereby enjoin upon you, that you
        follow the teaching of Blessed Thomas as the true and
        Catholic doctrine, and that you labor with all your force
        to profit by the same."[8]

1406   **Innocent VII**
        Const. *Duecens reputamus*
        Pope Innocent VII confirms the doctrine of the Friars
        Preachers, which is the doctrine of St. Thomas.[9]

1451   **Nicholas V**
        Brief to the Friars of the Order of Preachers
        In this Brief, Pope Nicholas V celebrates the wisdom of
        St. Thomas Aquinas, and honors the Dominicans for re-
        maining faithful to his teaching.[10]

1537-   **Council of Trent**
1563   According to Pope Leo XIII, "the chief and special glory
        of Thomas, one which he has shared with none of the
        Catholic Doctors, is that the Fathers of Trent made it part
        of the order of conclave to lay upon the altar, together with
        Sacred Scripture and the decrees of the supreme Pontiffs,
        the '*Summa*' of St. Thomas, whence to seek council, rea-
        son, and inspiration."[11]
        As Pope Pius XI confirms, "the Fathers of Trent resolved
        that two volumes only, Holy Scripture and the *Summa
        Theologica*, should be reverently laid open on the altar dur-
        ing their deliberations."[12]

---

[8] Const. *5a dat. Die* Aug. 3, 1368 ad Concell, Univ. Tolo; as quoted by Leo XIII in
   Aet. Pat. #21.

[9] Cf. Maritain, Append. II, page 220.

[10] Cited in *Aet. Pat.* #21.

[11] Cited in Leo XIII's *Aet. Pat.* #22.

[12] Cited in Pius XI's *Stud. Doc.* #11.

1567   **St. Pius V**
       Const., Bull, *Mirabilis Deus*
       St. Pius V is the first to proclaim the feast of St. Thomas
       as Doctor.[13]
       "But in as much as, by the providence of Almighty God,
       the power and truth of the philosophy of the Angelic
       Doctor, ever since his enrollment amongst the citizens of
       Heaven, have confounded, refuted, and routed many sub-
       sequent heresies, as was so often clearly seen in the past
       and was lately apparent in the sacred decrees of the Council
       of Trent. We order that the memory of the Doctor by
       whose valor the world is daily delivered from pestilent er-
       rors be cultivated more than ever before with feelings of
       pious and grateful devotion."[14]
       St. Pius V was the first to call Aquinas "Doctor of the
       Church" and "Angelic Doctor."[15]

1570   St. Pius V also ordered an edition of the complete works
       of St. Thomas.[16]

       Bull *In eminenti*
       He also said of Aquinas that "his theological doctrine, ac-
       cepted by the Catholic Church, *outshines every other as
       being safer and more secure.*"[17]

1588   **Sixtus V**
       Bull *Triumphantis*
       "By the divine favor of Him who alone gives the spirit of
       science, and wisdom, and understanding, and who through
       all ages, as there may be need, enriches His Church with

---

[13] Cf. Maritain, Append. II, page 220.
[14] As cited by St. Pius X in *Doc. Angel.* and also cited by Leo XIII in *Aet. Pat.* #21.
[15] Pius XI also cites this in *Stud. Doc.* #11; Pope John Paul II also reiterates this in his *Address to the International Society of St. Thomas Aquinas* #4 given in 1979.
[16] Cf. Maritain, Append. II, page 220.
[17] Bull *In eminenti*, July 29, 1570, op. cit., 99.

new blessings and strengthens it with new safeguards, there was founded by our fathers, men of eminent wisdom, the scholastic theology, which two glorious doctors in particular, the angelic St. Thomas and the seraphic St. Bonaventure, illustrious teachers of this faculty,... with surpassing genius, by unwearied diligence, and at the cost of long labors and vigils, set in order and beautified, and, when skillfully arranged and clearly explained in a variety of ways, handed down to posterity."[18]

Pope Sixtus V discussed that what gave scholastic theology its irreducible power against the enemies of truth was "that ready and close coherence of cause and effect, that order and array as of a disciplined army in battle, those clear definitions and distinctions, that strength of argument and those keen discussions, by which light is distinguished from darkness, the true from the false, expose and strip naked, as it were, the falsehoods of heretics wrapped around by a cloud of subterfuges and fallacies."[19]

1594   **Clement VIII**
Pope Clement VIII recommends the Fathers of the Society of Jesus to adhere to St. Thomas.[20]

1603   **Bull *Sicut Angeli***
"The proof of his doctrine is the great number of books which he wrote in a very short time, in practically every branch of learning, with remarkable order and wonderful planning, and *with no error at all*. While writing these works he had the holy Apostles Peter and Paul speaking to him and at the command of God they explained certain passages to him. When he finished his works, he heard them approved by the express word of Christ the Lord."[21]

---

[18] As quoted by Leo XIII in *Aet. Pat.* #14.
[19] As quoted by Leo XIII in *Aet. Pat.* #16.
[20] Cf. Maritain, Appen. II, pages 220-221.
[21] Bull *Sicut Angeli*, Nov. 22, 1603, op. cit., 112.

1607/ **Paul V**

1614 **Bull *Splendidissiums athleta***
In speaking about Aquinas' works: "By the shield of whose works the Church Militant happily escaped the darts of heretics."[22]

Bull *Cum sicut*
Called Aquinas "defender of the Catholic Church and conqueror of heretics."[23]

1694 **Innocent XII**
In this Letter in the form of a Brief, Pope Innocent XII addresses the University of Louvain enjoining them to follow the teaching of St. Thomas Aquinas.[24]

1718 **Clement XI**
Const. *Inscrutabili*
Pope Clement XI gives his solemn approbation to the statutes of the Academy of St. Thomas in Rome.[25]

1724 **Benedict XIII**
Bull *Demissas preces*
"Pursue with energy your Doctor's works, more brilliant than the sun and written without the shadow of error. These works made the Church illustrious with wonderful erudition, since they march ahead and proceed with unimpeded step, protecting and vindicating by that surest rule of Christian doctrine, the truth of our holy religion."[26]

---

[22] Bull *Splendidissiums athleta*, Sept. 17, 1607, op. cit., 117.

[23] Bull *Cum sicut*, Oct. 20, 1614, ibid.

[24] In this he followed the example of Urban V (1368); also cited by Leo XIII in *Aet. Pat.* #21.

[25] Cf. Maritain, Append. II, page 221.

[26] Bull *Demissas preces*, Nov. 6, 1724, op. cit. 147.

1720s **Bull *Pretiosus***
Benedict XIII heaped pontifical indulgences upon "the society of the *Angelic Militia* founded under the patronage
of Thomas for the preservation and maintenance of holy
chastity."[27]

1730s **Clement XII**
Bull *Verbo Dei*
In this Bull, Clement affirms "that most fruitful blessings
have spread abroad from his (Aquinas') writings over the
whole Church, and that he is worthy of the honor which
is bestowed on the greatest doctors of the Church."[28]

1752 **Benedict XIV**
"Numerous Roman Pontiffs, Our Predecessors, have borne
glorious testimony to his (Aquinas') philosophy. We also,
in the books which we have written on various topics, after by diligent examination perceiving and considering the
mind of the Angelic Doctor, have always adhered and sub-
scribed with joy and admiration to his philosophy, and
candidly confess that whatever good is to be found in Our
own writings is in no way to be attributed to Us, but entirely to so eminent a teacher."[29]

Brief to Dionysian College in Granada
Benedict XIV enjoins them to follow the teachings of St.
Thomas Aquinas.[30]

"That henceforth none of the Masters or Lectors of the College of St. Dionysius shall read, hand down or explain any
other doctrine to their students in that College."[31]

---

[27] As cited by Pius XI in *Stud. Doc.* #25.
[28] Quote taken from Leo XIII in *Aet. Pat.* #21.
[29] *Acta Cap. Gen. O.P.*, vol. XI, p. 196; St. Pius X (1914) adopts this statement from
Benedict XIV concerning the writings of St. Thomas Aquinas, more particularly
the *Summa Theologiae*, as a summary of all the commendations bestowed upon him.
[30] Cited by Leo XIII in *Aet. Pat* #21.
[31] *Brief to Dionysian College.*

1756 **Constitution *Sollicita***
"The other praises of the holy Doctor are surpassed by this, that he never despised his opponents or seemed to vilify or betray them but treated all courteously and very humanely. If he came upon any of their expressions which were inaccurate, ambiguous or obscure, he would temper his criticism with a smooth and benign interpretation. If the cause of religion or faith demanded that he investigate and refute their opinion, he would accomplish the refutation with so much discretion that he deserved no less praise for his manner of disagreement than for his assertion of the Catholic truth."[32]

1777 **Pius VI**
Allocution to the Dominican General Chapter
"In many schools Thomas Aquinas was rightly called the Sun of doctrine and the standard for theologians, because he taught only what was consistent with Sacred Scripture and the Fathers. Everything he wrote is worthy, as it is piously said, of divine confirmation. And so Our predecessors commended his doctrine with outstanding praises as the shield of Christian religion and the resolute guardian of the Church. Recently, Benedict XIV, whose wisdom We thoroughly admired, ordered Thomistic doctrine to be restored in the College of St. Dionysius the Areopagite outside Granada, and proposed the penalty of interdict for anyone who departed from it."[33]

---

[32] Constitution *Sollicita*.
[33] *Allocution to the Dominican General Chapter*, the Pontiff presiding, May 17, 1777, op. cit., 170.

1855   **Pius IX**
       False Traditionalism
       When the French philosopher Augustin Bonnetty, in re-
       action to Kantian rationalism began to spread errors of
       traditionalism, which accused, among other things, the
       writings of St. Thomas of leading to rationalism, Pope Pius
       IX's Sacred Congregation of the Index asked him to agree
       to a set of propositions which vindicated the rights of hu-
       man reason.
       The fourth proposition upheld the authentic philosophy
       of St. Thomas Aquinas: "The method used by St. Thomas
       and St. Bonaventure and other scholastics after them does
       not lead to rationalism nor has it been the reason why
       philosophy in today's schools is falling into naturalism and
       pantheism. These doctors and teachers are not to be
       blamed for using this method, especially since they used
       it with the approbation or at least with the silent approval
       of the Church."[34]

1870   *Letter to the Dominican Raymond Bianchi* dated June 9
       Pope Pius IX observed "that the Church, in the ecumeni-
       cal councils held after his (Aquinas') death, so used his
       writings that many of the decrees propounded found their
       source in his works; sometimes his very words were used
       to clarify Catholic dogmas or to destroy rising errors."[35]

1878   **Leo XIII**
       **Encyclical *Inscrutabli Dei Consilio* (*On the Evils of*
       Society)**
       "Philosophy seeks not the overthrow of divine revelation,
       but delights rather to prepare its way, and defend it against

---

[34] Quote taken from Clarkson's *The Church Teaches* (1955), 19; cf. also ND 105;
Denz. 2814.
[35] Cf. Berthier's *Sanctus Thomas Aquinas, 'Doctor Communis Ecclesiae'* (1914) 177;
also quoted in the *New Catholic Encyclopedia*, vol. 14, p. 110.

assailants, both by example and in written works, as the great Augustine and the Angelic Doctor, with all other teachers of Christian wisdom, have proved to us.[36]

1879   **Encyclical *Aeterni Patris* (*On the Restoration of Christian Philosophy*)**[37]

"The doctors of the Middle ages, who are called Scholastics, addressed themselves to a great work — that of diligently collecting, and sifting, and storing up, as it were, in one place, for the use and convenience of posterity the rich and fertile harvests of Christian learning scattered abroad in the voluminous works of the holy Fathers."[38]

"Among the Scholastic Doctors, the chief and master of all towers Aquinas, who, as Cajetan observes, because 'he most venerated the ancient doctors of the Church, in a certain way seems to have inherited the intellect of all.'[39] ...he is rightly and deservedly esteemed the special bulwark and glory of the Catholic faith.[40] With his spirit at once humble and swift, his memory ready and tenacious, his life spotless throughout, a love of truth for its own sake, richly endowed with human and divine science, like the sun he heated the world with the warmth of his virtues and filled it with the splendor of his teaching."[41]

"Moreover, the Angelic Doctor... single-handed... victoriously combated the errors of former times, and supplied

---

[36] Paragraph 13.

[37] In this encyclical, Pope Leo XIII directs Catholic theologians and philosophers to maintain, as their approved sources, the writings of St. Thomas Aquinas and Scholastic principles. To combat the movements of rationalism, secular liberalism, Kantian subjectivism, and historicism Leo XIII restored the dignity of Aquinas as the master of truth, which soon initiated the Neo-Scholastic movement beginning in Rome and Louvain.

[38] Paragraph 14.

[39] Quoted in Pius XI's *Stud. Ducem* #5.

[40] Also quoted and translated "the pre-eminent guardian and glory of the Catholic Church" by John Paul II in his *Address on the 100th Anniv. of Aet. Pat.* #13.

[41] Paragraph 17.

invincible arms to put those to rout which might in after-times spring up."[42]

"For these reasons most learned men... gave themselves up not so much to be instructed in his angelic wisdom as to be nourished upon it."[43]

"A last triumph was reserved for this incomparable man — namely, to compel the homage, praise, and admiration of even the very enemies of the Catholic name... [from whom some have said that] if the teaching of Thomas Aquinas were only taken away, they could easily battle with all Catholic teachers, gain the victory, and abolish the Church.[44] A vain hope, indeed, but no vain testimony."[45]

"Sacred theology... may be assisted and illustrated by all kinds of erudition, though it is absolutely necessary to approach it in the grave manner of the Scholastics, in order that, the forces of revelation and reason being united in it, it may continue to be 'the invincible bulwark of the faith.'"[46]

Leo XIII commends those who "aim at restoring the renowned teaching of Thomas Aquinas and winning it back to its ancient beauty."[47]

The pope then confesses that his "first and most cherished idea is that you (venerable brethren) should all furnish to studious youth a generous and copious supply of those purest streams of wisdom flowing inexhaustibly from the precious fountainhead of the Angelic Doctor."[48]

The hope, as he saw it, was for a more wholesome doctrine to be taught "in the universities and high schools —

---

[42] Paragraph 18.
[43] Paragraph 19.
[44] Bucer.
[45] Paragraph 23.
[46] Paragraph 24.
[47] Paragraph 25.
[48] Paragraph 26.

one more in conformity with the teaching of the Church, such as is contained in the works of Thomas Aquinas."[49] "For, the teachings of Thomas... have very great and invincible force to overturn those principles of the new order which are well known to be dangerous to the peaceful order of things...."[50]

"We exhort you, venerable brethren, in all earnestness to restore the golden wisdom of St. Thomas, and to spread it far and wide for the defense and beauty of the Catholic faith, for the good of society, and for the advantage of all the sciences.... Let carefully selected teachers endeavor to implant the doctrine of Thomas Aquinas in the minds of students, and set forth clearly his solidarity and excellence over others. Let the universities already founded or to be founded by you illustrate and defend this doctrine, and use it for the refutation of prevailing errors. But, lest the false for the true, or the corrupt for the pure be drunk in, be watchful that the doctrine of Thomas be drawn from his own fountains, or at least from those rivulets which, derived from the very fount, have thus far flowed, according to the established agreement of learned men, pure and clear; be careful to guard the minds of youth from those which are said to flow thence, but in reality are gathered from strange and unwholesome streams."[51]

"Therefore... let us follow the example of the Angelic Doctor, who never gave himself to reading or writing without first begging the blessing of God, who modestly confessed that whatever he knew he had acquired not so much by his own study and labor as by the divine gift."[52]

---

[49] Paragraph 28.
[50] Paragraph 29.
[51] Paragraph 31.
[52] Paragraph 33.

1879   **Letter *Jampridem***
This Letter proclaims his intention to restore the Roman Academy of St. Thomas and to publish Aquinas' complete works.[53]

1880   **Motu Proprio *Placere Nobis***
In this *motu proprio* he orders a new edition of the complete works of St. Thomas,[54] intending "that the excellent wisdom of the Angelic Doctor flow far and wide. There is nothing more suitable to oppose the perverse notions of our times. There is no more powerful agent for conserving the truth."[55]

1880   **Alloc. *Pergratus Nobis***
Pope Leo XIII proclaims the necessity of studying the philosophy of St. Thomas in this document.[56]

1880   ***Cum hoc sit***
Apostolic Letter Commemorating the First Anniversary of *Aeterni Patris*
"And those who are doing any work in sacred science so sharply attacked at present, have a source in the volumes of St. Thomas whence they can fully demonstrate the bases of Christian faith, whence they can convince others of supernatural truth, and whence they can repel the vicious attacks of the enemy upon our holy religion."[57]

---

[53] Cf. Maritain, Append. II, page 221.

[54] Cf. Maritain, Append. II, page 221.

[55] Motu propio *Placere nobis*, on the complete edition of the works of St. Thomas Aquinas, Jan. 18, 1880, cf. Berthier, op. cit., 200.

[56] Cf. Maritain, Append. II, page 221.

[57] Aug. 4, 1880, op. cit., I, 114.

"His doctrine is so inclusive that he has embraced within himself as in a sea all the wisdom flowing from the ancients. Whatever truth was spoken or discussed by pagan philosophers, by the Fathers and Doctors of the Church, by great men who lived before him, he not only thoroughly investigated but augmented, perfected and disposed with such a clear penetration of ideas, such an accurate system of argumentation, such an economy of speech, that he appears only to have left the power to imitate but not to excel…. He stands invincible, strengthening his arguments by the force of reason, and striking great terror in the minds of his adversaries."[58]

"The holy Doctor clearly proves that truths springing from the natural order cannot contradict those which are believed by faith: consequently, the support and cultivation of the Christian faith is not a mean and servile function of reason, but rather its noble obedience by which the mind is aided educated in a loftier realm of truth. Finally, science and faith both coming from God should not exercise a rivalry of dissension but, bound together by the ties of friendship, should offer help to each other. An outstanding example of this wonderful harmony and concordance is found in all the writings of St. Thomas. In them that harmony shines brilliantly; at one time reason predominates, with faith leading the way in the investigation of nature; at another time faith takes the lead defended and supported by reason, in such a way that each maintains inviolate its proper force and dignity. When a problem so demands, both join together, having made a compact, as it were, to destroy the enemies of each."[59]

On the first anniversary of *Aeterni Patris*, in *Cum hoc sit*,

---

[58] Brief *Cum hoc sit*, loc. cit., 112.
[59] Ibid.

he appoints St. Thomas universal patron of Catholic schools[60] and gives Aquinas the title, "Heavenly Patron of the Highest Studies."[61]

1881   **Letter to the Patriarch of Venice**
"The more the clergy is penetrated by the doctrine of St. Thomas, the more it will go forth instructed with stronger bases for a solid faith, and so much the more fruitful and useful will be its ministry to the faithful. Furthermore, those who impede Catholic truth with fallacious arguments will find its defenders better prepared, and supplied with excellent weapons for a strenuous defense."[62]

1881   Encyclical *Licet Multa (On Catholics in Belgium)*
"In what concerns yourselves, Dear Son and Venerable Brethren, use all your vigilance so that all men of science, and those, most especially, to whom you have confided the charge of teaching youth, be of one accord, and unanimous in all those questions upon which the teaching of the Holy See allows no freedom of opinion. And as to points left to the discussion of the learned, may their intellects, owing to your inspiration and your advice, be so exercised upon them that the divergences of opinion destroy not union of heart and concord of will. On this subject the Sovereign Pontiff, Benedict XIV, our immortal predecessor, has left in his Constitution 'Sollicita ac provida,' certain rules for men of study, full of wisdom and authority. He has even proposed to them, as a model to imitate in this matter, St. Thomas Aquinas, whose moderation of language and maturity of style are maintained as well in the combat against adversaries, as in the exposition of doctrine and the proofs

---

[60] Cf. Maritain, Append. II, page 222.
[61] As quoted by John Paul II in his *Address on the 100th Anniv. of Aet. Pat.*
[62] March 26, 1881, op. cit., 217-218.

destined for its defense. We wish to renew to learned men
the recommendations of our predecessor, and to point out
to them this noble model, who will teach them not only
the manner of carrying on controversy with opponents, but
also the character of the doctrine to be held and developed
in the cultivation of philosophy and theology. On many
occasions, Dear Son and Venerable Brethren, we have
expressed to you our earnest desire of seeing the wisdom
of St. Thomas reinstated in Catholic schools, and everywhere treated with the highest consideration. We have likewise exhorted you to establish in the University of Louvain
the teaching of higher philosophy in the spirit of St. Thomas. In this matter, as in all others, we have found you
entirely ready to condescend to our wishes and to fulfill
our will. Pursue then, with zeal, the task which has been
begun, and watch with care that in this same University
the fruitful sources of Christian philosophy, which spring
from the works of St. Thomas, be open to students in a
rich abundance, and applied to the profit of all other
branches of instruction. In the execution of this design, if
you have need of our aid or our counsels, they shall never
be wanting to you."[63]

1886   **Letter *Qui te***
Leo XIII discusses his desire that "the philosophy of St.
Thomas may flourish incorrupt and entire in schools, which
is very dear to Our heart," and that... "on the *Summa* of
St. Thomas Aquinas, so that his readers might not allow
the text of the Angelic Doctor to escape from their hands.
In this way only and not otherwise will the genuine doctrine of St. Thomas flourish in the schools, which is a goal
very close to Our heart. *For the method of teaching which
relies upon the authority and judgment of several masters has*

---

[63] Encyclical, Aug 3, 1881.

a changeable basis, in that mutually contradictory opinions arise which cannot be reconciled with the mind of St. Thomas. Then, too, such diverse opinions nourish dissension and disagreement which can no longer disturb Catholic schools without great harm to Christian knowledge. We desire teachers of Sacred Theology, imitating the Tridentine Fathers, should wish to have the *Summa* of St. Thomas open on their desks before them, whence they may find counsel, arguments and theological conclusions. From such schools the Church may rightly expect fearless soldiers who can destroy error and defend Catholicism."[64]

1886   *Letter to Cardinals Simeoni and Zigliara*
[Truly,] "anyone seriously interested in Philosophy and Theology and desirous of attaining some proficiency in those disciplines needs nothing more than a greater familiarity with the *Summa contra Gentiles* and the *Summa Theologiae.*"[65]

1891   Apostolic Letter *On the Mexican Hierarchy*
"This point is vital, that Bishops expend every effort to see that young men, destined to be the hope of the Church, should be imbued with the holy and heavenly doctrine of the Angelic Doctor. In those places where young men have devoted themselves to the patronage and doctrine of St. Thomas, true wisdom will flourish, drawn as it is from solid principles, and explained by reason in an orderly fashion!"[66]

1892   Brief *Gravissime Nos*
In this Brief, he invites members of the Society of Jesus to follow the teaching of St. Thomas.[67]

---

[64] Also quoted by St. Pius X in *Doc. Angel.*; Letter of June 19, 1886, op, cit., 228.
[65] Oct. 2, 1886, op. cit., 230.
[66] June 23, 1891, op. cit., 239.
[67] Cf. Maritain, Append. II, page 222.

1892   *Letter to Rev. P.J. Berthier*
       "We know that the Catholic clergy will be more solidly
       penetrated by divine science the more fully and thoroughly
       it is imbued with the doctrine of St. Thomas Aquinas."[68]

1893   Encyclical *Providentissimus Deus (On the Study of
       Sacred Scripture)*
       The great contribution of St. Thomas Aquinas and the
       other Scholastics is discussed by Pope Leo XIII in his En-
       cyclical on Sacred Scripture, as he states emphatically: "To
       them we owe the accurate and clear distinction, such as
       had not been given before of the various senses of the sa-
       cred words; the assignment of the value of each 'sense' in
       Theology; the division of books into parts, and the sum-
       maries of the various parts…. The valuable work of the
       scholastics in Holy Scripture is seen in their theological
       treatises and in their scripture commentaries; and in this
       respect the greatest name among them all is St. Thomas
       Aquinas."[69]
       In discussing his view that students in academies and
       schools should be primarily occupied with the learning of
       dogma from the Articles of Faith and from the proofs con-
       tained in Holy Scripture, Leo XIII then declares that "It is
       this view of doctrinal teaching which is laid down and rec-
       ommended by the prince of theologians, St. Thomas
       Aquinas." He goes on to recommend that "The best prepa-
       ration will be a conscientious application to philosophy and
       Theology under the guidance of St. Thomas of Aquinas."[70]

1893   Letter to the quarterly *Divus Thomas*
       "From the very beginning of Our Pontificate, driven by a
       knowledge of serious evils, We have often striven that the

---

[68] Aug. 29, 1892, op. cit., 242.

[69] I.B. 26.

[70] II., C., 2.

studies of Philosophy and Theology should be reintegrated according to the time-honored scholastic system of St. Thomas, and that the discipline of his scholastic method should be established as handmaid and companion to the truth of faith. We now rightly rejoice that this has been accomplished in practically every Catholic School."[71]

1893   **Letter of July 31**
"Theology proceeding correctly and well according to the plan and method of Aquinas in accordance with Our command. Every day We become more clearly aware how powerfully Sacred Doctrine taught by its Master and Patron, Thomas, affords the greatest possible utility for both clergy and laity."[72]

1895   **Apostolic Letter *Constitutiones***
Pope Leo XIII approves the new statutes of the Roman Academy of St. Thomas in this Apostolic Letter.[73]

1898   **To the Friars Minor**
He invites the Friars Minor to follow the teaching of St. Thomas.[74]

1899   **Encyclical *Depuis le jour***
"The book par excellence whence students can study Scholastic Theology with much profit is the Summa Theologiae of St. Thomas Aquinas…. It is our wish, therefore, that professors be sure to explain to all their pupils its method, as well as the principal articles relating to Catholic faith."[75]

---

[71] Cf. Berthier, op. cit., 259. Cf. also Letter to the quarterly *Divus Thomas*, Feb. 7, 1893, ibid., 253.
[72] Op. cit., 254.
[73] Cited in Maritain, Append. II, page 222.
[74] Cf. Maritain, Append. II, page 222.
[75] On the education of the clergy in France, Sept. 8, 1899, Acts, VI, 100.

1901 **Letter of Sept. 5**
"…as leader and master our remarkable Thomas, who is easily the prince of Sacred Science."[76]

1904 **St. Pius X**
Apostolic Letter *In praecipuis* to the Roman Academy of St. Thomas
"restored the Angelic Doctor… as the leader and master of Theology, whose divine genius fashioned weapons marvelously suited to protect the truth and destroy the many errors of the times. Indeed, those principles of wisdom useful for all time, which the holy Fathers and Doctors passed on to us, have been organized by no one more aptly than by Thomas, and no one has explained them more clearly."[77]

1906 **Encyclical *Pieni l'animo***
"Studies in Philosophy, Theology and cognate sciences, especially Sacred Scripture, should be made in conformity with the pontifical directives and the study of Saint Thomas, so often recommended by Our revered predecessor and by Us."[78]

1906 **Letter to the Bishop of St. Gall**
"Theology in the University of Fribourg in Switzerland was being guided by Dominican brethren who, following a true appraisal of science, especially of sacred science, clothe themselves with the security of true teaching, for they have their own brother in Theology, that divine light, Thomas Aquinas, who is not only the prince but also the leader and

---

[76] Op. cit., 269.
[77] *In praecipuis* to the Roman Academy of St. Thomas, Jan. 23, 1904, *Acta Pii X*, ed. Bonne Presse, I, 124.
[78] July 28, 1906, ASS, 324.

master of sacred schools. This is as Our predecessor Leo XIII ordered and We confirm that order with the certainty of fruitful results."[79]

1907   **Pascendi Dominici Gregis (On the Doctrine of the Modernists)**
"In the first place, with regard to studies, We will and strictly ordain that scholastic philosophy be made the basis of the sacred sciences.... And let it be clearly understood above all things that when We prescribe scholastic philosophy We understand chiefly that which the Angelic Doctor has bequeathed to us, and We, therefore, declare that all the ordinances of Our predecessor on this subject continue fully in force, and, as far as may be necessary, We do decree anew, and confirm, and order that they shall be strictly observed by all.... Further, We admonish professors to bear well in mind that they cannot set aside St. Thomas, especially in metaphysical questions, without grave disadvantage."[80]

1907   **Letter to Fr. Pegues**
"Indeed those who depart from Thomas, especially in Theology, 'seem to effect ultimately their own withdrawal from the Church.'"[81]

1908   **Letter to the Professors of the Theological Faculty of Fribourg**
"That no one, in any way whatsoever, depart from the regulations of the Church in the matter of teaching. Rejecting modernistic fallacies, let them deal only with the sources

---

[79] Feb. 6, 1906, cf. Berthier, op. cit., 274.
[80] Paragraph 45, latter part quoted also in Pius XI's *Stud. Ducem #16* as "To deviate from Aquinas in metaphysics especially, is to run grave risk," and is later re-stated by St. Pius X in *Doctoris Angelici*.
[81] Nov. 17, 1907, op. cit., 276.

of Sacred Doctrine and well-based Philosophy from the
rich vein of the Angelic Doctor."[82]

1910 **Letter *Sacrorum Antistitum***
"So far as studies are concerned, it is Our will and We
hereby explicitly ordain that the Scholastic philosophy be
considered as the basis of sacred studies.... And what is of
capital importance in prescribing that Scholastic philosophy is to be followed, We have in mind particularly the
philosophy which as been transmitted to us by St. Thomas Aquinas."[83]
"We warn teachers to keep this religiously in mind, that
disregarding Aquinas even slightly cannot be done without great harm. A small error in the beginning, to use the
words of Aquinas in the prologue to his *De ente et essentia*,
becomes very great in the end."[84]

1910 ***Letter to Fr. Lottini***
"In this particular matter no safer principle can be employed than to follow Thomas as leader and master. Those
who write of divine things according to his mind draw great
light and strength from this source."[85]

1913 ***Letter to Fr. Cormier***
"We consider of very great value the doctrine of St. Thomas Aquinas, with which We especially wish all students
to be imbued, in order that they may sweep out depraved
ideas of divine and human things, which insinuate themselves everywhere, and being solidly based in Christian
truth themselves, they may implant it deeply in the hearts
of all."[86]

---

[82] July 11, 1908, op. cit., 277.
[83] As quoted by St. Pius X in *Doctoris Angelici*.
[84] Sept. 1, 1910, AAS 2, 656-657.
[85] Aug. 8. 1910, AAS 2, 724.
[86] Aug. 4, 1913, op. cit., 280.

1914   **Motu Proprio *Praeclara***
"As we have said, one may not desert Aquinas, especially in philosophy and theology, without great harm; following him is the safest way to a knowledge of divine things."[87] "His golden doctrine lights up the mind with his own brilliance, his path and method lead to the deepest knowledge of divine things, without any danger of error."[88] "That the privilege of conferring all the academic degrees in philosophy and theology may bear more abundant fruit for the Order and the Church, We desire and command that the Professors of the College of St. Anselm always follow the doctrine of Aquinas in philosophy and theology, and use the text itself in their lectures to the students of Theology who are working for degrees."[89]

1914   **Motu Proprio *Doctoris Angelici (The Study of Thomistic Philosophy in Catholic Schools)***
As a clarification to his previous statement concerning the philosophy of St. Thomas Aquinas in *Sacrorum Antistitum,* St. Pius X states in this motu proprio:
"In recommending St. Thomas to Our subjects as supreme guide in the Scholastic philosophy, it goes without saying that Our intention was to be understood as referring above all to those principles upon which that philosophy is based as its foundation."[90]
"St. Thomas perfected and augmented still further by the almost angelic quality of his intellect all [the] superb patrimony of wisdom which he inherited from his predecessors (the Fathers and doctors of the Church) and applied it to prepare, illustrate and protect sacred doctrine... Sound

---

[87] June 24, 1914, AAS 6, 335.
[88] Ibid., 134.
[89] Loc. cit.
[90] There are no paragraph numbers for this document, so the citations are simply taken and listed in order as appeared in the document.

reason suggests that it would be foolish to neglect it... the capital theses in the philosophy of St. Thomas are not to be placed in the category of opinions capable of being debated one way or another, but are to be considered as the foundations upon which the whole science of natural and divine things is based; if such principles are once removed or in any way impaired, it must necessarily follow that students of the sacred sciences will ultimately fail to perceive the meaning of the words in which the dogmas of divine revelation are proposed by the magistracy of the Church."

"We therefore desired that all teachers of philosophy and sacred Theology should be warned that if they deviated so much as a step, in metaphysics especially, from Aquinas, they exposed themselves to grave risk.... If the doctrine of any writer or Saint has ever been approved by Us or Our Predecessors with such singular commendation... it may easily be understood that it was commended to the extent that it agreed with the principles of Aquinas or was in no way opposed to them."

"...it is of the first importance that the old system of lecturing on the actual text of the *Summa Theologica* — which should never have been allowed to fall into disuse —be revived.... For ever since the happy death of the saintly Doctor, the Church has not held a single Council, but he has been present at it with the wealth of his doctrine."[91]

"...it is Our will and We hereby order and command that teachers of sacred Theology... use the *Summa Theologica* of St. Thomas as the text of their predilections and comment upon it... and let them take particular care to inspire their pupils with a devotion for it."

"In future, therefore, no power to grant academic degrees in sacred Theology will be given to any institution unless Our prescription is religiously observed therein."

---

[91] Pius XI quotes this statement in *Stud. Ducem* #11.

"This is Our Order, and nothing shall be suffered to gainstay it."

Decree *XXIV Thomist Theses:* Sacred Congregation of Studies

A month after St. Pius X issued *Doctoris Angelici*, his Sacred Congregation of Studies issued "the principles and main theses of the holy Doctor" to be followed.

1914   **Motu Proprio *Non Multo Post***

In this Letter Pius X wrote concerning Aquinas to the Roman Academy of St. Thomas.[92]

"Along with Our predecessors We are equally persuaded that the only philosophy worth our efforts is that which is according to Christ (Coloss. II, 8). Therefore, *the study of philosophy according to the principles and system of Aquinas must certainly be encouraged* so that the explanation and invincible defense of divinely revealed truth may be as full as human reason can make it. And so, We wish this Academy of St. Thomas to be under Our care not less than it was under the care of Our predecessors."[93]

1914   ***Letter to Humbert Everest***

"To publish the immortal works of Aquinas is the same as divulging in writing the most complete human and divine knowledge, and offering to everyone desirous of knowledge the best method of philosophy to unlock sacred truths and effectively to destroy errors."[94]

1914   And so it is only right that we read in the eulogy of Pius X, placed at the foot of his coffin: "he zealously promoted the teaching of Thomas Aquinas."[95]

---

[92] Cited in Maritain, Append. II, page 222.

[93] Motu proprio *Non multo post*, loc. cit., 6-7.

[94] *Letter to Humbert Everest*, O.P. of Feb. 24, 1912, AAS 4, 164-165.

[95] AAS 6, 430.

1915   **Decree of the Sacred Congregation of Studies**
"The Roman Academy of St. Thomas has this particular purpose to explain, defend and protect the philosophy of the Angelic Doctor. Moreover, teachers, at least once every week during the academic year, should read the works of St. Thomas on philosophy, especially the commentaries on Aristotle and Boethius."[96]

1916   **Benedict XV**
Letter to Fr. Hugon
"It is a holy and salutary practice, and practically necessary in Catholic schools where young men are acquiring a knowledge of philosophy and theology, to have Thomas Aquinas as the supreme master. Therefore, what has been most wisely determined in this matter by Our predecessors, especially Leo XIII and Pius X of happy memory, is to be retained whole and inviolate at all costs. In addition, we consider it extremely useful if the Angelic Doctor were to step out from the very sanctuary of the school, as it were, and proffer the almost divine light of his brilliance to all who desire to be more deeply learned in their religion. For it is clear that the Modernists, as they are called, have fallen into such a great variety of opinions, all distant from the faith, precisely because they have neglected the principles and teaching of St. Thomas."[97]

1916   **Concerning the Dominicans**
Benedict XV stated that they "must be praised, not so much for having been the family of the Angelic Doctor, as for having never afterwards departed so much as a hair's breadth from his teaching."[98]

---

[96] March 12, 1915. AAS 7, 128, 129.
[97] May 5, 1916, AAS 8, 174.
[98] AAS 8, 1916, p. 397; also quoted in Pius XI's *Stud. Ducem* #31.

Congregation of Seminaries and Universities
Answers given on the XXIV theses.[99]

1916   *Decree*
"The purpose of this Academy is to explain, protect and spread the doctrine of the Angelic Doctor especially in philosophy, and follow strictly what was set down in the Encyclical *Aeterni Patris.* The chief works of the Academy are these: to join their studies and forces with the other academies of the same Institute so as to establish Christian philosophy everywhere according to the principles of Aquinas."[100]

1916   *Letter to Fr. Theissliing*
"Who is there devoted to serious study, with love for Holy Church joined to zeal for learning, who does not most faithfully cherish Thomas Aquinas, whose doctrine by the gift of divine providence furnishes so dependable a light for the Church to strengthen the truth and destroy error forever? To the credit of the Order of Preachers we must add this praise, not so much that it nourished the Angelic Doctor, but that never after, even in the slightest degree, has it deviated from his doctrine."[101]

1917   *Code of Canon Law*
Pope Benedict XV promulgated the Code of Canon Law and within it St. Thomas Aquinas was declared master: "Teachers shall deal with the studies of mental philosophy and Theology and the education of their pupils in such sciences according to the method (system or manner),

---

[99] Cited in Maritain, Append. II, page 222.
[100] Decree of the same Congregation approved by Benedict XV on Feb. 11, 1916 AAS 8, 364.
[101] *Letter to Fr. Theissliing,* Oct. 29, 1916, AAS 8, 397.

doctrine (philosophy) and principles of the Angelic Doctor and religiously adhere thereto."[102]

1918　***Letter of Nov. 17***

"We know as well as Our wise predecessors how to be zealous for the glory of Aquinas and We desire that this great Doctor, as he is the more viciously assailed by the heretics of our times, should on that account be more conscientiously regarded as leader and master by students for the Church in the study of philosophy and in sacred studies."[103]

1919　***Letter to Fr. Garrigou-Lagrange***

"That Aquinas has a phenomenal power for clarifying and defending Christian wisdom, is clear from your recent book *De Revelatione*. In your explanation of that part of fundamental theology called Apologetics you use the doctrine and method of St. Thomas in such a way that you singularly overcome not only the ancient but even the recent adversaries of the Christian faith."[104]

1919　***Letter To Fr. Pegues***

On the appearance of his French edition of the *Summa* in the form of a catechism. Using this occasion the Pontiff declared that Thomas is the Master and the Doctor of the whole Church, i.e., of all the faithful, clergy, laity, the wise and the unlearned, and of all time.

"The eminent commendations of Thomas Aquinas by the Holy See no longer permit a Catholic to doubt that he was divinely raised up that the Church might have a master whose doctrine should be followed in a special way at all

---

[102] Pope Pius XI, in his Encyclical *Studiorum Ducem* quotes this canon, 1366 sec. 2, twice (11, 30), and Pius XII quotes it in *Humani generis*, cf. Denz. 2322.

[103] Letter of Nov. 17, 1918, AAS 10, 480.

[104] Letter of Feb. 14, 1919, AAS 11, 121.

times. The singular wisdom of the man seems suitable to be offered directly not only to the clergy but to all who wish to extend their study of religion, and to the people generally as well. For nature brings it about that the more clearly a person approaches to the light, the more fully is he illuminated."[105]

1921   Encyclical *Fausto appetente die*
Indeed, he is the one "whom, as a son of Dominic, God considered worthy to illumine His Church";[106] "The Church declared that the doctrine of Thomas is its own."[107]

1922   Pius XI
Officiorum omnium
In his Apostolic Letter on the education of the clergy Pope Pius XI confirms St. Thomas Aquinas as their guide.[108]
Pius XI calls Aquinas, "the Angel of our Schools."[109]

1923   Encyclical *Studiorum Ducem*
On the sixth centenary of the canonization of St. Thomas. "Such a combination of doctrine and piety, of erudition and virtue, of truth, and charity, is to be found in an eminent degree in the angelic Doctor... for he both brings the light of learning into the minds of men and fires their hearts and wills with the virtues."[110]
"Thomas possessed all the moral virtues to a very high degree... his sanctity... chastity... aversion for fleeting pos-

---

[105] Letter of Feb. 9, 1919, AAS II, 71.
[106] June 29, 1921, AAS 13, 334.
[107] Encyclical *Fausto appetente die*, loc. cit., 332.
[108] Cited in Maritain, Append. II, page 223.
[109] *Ubi Arcano Dei Consiliuo* (On the Peace of Christ in the Kingdom of Christ), 23 December 1922.
[110] Paragraph 2.

sessions and a contempt for honours... two forms of wisdom, the acquired and the infused... humility, devotion to prayer, and the love of God."[111]

"This humility, therefore, combined with the purity of heart We have mentioned, and sedulous devotion to prayer, disposed the mind of Thomas to docility in receiving the inspirations of the Holy Ghost and following His illuminations, which are the first principles of contemplation. To obtain them from above, he would frequently fast, spend whole nights in prayer, lean his head in the fervour of his unaffected piety against the tabernacle containing the august Sacrament, constantly turn his eyes and mind in sorrow to the image of the crucified Jesus, and he confessed to his intimate friend St. Bonaventura that it was from that Book especially that he derived all his learning. It may, therefore, be truly said of Thomas what is commonly reported of St. Dominic, Father and Lawgiver, that in his conversation he never spoke but about God or with God."[112]

"This wisdom, therefore, which comes down from, or is infused by, God, accompanied by the other gifts of the Holy Ghost, continually grew and increased in Thomas, along with charity, the mistress and queen of all the virtues... so the love of God, continually increasing in Thomas along with that double wisdom induced in him in the end such absolute forgetfulness of self that when Jesus spoke to him from the cross, saying: 'Thomas, thou hast written well about me,' and asked him: 'What reward shall be given thee for all thy labour?' the saint made answer: 'None but thyself, O Lord!' Instinct with charity, therefore, he unceasingly continued to serve the convenience of others, not counting the cost, by writing admirable

---

[111] Paragraph 4.
[112] Paragraph 6.

books, helping his brethren in their labours, depriving himself of his own garments to give them to the poor, even restoring the sick to health as, for example, when preaching in the Vatican Basilica on the occasion of the Easter celebrations, he suddenly cured a woman who had touched the hem of his habit of a chronic hemorrhage."[113]

"In what other Doctor was this 'word of wisdom' mentioned by St. Paul more remarkable and abundant than in the Angelic Doctor? He was not satisfied with enlightening the minds of men by his teaching: he exerted himself strenuously to rouse their hearts... Nothing, however, shows the force of his genius and charity so clearly as the Office which he himself composed for the august Sacrament."[114]

"...it is easy to understand the pre-eminence of his doctrine and the marvelous authority it enjoys in the Church."[115]

"We so heartily approve the magnificent tribute of praise bestowed upon this most divine genius that We consider that Thomas should be called not only the Angelic, but also the Common or Universal Doctor of the Church; for the Church has adopted his philosophy for her own, as innumerable documents of every kind attest... that Thomas wrote under the inspiration of the supernatural spirit which animated his life and that his writings, which contain the principles of, and the laws governing, all sacred studies, must be said to possess a universal character."[116]

"In dealing orally or in writing with divine things, he provides theologians with a striking example of the intimate connection which should exist between the spiritual and

---

[113] Paragraph 8.
[114] Paragraph 9.
[115] Paragraph 10.
[116] Paragraph 11.

the intellectual life... The aim of the whole Theology of St. Thomas is to bring us into close living intimacy with God."[117]

"Sacred Studies, therefore, being directed by a triple light, undeviating reason, infused faith and the gifts of the Holy Ghost, by which the mind is brought to perfection, no one ever was more generously endowed with these than Our Saint... God was wont to listen to His suppliant so kindly that He dispatched the Princes of the Apostles at times to instruct him... For, according to Thomas, by far the most important benefit to be derived from sacred studies, is that they inspire a man with a great love for God and a great longing for eternal things."[118]

"His teaching with regard to the power or value of the human mind is irrefragable."[119]

"The arguments adduced by St. Thomas to prove the existence of God and that God alone is subsisting Being Itself are still today, as they were in the Middle Ages, the most cogent of all arguments... The metaphysical philosophy of St. Thomas... still retains, like gold which no acid can dissolve, its full force and splendor unimpaired."[120]

"There can be no doubt that Aquinas raised Theology to the highest eminence, for his knowledge of divine things was absolutely perfect... Thomas is therefore considered the Prince of teachers in our schools... because of his theological studies. There is no branch of theology in which he did not exercise the incredible fecundity of his genius."[121]

---

[117] Paragraph 12.
[118] Paragraph 13.
[119] Paragraph 15.
[120] Paragraph 16.
[121] Paragraph 17.

Fundamental Theology:

"For in the first place he established apologetics on a sound and genuine basis by defining exactly the difference between the province of reason and the province of faith and carefully distinguishing the natural and the supernatural orders."[122]

Dogmatic Theology:

"The other branch of Theology, which is concerned with the interpretation of dogmas, also found in St. Thomas by far the richest of all commentators, for nobody ever more profoundly penetrated or expounded with greater subtlety all the august mysteries."[123]

Moral Theology:

"He also composed a substantial moral theology, capable of directing all human acts in accordance with the supernatural last end of man. And as he is, as We have said, the perfect theologian, so he gives infallible rules and precepts of life not only for individuals, but also for civil and domestic society... It is therefore to be wished that the teachings of Aquinas... become more and more studied."[124]

Spiritual Theology:

"His eminence in the learning of asceticism and mysticism is no less remarkable; for he brought the whole science of morals back to the theory of the virtues and gifts... If anyone, therefore, desires to understand fully all the implications... of ascetical and mystical theology, he must have recourse in the first place to the Angelic Doctor."[125]

---

[122] Paragraph 18.
[123] Paragraph 19.
[124] Paragraph 20.
[125] Paragraph 21.

Biblical Theology:

"Everything he wrote was securely based upon Holy Scripture and that was the foundation upon which he built. For he was convinced that Scripture was entirely and in every particular the true word of God... he established the fecundity and riches of the spiritual sense."[126]

Sacramental Theology:

"Lastly, our Doctor possessed the exceptional and highly privileged gift of being able to convert his precepts into liturgical prayers and hymns and so became the poet and panegyrist of the Divine Eucharist... They are... a perfect statement of the doctrine of the august Sacrament transmitted by the Apostles... St. Thomas should also have received the title of the Doctor of the Eucharist."[127]

"Let Our young men especially consider the example of St. Thomas and strive diligently to imitate the eminent virtues which adorn his character, his humility above all, which is the foundation of the spiritual life, and his chastity. Let them learn... to abhor all pride of mind and to obtain by humble prayer a flood of divine light upon their studies.... If the purity of Thomas therefore had failed in the extreme peril into which, as we have seen, it had fallen it is very probable that the Church would never have had her Angelic Doctor."[128]

"But inasmuch as St. Thomas has been duly proclaimed patron of all Catholic Schools... let him be a model also for seminarians.... Let all the Faithful of Christ take the Angelic Doctor as a model of devotion to the august Queen of Heaven, for it was his custom often to repeat the 'Hail Mary' and to inscribe the sweet Name upon his pages, and let them ask the Doctor of the Eucharist himself to inspire

---

[126] Paragraph 22.
[127] Paragraph 23.
[128] Paragraph 24.

them with love for the divine Sacrament. Priests above all
will be zealous in so doing, as is only proper."[129]
"Again, if we avoid the errors which are the source and
fountain-head of all the miseries of our time, the teaching
of Aquinas must be adhered to more religiously than
ever."[130]
"...We now say to all such as are desirous of the truth: 'Go
to Thomas', and ask him to give you from his ample store
the food of substantial doctrine wherewith to nourish your
souls unto eternal life."[131]
"We desire those especially who are engaged in teaching
the higher studies in seminaries sedulously to observe and
inviolably to maintain the decrees of Our Predecessors....
Let them be persuaded that they will discharge their duty
and fulfill Our expectation when, after long and diligent
perusal of his writings, they begin to feel an intense devotion for the Doctor Aquinas and by their exposition of him
succeed in inspiring their pupils with like fervour and train
them to kindle a similar zeal in others."[132]
"Let everyone therefore inviolably observe the prescription
contained in the Code of Canon Law (1366, sec. 2)... and
may they conform to this rule so faithfully as to be able to
describe him in very truth as their master."[133]
"...in honouring St. Thomas something greater is involved
than the reputation of St. Thomas and that is the authority of the teaching Church."[134]
"Finally, that the studies to which Our young people de-
vote themselves may, under the patronage of Aquinas, daily

---

[129] Paragraph 26.
[130] Paragraph 27.
[131] Paragraph 28.
[132] Paragraph 29; cited also in Denz. 2191.
[133] Paragraph 30; cited also in Denz. 2192.
[134] Paragraph 31.

yield more and more fruit for the glory of God and the Church."[135]

1923   *Allocution to the Cardinals*
"...so to speak, a certain natural Gospel, an incomparably solid foundation for all scientific construction, since the chief characteristic of Thomism is its objectivity: its constructions or elevations are not those of a mind cut off from reality, but there are constructions of a spirit which follows the real nature of things.... The value of Thomistic doctrine will never seem less because this would require that the value of things become less."[136]

1924   **Apostolic Letter *Unigenitus Dei Filius***
"Let that, indeed, be inviolable for you which We published in agreement with Canon Law in Our Apostolic Letter on Seminaries and Clerical Studies, namely, that teachers, in teaching the principles of philosophy and theology, faithfully adhere to the scholastic method according to the principles and doctrines of Aquinas. Is anyone unaware how wonderfully suitable the scholastic discipline and angelic wisdom of Thomas is, which Our predecessors continually embellished with the most fulsome praise, for the purpose of explaining divine truths and refuting the errors of every age? The Angelic Doctor, so states Leo XIII, Our predecessor of immortal memory, in the encyclical *Aeterni Patris*, rich in divine and human knowledge, comparable to the sun, is responsible for the fact that he alone vanquished every error then in existence and supplied us with invincible weapons for destroying late errors which would continually arise."[137]

---

[135] Paragraph 34.
[136] Dec. 20, 1923, Loc. cit., cf. note 16.
[137] Apostolic Letter *Unigenitus Dei Filius* to the supreme moderators of Religious Orders and of other Societies of religious men, March 19, 1924, AAS 16, 144.

1924   **Letter to Cardinal Mercier**
         "By your explanation you protect the metaphysical prin-
         ciples of St. Thomas. To recede from them, even slightly,
         will cause great harm, as Our predecessor of happy
         memory, Pius X, warned."[138]

1925   **Allocution to the Professors and Students of the**
         Angelicum College
         "St. Thomas is the bard of the Eucharist and its Doctor:
         Cantor et Doctor Eucharisticus; a poet sweet, sublime, lu-
         minous even when he employs neither verse nor meter.
         When he treats of the Divine Eucharist he carries us to the
         center which was his center, to the secret which was his
         secret, to the source of his purity, to the celestial food
         which was his angelic nourishment."[139]
         "All these things are especially resplendent in his *Summa
         Theologiae* which 'is heaven seen from earth.'"[140]
         "Doctor of the whole Church, of every science, of all know-
         able things; a characteristic which approaches divine
         power. In few intellects has the participation of the divine
         intellect sparkled so brilliantly, for which reason we ask
         ourselves if the Eternal Creator ever left a deeper imprint
         upon other minds. In his teaching is found par excellence
         one of the characteristics of the book of life. In all circum-
         stances of life, for all problems which can arise that book
         has a word and a solution to proffer us. Such is the char-
         acter of the Holy Gospel because it is the word of God.
         Something of this divine characteristic is in St. Thomas in
         his classical works: the *Summa Philosophica* and the *Summa
         Theologica.* In these books, well read and carefully con-
         sulted, there is a word and a solution for all the questions

---

[138] March 26, AAS 16, 225.
[139] *Allocution to the professors and students of the Angelicum College,* Nov. 12, 1924,
     cf. *Xenia Thomistica,* III, 600-601, Rome, 1925.
[140] Ibid., 600.

that can be presented to us: a sure word and a word of genius; they are two books which summarize the entire universe, heaven and earth. *The Summa Theologica is heaven seen from earth, and the Summa contra Gentiles is earth seen from heaven....* It is for this reason that St. Thomas merited the name of Common Doctor."

"Let him, therefore, always be your light; let his books be your constant advisers; from his books always attain truth: if studied wisely and tirelessly, they will furnish the reply to all your questions with immense benefit for life."[141]

1931 *Deus Scientiarum Dominus*

Teachers of Catholic schools are to impart to their students "the full and coherent synthesis of philosophy according to the method and the principles of St. Thomas Aquinas; in the light of this teaching, furthermore, the different systems of the other philosophers are to be examined and judged."

"Sacred theology holds the chief place in a Theological Faculty. This study must be pursued by both a positive and a scholastic method. Therefore, when the truths of faith are explained and demonstrated from Scripture and tradition, their nature and close relation to the principles and doctrines of St. Thomas is to be investigated and clarified."[142]

1939 Pius XII

"It is that wisdom of Aquinas which collected the truths of human reason, illustrated them with brilliance, and most aptly and solidly unified them into a wonderful whole. It is the wisdom of Aquinas which is especially suited to declare and defend the dogmas of the faith. And finally it is his wisdom which was able to refute effectively the basic

---

[141] Op. cit., 599-600.
[142] May 24, 1931, AAS 23, 253.

errors continually arising, and conquer them invincibly. Wherefore, dear sons, bring to St. Thomas a heart full of love and zeal. With all your powers strive to explore with your intellect his excellent doctrine. Freely embrace whatever clearly pertains to it and is supported by a solid reason found in it."[143]

1942   ***Letter to Fr. Gillet***
"Aquinas, the Angelic and Common Doctor, like the sea receiving unto himself the rivers of wisdom from all who lived before his time, and whatever human reason had attained by thought and mental labor, so composed and ordered all of it in a wonderful manner and with brilliant clearness after exposing it to the supernal light emanating from the Gospel, that he seems to have left to his successors the power to imitate but to have taken away the power to surpass. The doctrine of Thomas not only was most apt for destroying ancient heresies, and for that reason stands forth as the champion of faith and firm bulwark of religion, but also offers the most powerful weapon for destroying thoroughly errors which are being reborn in perpetual succession and which wear the garb of newness.
"Therefore, all who attend Catholic schools of any type should cherish, revere and imitate Thomas Aquinas as a heavenly patron, those especially who study him in philosophy and theology, and specifically students divinely called to the priesthood and growing into the hope of the Church, ought to follow Thomas as leader and master, recalling that there is an innate excellence in Thomistic doctrine and a singular force and power to cure the evils which afflict our age."[144]

---

[143] June 24, 1939, AAS 31, 246.
[144] March 7, 1942, AAS 34, 97.

1943   Encyclical *Mystici Corporis (On the Mystical Body of Christ)*
        "You are familiar, Venerable Brethren, with the admirable and luminous language used by the masters of Scholastic Theology and chiefly by the Angelic and Common Doctor… and you know that reasons advanced by Aquinas are a faithful reflection of the mind and writings of the Holy Fathers, who moreover merely repeated and commented on the inspired word of Sacred Scripture."[145]

1943   Encyclical *Divino Afflante Spiritu (Inspired by the Divine Spirit)*
        "As in our age, indeed new questions and new difficulties are multiplied, so, by God's favor, new means and aids to exegesis are also provided. Among these it is worthy of special mention that Catholic theologians, following the teaching of the Holy Father and especially of the Angelic and Common Doctor, have examined and explained the nature and effects of biblical inspiration more exactly and more fully than was wont to be done in previous ages."[146]

1946   Encyclical *Humani generis*
        "If these matters are thoroughly examined, it will be evident why the Church demands that future priests be instructed in the philosophic disciplines 'according to the manner, doctrine and principles of the Angelic Doctor,'[147] since it knows well from the experience of many ages that the method and system of Aquinas, whether in training beginners or investigating hidden truth, stand out with special prominence; moreover, that his doctrine is in harmony, as in a kind of symphony, with divine 'revelation', and is most efficacious in laying safe foundations of faith,

---

[145] Paragraph 35.
[146] Paragraph 33.

and also in collecting usefully and securely the fruits of sound progress."[148]

1946 **Allocution to the Jesuit General Congregation**
He admonished the members of the Society of Jesus "to observe with all diligence their laws which command them to follow the doctrine of St. Thomas as being more solid, safe, approved and constant with their Constitutions."[149]

Allocution to the Dominican General Chapter
"...the Angelic Doctor is always a most skilled leader and is a never-failing light whose accomplishments will always remain fresh."[150]
"These things have the force of law, which bind all Catholic schools of philosophy and theology."[151]

1949 **Allocution to the Congress on Humanistic Studies**
"Humanism is now the order of the day. Undoubtedly is not an easy task to extract and recognize a clear idea of its nature in the course of its historical evolution. Nevertheless — although humanism has for long had the pretension of being formally opposed to the Middle Ages which preceded it — it is none the less certain that everything it contains of truth, of goodness, of the great and the eternal, belongs to the spiritual universe of the greatest genius of the Middle Ages, Saint Thomas Aquinas."[152]

[147] *CIC;* can. 1366,2.
[148] Denz. 2322 citing AAS 38, 1946, 387.
[149] *Allocution to the Jesuit General Congregation,* Sept. 17, 1946, AAS 38, 380.
[150] *Allocution to the Dominican General Chapter,* Sept. 22, 1946. AAS 38, 387-383.
[151] Ibid.
[152] *Allocution to the Congress on Humanistic Studies,* Rome, Sept. 25, 1949. AAS 41, 555.

1950   *Third International Thomistic Congress* in Rome

"This represents a safe path for you who are engaged in discussion and publication; follow the doctrine of St. Thomas Aquinas, which lights up the road like a brilliant ray of sun."[153]

"Heaven is distant from the earth in the same degree that the truths of divine revelation exceed the powers of the human mind. They are loftier than those powers of mind but not in the least contradictory or repugnant to them. They are above reason but not opposed to it. With infectious eagerness St. Thomas leads human intelligence, hesitating and dubious by reason of brilliant splendor, into the very temple of the mysteries of God. Producing the solution to the problems by the artistry of his arguments, he brings out the clear and splendid harmony existing between divine and human things. Always follow that inspiration by which the Angelic Doctor learned the truth, namely, by the greater effort of intelligence and by religious piety. Treat these matters thoroughly, insisting upon his method, by which he always defined the limits and content of his opinions, with no useless flow of words but with serious and solid discourse."[154]

1950   *Dominican Missal*

"In the Preface for the Mass of St. Thomas, which the Holy Father himself wrote, he gives thanks to God and addresses Him in these words: "Who wished to raise up in Thy Church the blessed Doctor Thomas, truly Angelic by reason of his pure life and sublime mind; that he might communicate his solid and salutary doctrine and illuminate the Church like the sun; whose wisdom, especially commended to all, is admired by the whole world."[155]

---

[153] Sept. 17, 1950, AAS 42, 734.
[154] Ibid., 735.
[155] *Dominican Missal*, Preface of the Mass of St. Thomas.

1960   **Pope John XXIII**
       Allocution of Sept 18
       In preparing for the Second Vatican Council, John XXIII
       established the importance of St. Thomas Aquinas in con-
       sidering the conciliar objectives: "But if all these things we
       desire so ardently are to come about the first thing neces-
       sary is to study the works of St. Thomas Aquinas carefully.
       And so we are very interested in seeing a steady growth in
       the number of people who find enlightenment and learn-
       ing in the works of the Angelic Doctor."[156]
       Pope John XXIII raised the Angelicum in Rome to the rank
       of a Pontifical University.

1965   **Vatican II**
       Optatum Totius (Decree on the Training of Priests)
       "In order to throw as full a light as possible on the myster-
       ies of salvation the student should learn to examine more
       deeply with the help of speculation and with St. Thomas
       as teacher all aspects of these mysteries."[157]

       Gravissimum Educationis (Declaration on Christian
       Education)
       "The Church likewise devotes considerable care to higher
       level education especially in universities and faculties. In-
       deed, in institutions under its control the Church endeav-
       ors systematically to ensure that the treatment of the in-
       dividual disciplines is consonant with their own principles,
       their own methods and with a true liberty of scientific in-
       quiry. Its object is that a progressively deeper understand-
       ing of them may be achieved, and by a careful attention
       to the current problems of these changing times and to the
       research being undertaken the convergence of faith and
       reason in one truth may be seen more clearly. This method

---

[156] Given September 18, 1960.
[157] Paragraph 16.

follows the tradition of the Doctors of the Church and especially St. Thomas Aquinas."[158]

Pope John Paul II commented on these two citations from Vatican II in 1979 when he commemorated the 100th Anniversary of Leo XIII's *Aeterni Patris:* "The words of the Council are clear: 'the Fathers saw that it is fundamental for the adequate formation of the clergy and of Christian youth that it preserve a close link with the cultural heritage of the past, and in particular with the thought of St. Thomas; and that this, in the long run is a necessary condition for the longed-for renewal of the Church.'"[159]

1974   **Paul VI**
        Apostolic Letter *Lumen Ecclesiae*
        In this Letter, Pope Paul VI calls Thomas "Doctor Communis Ecclesiae."

"Without doubt, Thomas possessed supremely the courage of the truth, a freedom of spirit in confronting new problems, the intellectual honesty of those who allow Christianity to be contaminated neither by secular philosophy nor by a prejudiced rejection of it. He passed therefore into the history of Christian thought as a pioneer of the new path of philosophy and universal culture."[160]

"The key point and almost the kernel of the solution which, with all the brilliance of his prophetic intuition, he gave to the new encounter of faith and reason was a reconciliation between the secularity of the world and the radicality of the Gospel, thus avoiding the unnatural tendency to negate the world and its values while at the same time keeping faith with the supreme and inexorable demands of the supernatural order."[161]

---

[158] Paragraph 10.
[159] Paragraph 15.
[160] Paragraph 8; also quoted by John Paul II in *Fides et Ratio* #43.
[161] Ibid.

Paul VI also calls Aquinas an "apostle of truth."[162]
"In accomplishing the work signaling the culmination of medieval Christian thought, St. Thomas was not alone. Before and after him many other illustrious doctors worked toward the same good... But without a doubt St. Thomas, as willed by divine Providence, reached the height of all 'scholastic' theology and philosophy, as it is usually called, and set the central pivot in the Church around which, at that time and since, Christian thought could be developed with sure progress."[163]

1979   John Paul II
Perennial Philosophy of St. Thomas for the Youth of Our Times

Soon after becoming pope, John Paul II, who had been a student of St. Thomas at the Angelicum from 1946-1948, gave an address at the conclusion of an international congress commemorating the hundredth anniversary of the publication of Pope Leo XIII's Encyclical *Aeterni Patris*. Some excerpts from his address are as follows:

He calls the Angelicum a "celebrated Roman center of Thomistic studies where one can say that Aquinas lives 'as in his own home'."[164]

Pope John Paul II outlined three extraordinary qualities found in St. Thomas:

(1) "...his complete submission of mind and heart to divine revelation;"

(2) "...his excellence as a teacher;"

(3) "...his sincere, total and lifelong acceptance of the teaching office of the Church... His writings make it clear that this reverential assent was not confined only

---

[162] Paragraph 8; also quoted by John Paul II in *Fides et Ratio* #44.

[163] Paragraph 13; also quoted by John Paul II in his *Address to the 80th Internat. Thom. Cong.* (1980), #2.

[164] Paragraph 1.

to the solemn and infallible teaching of the Councils and of the Supreme Pontiffs."[165]

About these qualities of St. Thomas, Pope John Paul II adds: "These three qualities mark the entire speculative effort of St. Thomas and make sure that its results are orthodox."[166]

"The philosophy of St. Thomas deserves to be attentively studied and accepted with conviction by the youth of our day by reason of its spirit of openness and of universalism, characteristics which are hard to find in many trends of contemporary thought."[167]

"Not even theology, then, can abandon the philosophy of St. Thomas."[168]

"...other trends in philosophy... can and indeed should be treated as natural allies of the philosophy of St. Thomas."[169]

"There is still one more reason why the philosophy of St. Thomas has enduring value: its prevailing characteristic is that it is always in search of the truth.... The reason why the philosophy of St. Thomas is pre-eminent is to be found in its realism and objectivity: it is a philosophy of what is, not of what appears", and John Paul II goes on to call the philosophy of St. Thomas the "handmaid of faith" (ancilla fidei).[170]

Concerning Leo XIII's admonition: "Let us follow the example of the 'Angelic Doctor,'"[171] Pope John Paul II declares: "That is what I also repeat this evening. This advice is indeed fully justified by the witness which he gave by his manner of living and which gave force to what he said

---

[165] Paragraph 14.
[166] Paragraph 15.
[167] Paragraph 6.
[168] Paragraph 6.
[169] Paragraph 7.
[170] Paragraph 8.
[171] *Aeterni Patris* #33.

as a teacher. He had indeed the technical mastery befitting a teacher, but, prior to this, his manner of teaching was that of a saint who lives the Gospel fully, of one for whom love is everything."[172]

"If we look for the driving force behind his commitment to a life of study, the secret urge which led him to consecrate himself through a total dedication, we find it in… a heart full of the love of God and of his neighbor… allow[ing] us to perceive, behind the thinker able to rise to the loftiest heights of speculation, the mystic accustomed to going straight to the very foundation of all truth to find the answer to the deepest questionings of the human spirit."[173]

"One who approaches St. Thomas cannot set aside this witness which comes from his life; he must rather follow courageously the path traced out by him and bind himself to follow his example if he would wish to taste the most secret and savory fruits of his teachings. This is the burden of the prayer which the liturgy places on our lips on his feastday and 'O God, since it was by Your gift that St. Thomas became so great a saint and theologian, give us the grace to understand his teaching and follow his way of life.'"[174]

1980   **The Method and Doctrine of St. Thomas in Dialogue with Modern Culture:**
Address to the Eighth International Thomistic Congress at the Conclusion of the Centenary Year of *Aeterni Patris*.
"The Church has given preference to the method and doctrine of the Angelic Doctor… not only for the completeness, balance, depth, and clarity of his style, but still more for his keen sense of fidelity to the truth, which can also

---

[172] Paragraph 10.
[173] Paragraph 10.
[174] Paragraph 10.

be called realism. Fidelity to the voice of created things so as to construct the edifice of philosophy: fidelity to the voice of the Church so as to construct the edifice of theology."[175]

"St. Thomas can be considered the true pioneer of modern scientific realism."[176]

"St. Thomas has always given respectful attention to all authors."[177]

"Furthermore, the basis of his attitude, sympathetic toward everyone, but without failing to be openly critical every time he felt he had to — and he did it courageously in many cases — is in the very concept of truth."[178]

"St. Thomas [is] not only the *Doctor Communis Ecclesiae*, as Paul VI calls him in his beautiful letter *Lumen ecclesiae*, but the *Doctor Humanitatis*, because he is always ready and available to receive the human values of all cultures.... St. Thomas put all the strength of his genius at the exclusive service of the truth, behind which he seems to want to disappear almost for fear of disturbing its brightness so that truth and not he may shine in all its brilliance."[179]

"The authority of St. Thomas' doctrine is here resolved and replenished in the authority of the Church's Doctrine. That is why the Church has proposed it as an exemplary model of theological research."[180]

"The Magisterium of the Church [chooses] St. Thomas as a sure guide in theological and philosophical disciplines."[181]

"The idea of St. Thomas as a cold intellectual, advanced by some, is disproved by the fact that the Angelic One

---

[175] Paragraph 2.
[176] Paragraph 3.
[177] Paragraph 3.
[178] Paragraph 3.
[179] Paragraph 3.
[180] Paragraph 4.
[181] Paragraph 4.

reduces knowledge itself to love of truth."[182]

"I urge you to continue, with great commitment and seriousness, to accomplish the goals of your Academy so that it can be a living, pulsing, modern center in which the method and doctrine of St. Thomas can be put into continuous contact and serene dialogue with the complex leavens of contemporary culture in which we live and are immersed."[183]

1980   **John Paul II's Congregation for Catholic Education:**
       Ratio Fundamentalis Institutionis Sacerdotalis
       (Spiritual Formation in Seminaries)
       "Dogmatic Theology should be presented in full and systematically. It should begin with an exposition of its biblical sources, followed by an explanation of the contribution which the Oriental and Latin Fathers have made to the formulation and handing down of the truths of revelation, and how dogma has developed through historical progression. Finally, there should be a full, speculative study, based on St. Thomas of the mysteries of salvation and their interrelation."[184]
       "Tradition and Sacred Scripture form one sacred deposit of God's word and this is committed to the Church's care. Consequently students should have a lively appreciation for this Tradition as it is found in the works of the Fathers, and should pay special attention to the doctrine of the Fathers and the other Doctors who are renowned in the Church. They should regard St. Thomas as one of the Church's greatest teachers while still esteeming authors of more recent times."[185]

---

[182] Paragraph 4.
[183] Paragraph 7.
[184] Paragraph 79.
[185] Paragraph 86.

1981   Encyclical *Laborem Exercens,* 90th Anniv. of
        Rerum Novarum (On Human Work)
        "In the course of the decades since the publication of the
        Encyclical *Rerum novarum,* the Church's teaching has al-
        ways recalled all these principles, going back to the argu-
        ments formulated in a much older tradition, for example,
        the well-known arguments of the *Summa Theologiae* of St.
        Thomas Aquinas."[186]

1983   *Code of Canon Law,* Chapter on the Formation of
        Clerics
        "Theological training is to be... imparted in the light of the
        faith and under the guidance of the magisterium.... There
        are to be classes in dogmatic theology which are always to
        be based upon the written word of God along with sacred
        tradition, in which the students may learn to penetrate ever
        more profoundly the mysteries of salvation, with St. Tho-
        mas as their teacher in a special way."[187]

1988   Pope John Paul II's Head of the Congregation for the
        Doctrine of the Faith, Cardinal Ratzinger (Benedict XVI)
        Cardinal Ratzinger spoke in his 1988 Erasmus Conference
        lecture entitled, "Biblical Interpretation in Crisis," where
        he challenged the so-called modern Thomists to re-evalu-
        ate their source as follows:
        "Take a look at later times: whole generations of Thomistic
        scholars have not been able to take in the greatness of his
        (St. Thomas') thought."[188]

---

[186] Paragraph 22.
[187] *Canon* 252, sec. 1, 3.
[188] Page 11.

1992   **Catechism of the Catholic Church**
It's worth noting that the new *Catechism* cites St. Thomas Aquinas 61 times. Aquinas is cited second only to St. Augustine who is cited 87 times.[189] Whereas, a recent edition of the *Roman Catechism* only cites Aquinas once, and in a footnote at that.[190]
Part Three of the *Catechism*, 'Life in Christ,' relies significantly on Aquinas' moral structure contained in his *Summa*, according to Cardinal Ratzinger (Benedict XVI).[191]

Encyclical *Pastores Dabo Vobis* (I Will Give You Shepherds)
"St. Thomas is extremely clear when he affirms that the faith is as it were the habitus of theology, that is its permanent principle of operation, and that the whole of theology is ordered to nourishing the faith."[192]

NCCB's *Program for Priestly Formation*
In this document of the American Bishops they declare that "the perennial philosophy of St. Thomas should be given the recognition which Church teaching accords it."[193]

---

[189] Cf. pages 742-743.

[190] Cf. section on Sacraments, footnote 20.

[191] Cf. pages 751-752. Part Three of the *Catechism*, 'Life in Christ,' relies heavily upon St. Thomas' moral structure. "The structure of this 'fundamental moral theology' follows the great intuition of the *Summa* of St. Thomas. Is this the choice of a particular theological school? The commission [which organized the *Catechism*] was convinced that it should take the *doctor communis* as guide, not as the founder of a school, but as the great teacher of Christian morality." Joseph Cardinal Ratzinger and Christoph Schönborn, *Introduction to the Catechism of the Catholic Church* (San Francisco: Ignatius Press, 1994), 87-88.

[192] Chapter V.

[193] 4th Edition.

1993   Encyclical *Veritatis Splendor (The Splendor of Truth)*
       "Going to the heart of the moral message of Jesus and the
       preaching of the Apostles, and summing up in a remark-
       able way the great tradition of the Fathers of the East and
       West, and of Saint Augustine in particular, Saint Thomas
       was able to write that the New Law is the grace of the Holy
       Spirit given through faith in Christ."[194]
       "The Church has often made reference to the Thomistic
       doctrine of natural law, including in her own teaching on
       morality."[195]

1994   *Crossing the Threshold of Hope,* book by Pope John
       Paul II
       "Saint Thomas, however, did not abandon the philoso-
       phers' approach. He began his *Summa Theologica* with the
       question 'An Deus sit?' — 'Does God exist?'[196] ...Even if
       today, unfortunately, the *Summa Theologica* has been
       somewhat neglected, its initial question persists and con-
       tinues to resound throughout our civilization."[197]
       "I think that it is wrong to maintain that Saint Thomas'
       position stands up only in the realm of the rational. One
       must, it is true, applaud Etienne Gilson when he agrees
       with Saint Thomas that the intellect is the most marvel-
       ous of God's creations, but that does not mean that we
       must give in to a unilateral rationalism. Saint Thomas cel-
       ebrates all the richness and complexity of each created
       being, and especially of the human being. It is not good
       that his thought has been set aside in the post-conciliar
       period; he continues in fact, to be *the master of philosophi-
       cal and theological universalism.*"[198]

---

[194] Paragraph 24.
[195] Paragraph 44.
[196] Cf. I, q. 2, a. 3.
[197] Page 29.
[198] Page 31.

1998   Encyclical *Fides et Ratio (Faith and Reason)*
On the development of the complementarity of faith and
reason, Pope John Paul II states: "A quite special place in
this long development belongs to St. Thomas ...Both the
light of reason and the light of faith come from God, he
argued; hence there can be no contradiction between
them."[199]
"More radically, Thomas recognized that nature, philosophy's proper concern, could contribute to the understanding of divine revelation."[200]
"Although he made much of the supernatural character of
faith, the Angelic Doctor did not overlook the importance
of its reasonableness; indeed he was able to plumb the
depths and explain the meaning of this reasonableness."[201]
"This is why the Church has been justified in consistently
proposing St. Thomas as a master of thought and a model
of the right way to do theology."[202]
"Another of the great insights of St. Thomas was his perception of the role of the Holy Spirit in the process by
which knowledge matures into wisdom. From the first
pages of his *Summa Theologiae*, Aquinas was keen to show
the primacy of the wisdom which is the gift of the Holy
Spirit and which opens the way to a knowledge of divine
realities."[203]
"...St. Thomas was impartial in his love of truth. He sought
truth wherever it might be found and gave consummate
demonstration of its universality. In him, the Church's
magisterium has seen and recognized the passion for truth;
and, precisely because it stays consistently within the ho-
rizon of universal, objective and transcendent truth, his

---

[199] Paragraph 43.
[200] Paragraph 43.
[201] Paragraph 43.
[202] Paragraph 43.
[203] Paragraph 44.

thought scales 'heights unthinkable to human intelligence.'"[204]

"With the rise of the first universities, theology came more directly into contact with other forms of learning and scientific research. Although they insisted upon the organic link between theology and philosophy, St. Albert the Great and St. Thomas were the first to recognize the autonomy which philosophy and the sciences need if they were to perform well in their respective fields of research."[205]

Discussing the timeless relevance of Leo XIII's *Aeterni Patris*, Pope John Paul II states: "More than a century later, many of the insights of his encyclical letter have lost none of their interest from either a practical or pedagogical point of view — most particularly his insistence upon the incomparable value of the philosophy of St. Thomas. A renewed insistence upon the thought of the Angelic Doctor seemed to Pope Leo XIII the best way to recover the practice of a philosophy consonant with the demands of faith."[206]

"The positive results of the papal summons [of Leo XIII] are well known. Studies of the thought of St. Thomas and other Scholastic writers received new impetus. Historical studies flourished, resulting in a rediscovery of the riches of medieval thought, which until then had been largely unknown; and there emerged new Thomistic schools. With the use of historical method, knowledge of the works of St. Thomas increased greatly, and many scholars had courage enough to introduce the Thomistic tradition into the philosophical and theological discussions of the day. The most influential Catholic theologians of the present century, to whose thinking and research the Second Vatican Council was much indebted, were products of this revival

---

[204] Paragraph 44; with internal quote from Leo XIII's *Aeterni Patris*.
[205] Paragraph 45.
[206] Paragraph 57.

of Thomistic philosophy. Throughout the 20th century, the Church has been served by a powerful array of thinkers formed in the school of the Angelic Doctor."[207]

"It has been necessary from time to time... to reiterate the value of the Angelic Doctor's insights and insist on the study of his thought... because the magisterium's directives have not always been followed with the readiness one would wish. In the years after the Second Vatican Council, many Catholic faculties were in some ways impoverished by a diminished sense of the importance of the study not just of Scholastic philosophy, but more generally of the study of philosophy itself."[208]

"It should be clear... why the magisterium has repeatedly acclaimed the merits of St. Thomas' thought and made him the guide and model for theological studies... The magisterium's intention has always been to show how St. Thomas is an authentic model for all who seek the truth. In his thinking, the demands of reason and the power of faith found the most elevated synthesis ever attained by human thought."[209]

1999   **Apostolic Letter *Inter Munera Academiarum***
Pope John Paul II confirms that St. Thomas Aquinas remains the "eminent model" of theological and philosophical studies. The letter approves the new statutes of the Pontifical Academy of Saint Thomas Aquinas and the Pontifical Academy of Theology.

Address to the Academicians of the Pontifical University of the Holy Cross
"Contemplation of the union of the human and the divine in Christ, particularly in the crucified Christ, will not fail

---

[207] Paragraph 58.
[208] Paragraph 61.
[209] Paragraph 78.

to help you integrate the various fields of knowledge, to foster interdisciplinary study and to open you to the whole truth. In this task you will also find sound guidance in St. Thomas Aquinas, in whose thinking 'the demands of reason and the power of faith found the most elevated synthesis ever attained by human thought, for he could defend the radical newness introduced by Revelation without ever demeaning the venture proper to reason' (*Fides et Ratio*, 78)... I encourage you to pursue the commitment you have made to deepening your knowledge of doctrine, a commitment enlivened by a constant yearning for holiness."[210]

2000   ***Address on the Jubilee for Men and Women of Learning***
"Men and women of learning, be builders of hope for all humanity! May God accompany you and make fruitful your efforts at the service of genuine human progress. May Mary, Seat of Wisdom, protect you. May St. Thomas Aquinas and the other holy men and women who, in various fields of learning have made a remarkable contribution to an ever deeper knowledge of created reality in light of the divine mystery, intercede for you."[211]

2005   **Benedict XVI**
Address to the University of the Sacred Heart
"[Every Catholic university must be] a great laboratory in which, according to the different disciplines, new ways of research are always celebrated in a stimulating dialogue between faith and reason, which seeks to recover the harmonious synthesis reached by Thomas Aquinas and the other great Christian thinkers."[212]

---

[210] Address to the Academians of the Pontifical University of the Holy Cross, "*The Cross Illumines All of Human Life*," 5/29/99.

[211] Jubilee for Men and Women of Learning (5/25/00), Paragraph 6.

[212] Address to the University of the Sacred Heart, Rome, November 25, 2005.

Summary of Views of Commentators on *Sacra Doctrina*, STh I, 1

Name	Model of *Sacra Doctrina*	
Cajetan[1]	Revealed knowledge prescinding from its specification as faith or Theology	
Sylvius[2]	The science of Theology	
John of St. Thomas[3]	Art. 1	Theology as doctrine
	Art. 2-7	Theology as science
	Art. 8-9	Theology as doctrine
Báñez	Art. 1	Divine Revelation is necessary for salvation
	Q. 1 (except part of art. 1) Scholastic Theology	
Billuart	Art. 1	Theology itself
	Art. 2-8	Theology as a science
	Art. 9-10	Sacred Scripture constitutes a good part of Theology
	In general all of q. 1 is about Theology	
Buonpensiere[4]	Art. 1	The certain knowledge of truths produced by the supernatural light of Revelation

---

[1] Van Ackeren, *Sacra Doctrina*, 52.
[2] Van Ackeren, 52.
[3] Van Ackeren, 52.
[4] Weisheipl, "The Meaning of Sacra Doctrina in *Summa Theologiae* I, q. 1", 60.

	Art. 2-5	Deductions from principles concluded by theologians
	Art. 8	Method of theologian is argumentation
	Art. 9-10	The most important *loci theologici* is Sacred Scripture
R. Garrigou-Lagrange[5]	Art. 1	a. Cf. Cajetan b. Faith c. Theology as science
	Art. 2-7	Theology as science
	Art. 8-9	(?)

Van der Ploeg Holy Scripture is the highest part of *sacra doctrina*, which also includes Theology

Chenu An ambiguous term having a general sense of Revelation, a technical sense of theological science, as well as a Scriptural sense. Its various meanings cannot be parceled out to particular questions.[6]

Art. 9-10   Do not belong to q.1 properly, but only included as deference to medieval period

Bonnefoy Equates with Scripture and Theology
Seen as the body of immediately revealed truths imposed on our faith[7]
Identical to Scripture in origin, certitude, object and content
Distinct from Scripture in order of exposition and difference of language

Congar Christian instruction proceeding from Divine Revelation[8]: Scripture, catechesis, preaching, and Theology in its scientific form are all parts or functions of *sacra doctrina*
Supreme wisdom and supreme science

5   Van Ackeren, 52.
6   Van Ackeren, 52.
7   Van Ackeren, 52.
8   Van Ackeren, 52.

Van Ackeren	The action of "sacred instruction" Exclusively the action of a teacher received in a disciple terminating in the knowledge of salvation (instruction in divine knowledge by way of Revelation) One of the instrumental causes of the "action" is Scripture "Action" ultimately proceeds from God as principal cause "Divine Revelation" passed on by "Catholic education" (Theology and catechesis)
Muniz	Theology, including Scripture, throughout q.1
Persson	Christian Theology as a science (begins with known principles and draws new conclusions from them) and holy teaching Directly related to Scripture, though Scripture is the object of faith while *sacra doctrina*, with reason and faith, draws rational and human truth from it
White	Holy Teaching Includes Theology, but more a catechetical enterprise, emphasizing that it is Kerygmatic, evangelistic, pastoral, and pedagogical in nature God is first the Teacher and the Taught, thus *sacra doctrina* is God's teaching itself, primarily found in Scripture No distinction between Theology and catechesis
Gilby	Has two senses: passive (the content of teaching and learning) and active (the action of a teacher educating a student) Covers every cognitive response to the Word of God, i.e., Revelation, Scripture, habit of faith, theological science Can be defined as Theology in its modern sense
Weisheipl	Wisdom about God, derived from Divine Revelation, accepted in faith, which directs toward eternal beatitude Includes *scientia, Sacra Scriptura, theologia* The good news of salvation, *evangelion*

Ernest	An *impressio* of divine science
O'Brien	A Christian Theology attained via intellectual discipline through study
	Bi-modal dimension
	God's communication and man's teaching in keeping with Divine Revelation
Merkt	Not Theology in the modern sense
	Scientia: drawing conclusions from known truths, both of which are objects of faith, the deduced truths becoming part of Tradition and passed on via catechesis and Theology
Davies	True teaching revealed by God, or "holy teaching" necessary for salvation
	Theology, but only in the true sense of the word, namely discourse about God
	Contained in Scripture and the Creeds (Tradition)
Kreeft	Theology
	Scripture (including articles of faith): its data, or material cause of its data
	Science: its formal cause
	The truth about God: its speculative end or final cause
	Salvation through this truth: its practical end or final cause
Johnson	The highest human <u>wisdom</u>: stamp of God's knowledge in us
	Sacred Theology
	Acquired through study
	Scripture is its source (Is 64:4 and 2 Tm 3:26)
Shanley	7. A teaching following on Divine Revelation
	8. A teaching in keeping with, conformed to Divine Revelation
	Emphasizes necessity of faith
	seen as a knowledge of the mind in love with God and a sharing in God's own life
	Admits *sacra doctrina* includes Scripture, Theology, scientia, and wisdom

Donneaud	*Sacra doctrina* does not mean 'theology' but it has a much broader reality: namely the ensemble of Christian teaching based on divine revelation.
Neumayr	Divine Wisdom itself Necessary in every way for our salvation A knowledge of God which forms the articles of faith Shares in the very knowledge of God in Himself through faith A taste of the light of glory, the beatific vision 1) Divine contemplation and 2) contemplative communication of the Divine Wisdom of God
Bowring	For St. Thomas, at least implicitly in his writings (though explicitly nuanced further in later centuries), *sacra doctrina* invariably means "sacred doctrine" — sacred, revealed and reasoned, divine truth, which taken as a whole, makes up the one, comprehensive and unified propositional summation of the Deposit of Faith given to the Church by Jesus Christ and His Apostles, known through natural law and divine Revelation, containing the twofold Source of the Word of God — Sacred Tradition and the inspired Sacred Scriptures — both of which rely upon the infallible Magisterium as their sole official interpreter; which includes (1) dogmatic doctrine, all divinely revealed truths infallibly pronounced and solemnly declared to be found in Revelation; (2) definitive doctrine, everything definitively proposed by the Church regarding faith and morals (as revealed doctrine or at least as intimately and intrinsically connected with formally and divinely revealed truth), and (3) authoritative, non-definitive doctrine, including all of the Church's teachings regarding faith and morals which have been presented as true or at least as sure; a deposit which is transmitted by holy teaching (with a pedagogy that respects the natural order of learning

and utilizes a genuine inculturation) via Christian catechesis and sacred theology by baptized faithful who are authentic living witnesses, through reasoning, prayer, contemplation and love-inspired exposition; altogether acquired (or infused) so as to attain holy wisdom in accordance with a living theological faith in Christ and His Church, the hope of eternal life, and communion with divine Love; thus as the Word made flesh, in His humanity Christ is the personification of sacred doctrine, and now through the Church sacred doctrine is the "icon" of Jesus Christ; in other words, Jesus Christ, in a certain sense, is Sacred Doctrine personified; the mirror that Catholic sacred doctrine reflects is nothing other than Christ.

Bibliography

Ashley, Fr. Benedict. Introduction. *The Common Things: Essays on Thomism and Education*, Ed. Daniel McInerny. Washington, DC: Catholic UP, 1999.

Augustine. *Confessions* [*Confessiones*].

_____. *The First Catechetical Instruction* [*De Catechizandis Rudibus*]. Trans. Rev. Joseph P. Christopher, PhD. Westminster: The Newman Bookshop, 1946.

_____. *On Christian Doctrine* [*De Doctrina Christiana*].

_____. *On the Trinity* [*De Trinitate*].

Balthasar, Hans Urs von. *In the Fullness of Faith*. Trans. Graham Harrison. San Francisco: Ignatius Press, 1988.

Báñez, Dominic. *Commentaria in I Partem D. Thomae*.

Belloc, Hilaire. "What was the Church of the Roman Empire?" *Europe and the Faith*. New York: Missionary Society of St. Paul, 1920.

Bessarion. *Adversus calumniatorem Platonis*.

Billuart, C. R. *Summa Sancti Thomae hodiernis Academicarum moribus accomodata*. Paris, n.d.

Bokenkotter, Thomas. *Essential Catholicism: Dynamics of Faith and Belief*. New York: Doubleday, 1985.

Bonnefoy, J., OFM. *La nature de la theologie selon Saint Thomas d'Aquin*. Paris: J. Vrin - Bruges, Ch. Beyaert, 1939: 88.

_____. "La theologie comme science et l'explication de la foi selon S. Thomas d'Aquin." *Ephemerides Theologicae Lovanienses*, XIV (1937), 421-446; 600-631; XV (1938), 491-516.

_____. "La methodologie theologique de saint Thomas," *Revista Espanola de Teologia,* X (1950), 41-81.

Bowring, Kelly. "The Case for a National Catechism." *National Catholic Register* Vol. 74 No. 36 (Sept. 6, 1998): 9.

_____. "Will Theology Regain Its Soul in America?" *The Catholic Faith* Vol. 7, No. 6 (Nov./Dec., 2001): 28-30.

_____. "How Will the Renewal of Catholic Higher Education Succeed?" *National Catholic Register* (Sept. 22, 2002); *Fellowship of Catholic Scholars Quarterly* (Summer 2002).

_____. "Letter to the Editor: Response to Secular Universities That Are Catholic." *The Chronicle of Higher Education* Vol. 51, Issue 41 (June 17, 2005).

_____. *The Holy Keeping. Faithful Exposition of the Deposit of Faith: A Hermeneutic of Sacred Doctrine within the Ministry of Catechesis* (Doctoral dissertation) Angelicum, Rome, 2002.

Boyer, Charles, SJ. "Theological Pluralism." *L'Oss. Rom. - English Edition.* 12 Aug. 1971: 6ff.

Bradley, Robert, SJ. *The Roman Catechism in the Catechetical Tradition of the Church.* Lanham: University Press, 1990.

Braxton. Edward K. Presentation. NCEA/CACE Conference 10/20/98.

Buechlein, Daniel. *Oral Report to the General Assembly of Bishops,* June 19, 1997, [Document on line] http://www.nccbuscc.org/catechism/document/oralrpt.htm (Internet) Accessed July 24, 2001.

Buonpensiere, H. *Commentaria in I P. Summa Theologiae (De Deo Uno).* Rome, 1902.

Cano, Melchior. *De Locis Theologicis.* Rome, 1900.

Canon Law Society of America. *Code of Canon Law.* Washington, DC: CLSA, 1983.

Catechism of the Catholic Church, 2nd ed., trans. United States Catholic Conference, 1997.

Catholics United for the Faith. *Our New Catechisms: A Critical*

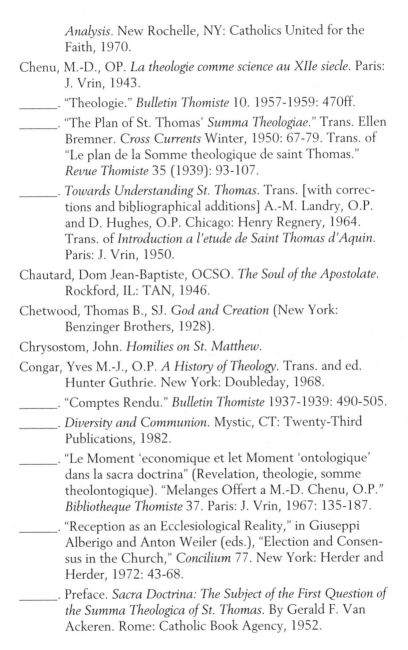

Analysis. New Rochelle, NY: Catholics United for the Faith, 1970.

Chenu, M.-D., OP. *La theologie comme science au XIIe siecle.* Paris: J. Vrin, 1943.

_____. "Theologie." *Bulletin Thomiste* 10. 1957-1959: 470ff.

_____. "The Plan of St. Thomas' *Summa Theologiae.*" Trans. Ellen Bremner. *Cross Currents* Winter, 1950: 67-79. Trans. of "Le plan de la Somme theologique de saint Thomas." *Revue Thomiste* 35 (1939): 93-107.

_____. *Towards Understanding St. Thomas.* Trans. [with corrections and bibliographical additions] A.-M. Landry, O.P. and D. Hughes, O.P. Chicago: Henry Regnery, 1964. Trans. of *Introduction a l'etude de Saint Thomas d'Aquin.* Paris: J. Vrin, 1950.

Chautard, Dom Jean-Baptiste, OCSO. *The Soul of the Apostolate.* Rockford, IL: TAN, 1946.

Chetwood, Thomas B., SJ. *God and Creation* (New York: Benzinger Brothers, 1928).

Chrysostom, John. *Homilies on St. Matthew.*

Congar, Yves M.-J., O.P. *A History of Theology.* Trans. and ed. Hunter Guthrie. New York: Doubleday, 1968.

_____. "Comptes Rendu." *Bulletin Thomiste* 1937-1939: 490-505.

_____. *Diversity and Communion.* Mystic, CT: Twenty-Third Publications, 1982.

_____. "Le Moment 'economique et let Moment 'ontologique' dans la sacra doctrina" (Revelation, theologie, somme theolontogique). "Melanges Offert a M.-D. Chenu, O.P." *Bibliotheque Thomiste* 37. Paris: J. Vrin, 1967: 135-187.

_____. "Reception as an Ecclesiological Reality," in Giuseppi Alberigo and Anton Weiler (eds.), "Election and Consensus in the Church," *Concilium* 77. New York: Herder and Herder, 1972: 43-68.

_____. Preface. *Sacra Doctrina: The Subject of the First Question of the Summa Theologica of St. Thomas.* By Gerald F. Van Ackeren. Rome: Catholic Book Agency, 1952.

Congregation for Catholic Education. *Instruction on the Study of the Fathers of the Church* (1989).

_____. *Lay Catholics in Schools: Witness to Faith* (1982).

_____. *The Catholic School* (1977).

_____. *The Religious Dimension of Education in a Catholic School* (1988).

_____. *The Theological Formation of Future Priests* (1976).

Congregation for the Clergy. *General Catechetical Directory.* Washington, DC: United States Catholic Conference, 1971.

_____. *General Directory for Catechesis.* Washington, DC: USCC, 1998.

Congregation for the Doctrine of the Faith. *Instruction on the Ecclesial Vocation of the Theologian* [*Donum Veritatis*] (1990).

_____. *Commentary on the Concluding Formula of the 'Professio Fidei'* (1998).

_____. *On the Unicity and Salvific Universality of Jesus Christ and the Church* [*Dominus Iesus*] (2000).

Congregation for the Evangelization of Peoples. *Guide for Catechists* (1993).

Conley, Kieran. *A Theology of Wisdom: A Study in St. Thomas.* Dubuque: The Priory Press, 1963.

Coriden, James A. "The Canonical Doctrine of Reception." *The Jurist* 50 (1990).

Davies, Brian, OP. "Is *Sacra Doctrina* Theology?" *New Blackfriars* 71 (1990): 141-146.

Denzinger-Schonmetzer, *Enchiridion Symbolorum.*

De Guibert, J., SJ. *De Ecclesia Christi.* Rome: n.p., 1928: 386ff.

De Vitoria, Francis. "The Manuscripts of Master Francis de Vitoria," by Fr. Beltran de Heredia, OP, in *La Ciencia Tomista*, XXXVI (1927).

Di Noia, J.A., OP. "American Catholic Theology at Century's End: Postconciliar, Postmodern, Post-Thomistic." *The Thomist* 54 (1990): 500-518.

_____. "Authority, Public Dissent and the Nature of Theological Thinking." *The Thomist* 52 (1988): 185-207.

Donneaud, OP, Henry. "Insaisissable *sacra doctrina?*" *Revue Thomiste* (1998): 179-224.

Dubay, Thomas. *Faith and Certitude.* San Francisco: Ignatius Press, 1985.

Dulles, Avery, SJ. "Evangelizing Theology," *First Things* 62 (March 1996).

_____. "Vatican II and Scholasticism." *New Oxford Review* 57 (May 1990): 8ff.

Erdozain, Luis. "The Evolution of Catechetics: A Survey of Six International Study Weeks on Catechetics." Ed. Michael Warren. *Sourcebook for Modern Catechetics.* Winona, MN: St. Mary's Press, 1983.

Ernest, Cornelius, OP. "Metaphor and Ontology in *Sacra Doctrina.*" *The Thomist* 38 (July 1974): 404ff.

Fernandez, Francis. *In Conversation with God,* vol. 3. New York: Scepter, 1994.

Gardeil, H-D. OP, and M-D Chenu, OP. *La Theologie Ia, Prologue et Question 1.* Paris: Les Editions du Cerf, 1997.

_____. *Le Donne revele et la theologie.* Paris: n.p., 1910.

Garrigou-Lagrange, Reginald, OP. *The One God.* Trans. Dominic Bede Rose. St. Louis: B. Herder, 1946.

Geenan, G., OP. "The Place of Tradition in the Theology of St. Thomas." *The Thomist* XV (Jan. 1952): 110-135.

George, Francis. "The Catholic Mission Today in Higher Education." *Origins* Vol. 27, No. 21 (Nov. 6, 1997): 352-358.

George, Marie I. "Mind Forming and *Manuductio* in Aquinas." *The Thomist* 57 (1993): 201-213.

Gilby, Thomas, OP. "Appendix 5: *Sacra Doctrina.*" Blackfriars' *Summa Theologiae.* New York: McGraw-Hill, 1963: 58-66.

Gillet, Stanislaus M., OP. *A Study of Saint Thomas.* Trans. Gerald Christian, OP. Washington, DC: Dominican House of Studies Library, n.d.

Gilson, Étienne. *Reason and Revelation in the Middle Ages.* New York: Charles Scribner's Sons, 1938.

Gui, Bernard. *Legenda S. Thomae Aquinatis.*

Hahn, Scott. "*Prima Scriptura.*" *The Church and the Universal Catechism.* Ed. Anthony Mastroeni. Steubenville: Franciscan University Press, 1992.

Hardon, John A., SJ. "General Catechetical Directory." *Pocket Catholic Dictionary.* New York: Image, 1985.

_____. *The Treasury of Catholic Wisdom.* NY: Doubleday, 1987.

_____. *With Us Today.* Ypsilanti, MI: Ave Maria University Communications, 2000.

Heath, Mark. "Thomistic Theology and Religious Education." *Theologies of Religious Education.* Ed. R.C. Miller, 38ff.

Hill, Brennan and William Madges. *The Catechism: Highlights & Commentary.* Mystic, CT: Twenty-Third Publications, 1994.

Hitchcock, James. *Catholicism and Modernity.* New York: Seabury Press, 1979.

Hofinger, J., SJ, and Francis Buckley, SJ. *The Good News and Its Proclamation.* Notre Dame: University of Notre Dame Press, 1968.

Jenkins, John. *Knowledge and Faith in Thomas Aquinas.* Cambridge: University Press, 1997.

John XXIII, Encyclical *Ecclesiam Suam.*

John Paul I, Angelus, 9/17/78.

John Paul II. *Crossing the Threshold of Hope.* New York: Alfred A. Knopf, 1994.

_____. *Ecclesia in America* (1999).

_____. Encyclical *Faith and Reason* [*Fides et Ratio*] (1998).

_____. Apostolic Constitution *From the Heart of the Church* [*Ex Corde Ecclesiae*] (1990).

_____. Apostolic Exhortation *On Catechesis in Our Time* [*Catechesi Tradendae*] (1979).

_____. Encyclical *Redeemer of Man* [*Redemptor Hominis*] (1979).

_____. Apostolic Constitution *The Deposit of Faith* [*Fidei Depositum*] (1992).

_____. Encyclical *The Splendor of Truth* [*Veritatis Splendor*] (1993).

_____. Apostolic Letter Motu Proprio *To Protect the Faith* [*Ad Tuendam Fidem*] (1998).

_____. *The Method and Doctrine of St. Thomas in Dialogue with Modern Culture* (1980).

John of St. Thomas, *Cursus Theologicus*, III Tom. Parisis-Tornaci-Romae: Desclée et Sociorum, 1931.

Johnson, Mark F. "God's Knowledge in Our Frail Mind: The Thomistic Model of Theology." *Angelicum* (1999): 25-45.

_____. "The Sapiential Character of the First Article of the *Summa theologiae*." *Philosophy and the God of Abraham*. Ed. by James Long. Toronto: Pontifical Institute of Medieval Studies, 1991: 87-98.

Kelly, Francis D. *The Mystery We Proclaim*, 1st and 2nd ed. Huntington: Our Sunday Visitor, 1993.

Kelly, George. *Who Should Run the Church: Social Scientists, Theologians or Bishops?* Huntington: Our Sunday Visitor, 1976.

Kelly, J. N. D. *Early Christian Creeds*, 3rd ed. London: Longman, 1972.

Kevane, Msgr. Eugene M. *Augustine the Educator: A Study in the Fundamentals of Christian Formation*. Westminster: The Newman Press, 1964.

_____. *Catechism of Christian Doctrine*, ordered by St. Pius X, ed. Eugene Kevane. Arlington: Center for Family Catechetics, 1980.

_____. *Creed and Catechetics: A Catechetical Commentary on the Creed of the People of God*. Westminster: Christian Classics, 1978.

_____. *Jesus the Divine Teacher*. Steubenville: Franciscan University Press, 1991.

Kloppenburg, Bonaventure, OFM. *The Ecclesiology of Vatican II,* trans. Matthew J. O'Connell. Chicago: Franciscan Herald Press, n.d.

Komonochak, Joseph. "Thomism and the Second Vatican Council." *Continuity and Pluralism in the Catholic Theology.* Ed. Anthony Cernara. Fairfield: Sacred Heart University, 1998: 53-73.

Kreeft, Peter. *A Summa of the Summa.* San Francisco: Ignatius Press, 1990.

Latourelle, Rene and Rino Fisichella. *Dictionary of Fundamental Theology.* New York: Crossroad, 1995.

Laux, John. *Church History.* Rockford: TAN Books, 1989.

Leo XIII. *Militantis Ecclesiae* (1897).

_____. Encyclical *On the Education of the Clergy* [*Depuis Le Jour*] (1899).

Lieblich, Julia. "Catholic colleges mum on teacher 'loyalty oath.'" *Chicago Tribune* (June, 7, 2002).

Lonergan, Bernard. *Method in Theology.* New York: Seabury Press, 1979.

Maritain, Jacques. *The Peasant of the Garonne.* New York: Holt, Rinehart, and Winston, 1968.

Marthaler, Berard. "The Genesis and Genius of the *General Catechetical Directory.*" Ed. Michael Warren. *Sourcebook for Modern Catechetics.* Winona, MN: St. Mary's Press, 1983.

_____. "The Modern Catechetical Movement in Roman Catholicism: Issues and Personalities." Ed. Michael Warren. *Sourcebook for Modern Catechetics.* Winona, MN: St. Mary's Press, 1983.

Masterson, Reginald, OP, ed. *Theology in the Catholic College.* Dubuque, IA: The Priory Press, 1961.

McBride, Alfred, O. Praem. "Why We Need the New Catechism: Vatican II Promise and Post-Vatican II Reality." *The Church and the Universal Catechism.* Ed. Anthony Mastroeni. Steubenville: Franciscan University Press, 1992.

McBrien, Richard. "Why I Shall Not Seek a Mandate." *America* Vol. 182, No. 4 (Feb. 12, 2000).

McCool, Gerald, SJ. *From Unity to Pluralism: The Internal Evolution of Thomism.* New York: Fordham University Press, 1989.

McGuire, Brian. "Mandatum Won't Guarantee Fidelity in Catholic Universities." *National Catholic Register* Vol. 77, No. 29 (July 22-28, 2001).

McHugh, John J., OP and Charles J. Callan, OP. *Catechism of the Council of Trent for Parish Priests.* New York: Joseph Wagner, 1923.

Merkt, J. *Sacra Doctrina and Christian Eschatology.* Diss. Ann Arbor, MI: UMI, 1983.

Miravalle, S.T.D., Mark. *Mary: Coredemptrix, Mediatrix, Advocate.* Santa Barbara: Queenship Publishing, 1993.

Moran, Gabriel. *Design for Religion.* New York: Herder and Herder, 1971.

_____. *Theology of Revelation.* New York: Herder and Herder, 1966.

Muniz, Francisco P., OP. *The Work of Theology.* Washington, DC: Thomist Press, 1953.

National Conference of Catholic Bishops. *Doctrinal Responsibilities: Approaches to Promoting and Resolving Misunderstandings between Bishops and Theologians* (1989).

_____. *Guidelines Concerning the Academic Mandatum in Catholic Universities* (USCCB, 2001).

_____. *The Application of Ex Corde Ecclesiae for the United States* (2000).

Neumayr, John W. "The Science of God and the Blessed." *Return to the Source* Vol. 1 No. 1 (Winter 1999): 27-36.

Neuner, J., SJ. and J. Dupuis, SJ, Eds. *Christian Faith.* New York: Alba House, 1998.

Newman, John Henry. *The Arians of the Fourth Century.* London: n.p., 1833.

_____. *The Idea of a University*. London: Longmans, Green and Co., 1893.

Nichols, Aidan, OP. *From Newman to Congar: The Idea of Doctrinal Development from the Victorians to the Second Vatican Council*. Edinburgh: T & T Clark, 1990.

O'Brien, Thomas C. "'Sacra Doctrina' Revisited: The Context of Medieval Education." *The Thomist* 41 (Oct. 1977): 476-509.

O'Connell, David, OP. *Notes from the Summa on God and His Creatures*. Providence: Providence College, 1956.

O'Meara, Thomas, OP. *Thomas Aquinas, Theologian*. Notre Dame: University of Notre Dame Press, 1997.

Patfoort, Albert. "*Sacra doctrina*, Theologie et unité de la *Ia Pars*." *Angelicum* 62 (1985): 306-319.

Paul VI. Apost. Exhort. *Paterna cum Benevolentia*. AAS 67 (1975).

_____. *Evangelization in the Modern World* [*Evangelii Nuntiandi*] (1975).

_____. *General Catechetical Directory* (1971).

Perrotta, Paul, OP. *Theology Summary: Part 1 of Summa of St. Thomas*. Somerset, OH: Rosary Press, n.d.

Persson, Per Erik. *Sacra Doctrina: Reason and Revelation in Aquinas*. Trans. Ross MacKenzie. Philadelphia: Fortress Press, 1970.

Pieper, Josef. *Guide to St. Thomas*, trans. Richard and Clara Winston. San Francisco: Ignatius Press, 1986.

_____. *The Silence of St. Thomas*. Trans. John Murray, SJ and Daniel O'Connor. New York: Pantheon, 1957.

Pius X. *Acerbo Nimus*.

_____. *An Exhortation on Catechetics to Catholic Parents and Teachers*.

_____. Encyclical, *Haerent animo* (1908).

_____. Letter, "La ristorazione."

Pius XI. *On the Sixth Centenary of the Canonization of St. Thomas* [*Studiorum Ducem*] (1923).

Pius XII. *On Human Origins* [*Humani Generis*], Encyclical (1950).

Rahner, Karl, SJ. "Pluralism in Theology and the Oneness of the Church's Profession of Faith." *Concilium* 46 (1969): 115ff.

_____. "Magisterium." *Sacramentum Mundi* (1969).

Ramirez, Santiago, OP. "The Authority of St. Thomas Aquinas." *The Thomist* 15 (Jan. 1952): 35ff.

Ratzinger, Joseph Cardinal (Benedict XVI). "Commentary on the Dogmatic Constitution on the Church" Ed. H. Vorgrimler. *Commentary on the Documents of Vatican II*, vol. I (1967).

_____. *Gospel, Catechesis, Catechism*. San Francisco: Ignatius Press, 1997.

_____ and Christoph Schönborn, *Introduction to the Catechism of the Catholic Church*. San Francisco: Ignatius Press, 1997.

_____. *Introduction to Christianity*. San Francisco: Ignatius Press, 2004.

_____. *The Nature and Mission of Theology*. San Francisco: Ignatius Press, 1995.

_____. *Principles of Catholic Theology: Building Stones for a Fundamental Theology*. San Francisco: Ignatius Press, 1987.

_____. *The Ratzinger Report*. San Francisco: Ignatius Press, 1985.

_____. "Thorn in the Flesh." *The Catholic World Report* Nov. 1992: 48-54.

Reith, Herman, CSC. *Freedom and Authority*. Notre Dame: BRC Printing, 1999.

Ryan, Mary Perkins, ed. *Helping Adolescents Grow Up in Christ*. New York: Paulist Press/Deus Books, 1967.

Salaverri, Joachim, SJ. *De Ecclesia Christi* no. 872, 874. Madrid, 1950: 757-758.

Schaeffer, Pamela. "Down to the Wire: The Mandatum Debate." *National Catholic Reporter* Vol. 37, No. 32 (June 15, 2001).

Schall, James V., SJ. *A Student's Guide to Liberal Education.* Wilmington, DE: ISI Books, 2000.

Schönborn, Christoph, OP. "Major Themes Underlying Principles of the Catechism of the Catholic Church." *Living Light* 30:1 (Fall 1993): 56ff.

Seckler, Max. *Le Salut et l'Historie: La pensee de Saint Thomas d'Aquin sur de l'histoire.* Paris: Editions de Cerf, 1967.

Shanley, Brian, OP. "*Sacra Doctrina* and the Theology of Disclosure." *The Thomist* 61 (1997): 163-187.

Sheen, Fulton J. *Mornings with Fulton Sheen.* Ed. Beverly Coney Heirich. Ann Arbor, MI: Servant Publications, 2000.

Sloyan, Gerard S. "Religious Education: From Early Christianity to Medieval Times." Ed. Michael Warren. *Sourcebook for Modern Catechetics.* Winona, MN: St. Mary's Press, 1983.

Sparrow, M.F. "Natural Knowledge of God and the Principles of *Sacra Doctrina.*" *Angelicum* 69 (1992): 471-491.

Stackpole, Robert A. *Jesus, Mercy Incarnate.* Stockbridge: Marian Press, 2000.

Sullivan, Thomas F. and John F. Meyers. *Focus on American Catechetics: A Commentary on the General Catechetical Directory.* Washington, DC: NCEA National Conference of Diocesan Directors of Religious Education, 1972.

Swetland, Stuart. "Catechetical Content for Our Culture." *The Church and the Universal Catechism.* Steubenville: Franciscan University Press, 1992.

Sylvius, Franciscus. *Opera omnia. Tomi VI. - Tome I: Commentarii in Totam Primam Partem S. Thomae Aquinatis Doctoris Angelici et Communis.* Antuerpiae, 1714.

The Holy Bible, RSVCE. San Francisco: Ignatius Press, 1996.

The Jesuit Ratio Studiorum of 1599. Trans. Allan P. Farrell, SJ. Washington, DC: Conference of Major Superiors of Jesuits, 1970.

The Roman Catechism. Trans. and annotated by Robert Bradley, SJ and Eugene Kevane. Boston: St. Paul, 1985.

Thomas Aquinas, OP. *De fide orthodoxa.*

_____. *Scriptum super Libros Sententiarum.*

_____. *Summa Theologiae,* Blackfriars edition. New York: McGraw-Hill, 1963.

_____. *In Boet. De Trinitiate.*

_____. *In De Trin.*

_____. *In L. Sent.*

_____. *In Post. Anal.*

_____. *The Catechetical Instructions of St. Thomas Aquinas.* Manila: Sinag-Tala, n.d.

Torrell, Jean-Pierre, OP. *St. Thomas Aquinas: vol. 1: The Person and His Work.* Trans. Robert Royal. Washington, DC: Catholic University Press, 1993.

Turner, Geoffrey. "St. Thomas Aquinas on the Scientific Nature of Theology." *New Blackfriars* 78 (1997): 464-476.

United States Catholic Conference. *National Catechetical Directory,* "Sharing the Light of Faith" (1979).

Valkenberg, Pim. *Did Not Our Hearts Burn? Place and Function of Holy Scripture in the Theology of St. Thomas.* Utrecht: n.p., 1990.

Van Ackeren, Geraldo. *Sacra Doctrina: The Subject of the First Question of the Summa Theologiae of St. Thomas.* Rome: Catholic Book Agency, 1952.

_____ and P. De Letter. "Theology." *NCE* 14 (1967): 39-58.

Van der Ploeg, J., OP. "The Place of Holy Scripture in the Theology of St. Thomas." *The Thomist* 38 (Jan. 1974): 402-421.

Vann, Gerald, OP. *The Aquinas Prescription (St. Thomas Aquinas).* Manchester, NH: Sophia Press, 1939.

Vatican Council I. Denzinger, *Enchiridion Symbolorum.*

Vatican Council II. *Declaration on Catholic Education [Gravissimum Educationis]* (1966).

_____. *Declaration on the Church in the Modern World [Gaudium et Spes]* (1965).

_____. *Decree on Ecumenism* [*Unitatis Redintegratio*] (1964).

_____. *Decree on the Pastoral Office of Bishops in the Church* [*Christus Dominus*] (1965).

_____. *Decree on the Training of Priests* [*Optatam Totius*] (1965).

_____. *Dogmatic Constitution on Divine Revelation* [*Dei Verbum*] (1965).

Von Hildebrand, Alice. "The Nature and Mission of a Catholic University," *Honors Convocation Address at Franciscan University of Steubenville*, 3/18/87.

Von Hildebrand, Dietrich. *Trojan Horse in the City of God: The Catholic Crisis Explained.* Manchester, NH: Sophia Institute, 1967.

Walgrave, Jan H., OP. *Selected Writings/Thematische Geschriften.* Louvain: UP, 1982.

Warren, Michael, ed., *Sourcebook for Modern Catechetics.* Winona, MN: St. Mary's Press, 1983.

Weigel, George. *Witness to Hope.* New York: Harper Collins, 1999.

Weisheipl, James, OP. *Friar Thomas D'Aquino: His Life, Thought, and Work.* Garden City, NY: Doubleday and Co., 1974.

_____. "The Meaning of Sacra Doctrina in *Summa Theologiae* I, q. 1." *The Thomist* 38 (Jan. 1974): 49-80.

White, Victor, OP. "Holy Teaching: The Idea of Theology According to St. Thomas." *Aquinas Papers No. 33.* London: Blackfriars, 1958: 4-20.

Wrenn, Michael J. *Catechisms and Controversies: Religious Education in the Postconciliar Years.* San Francisco: Ignatius Press, 1991.

Wrenn, Msgr. Michael and Kenneth D. Whitehead. *Flawed Expectations.* San Francisco: Ignatius Press, 1996.

PRAYER OF ST. THOMAS AQUINAS

Ineffable Creator,
Who out of the treasures of Your wisdom has appointed three
hierarchies of angels
and set them in admirable order high above the heavens
and has disposed the diverse portions of the universe in such
marvelous arrays;
You Who are called the true source of Light and supereminent
principle of Wisdom,
be pleased to cast a beam of Your radiance upon the darkness of
my mind
and dispel from me the double darkness of sin and ignorance in
which I was born.
You Who make eloquent the tongues of little children,
fashion my words
and pour upon my (mind and) lips the grace of Your benediction.
Grant me penetration to understand,
capacity to retain,
method and facility in study,
subtlety in interpretation,
and abundant grace of expression,
[always accurate in truth, expressed in love (Eph 4:15)].
Order the beginning,
direct the progress
and perfect the achievement of my work,
You Who are true God and man
and live and reign forever and ever.
Amen.

from Pope Pius XI's Encyclical, *Studiorum Ducem* (1923)